Multiculturalism in Contemporary Societies:
Perspectives on Difference and Transdifference

ERLANGER FORSCHUNGEN

Reihe A • Geisteswissenschaften • Band 101

Multiculturalism in Contemporary Societies: Perspectives on Difference and Transdifference

Herausgegeben von

Helmbrecht Breinig, Jürgen Gebhardt
und Klaus Lösch

Erlangen 2002

Die wissenschaftliche Buchreihe ERLANGER FORSCHUNGEN wurde
gegründet mit Mitteln der Jubiläumsspende der Siemens AG Erlangen

Die Deutsche Bibliothek – CIP-Einheitsaufnahme

Multiculturalism in contemporary societies : perspectives on difference and
transdifference / [Universitätsbibliothek Erlangen-Nürnberg].
Ed.: Helmbrecht Breinig. - Erlangen : Univ.-Bibliothek, 2002
(Erlanger Forschungen : Reihe A, Geisteswissenschaften ; Bd. 101)
ISBN 3-930357-51-8

Verlag:
Universitätsbund Erlangen-Nürnberg e.V.
Kochstraße 4, 91054 Erlangen

Auslieferung:
Universitätsbibliothek Erlangen-Nürnberg
Universitätsstraße 4, 91054 Erlangen

Lasersatz: Lehrstuhl für Amerikanistik, Erlangen
Druck: Heinrich Delp GmbH, Bad Windsheim

ISBN 3-930357-51-8

ISSN 0423-3433

Contents

Preface 7

Helmbrecht Breinig and Klaus Lösch
Introduction: Difference and Transdifference 11

Nathan Glazer
We Are All Multiculturalists Now 37

Homi K. Bhabha
On Cultural Respect 53

Nancy Fraser
Redistribution, Recognition, and Participation:
Toward an Integrated Conception of Justice 69

Iris Marion Young
Self-determination and Global Democracy:
A Critique of Liberal Nationalism 91

Alain-G. Gagnon
Problems and Limits of Multiculturalism:
A View from Québec 125

Juan Bruce-Novoa
Different Drummers, Same Beat:
Resistance as Assimilation 147

Werner Sollors
Beyond Multiculturalism? 163

Rüdiger Kunow
From "Roots" to "Routes":
Ethnic Fiction between Comfort Zones and Danger Zones 195

Gerald Vizenor
Interimage Simulations:
Fugitive Poses of Native American Indians 229

References 249

Index 265

Preface

The multicultural diversity of national or regional populations has become a universal phenomenon. Some countries or areas have been the home of a variety of ethnicities for many centuries, sometimes harmoniously, sometimes beset by various forms of conflict. However, international migration and other aspects of globalization but also the counter-tendencies of localization and renewed cultural diversification have made even those parts of the globe that used to consider themselves monocultural (for instance many European nation states) locations of cultural pluralism. Possibly they have always been that, and it is only the awareness of scholars and politicians with regard to the ensuing problems that has grown in recent years.

In many countries, the answer to multiculturality is multiculturalism, a collective term denoting approaches to (1) questions of definition still in need of clarification, such as culture, individual and group identity, individual and collective rights, the requirements of nations and transnational configurations, as well as to (2) questions of political and legal action in many contexts, from education to land rights or job opportunity measures. While the discussion in parts of Asia is widely ignored by Americans and Europeans alike, the North American debate on the cultural status of not only ethnic but also social minorities or underprivileged groups (defined, for instance by gender, sexual orientation or class) has carried over to Europe, although the multicultural awareness in the various countries is still differently focused. Yet while the United States and Canada have been involved in such public debates for many years, Germany has only recently awakened to this issue. The academic discussion in this country, too, is still lagging behind.

As a contribution to improving this situation, the North American Section of the Central Institute for Area Studies at the University of Erlangen-Nürnberg devoted its 1998-99 lecture series (the Friedrich Alexander University North America Colloquium, FAUNAC), to the topic of "Multicultural Societies on the Threshold of the Twenty-First Century: Intercultural and Transcultural Developments." A number of prominent experts from the United States, Canada, and Germany were invited to speak on various aspects of the multicultural agenda. This interdisciplinary series was made possible by a collaboration with the recently founded Bavarian-American Academy, Munich and the German-American Institute of Nuremberg.

Literary and cultural critics, political and social scientists, professors of law and philosophy as well as representatives of minority literatures came to Erlangen to present their views. Most of them agreed to make their papers available for publication. In some cases, where the lectures were condensed versions of longer publications already in progress, the authors graciously gave their permission to reprint the extended or revised versions. The resulting volume therefore contains some of the most substantial contributions made to the multiculturalism debate in recent years.

While most of the speakers considered the trend toward multicultural diversity an irreversible development in most parts of the world, their comments varied considerably with regard to the scope of the term and the phenomenon of "multiculturalism," to the ways by which intercultural interaction takes place, and to the respective rights and demands of nations, groups and individuals. They also differed in their perception of the necessity of measures needed to make societies more tolerant and to strike a balance between enriching cultural diversity and the desire for a unified and unifying national or even international culture.

In his paper, Nathan Glazer, Professor emeritus of Education and Sociology at Harvard University and one of the most prominent American social scientists of the last decades, casts a slightly skeptical glance at multiculturalism (in terms of ethnic diversity) and, taking up questions addressed in his book *We Are All Multiculturalists Now*, comments on the origin, academic success and future impact of the current trend as well as on similar tendencies in Europe. Homi K. Bhabha, Indian-born Professor of English who is also now at Harvard and a world-renowned cultural and postcolonial theorist, brings the contemporary migrational experience to bear on the question of belonging, the meaning of "one of Us," and the relevance of "choice" and "respect" in a situation characterized as the "interstitial moment and movement" between the local, the regional and the international. Nancy Fraser, Professor of Political and Social Science at New School University, New York, is known in Germany from the translated versions of her seminal books on the theory of gender, power and social justice. In her paper based on her "Tanner Lecture on Human Values," she postulates an integration of the politics of redistribution and of recognition in order to redress economic as well as cultural injustices, an approach based on a theory of "perspectival dualism." Iris M. Young, Professor of Political Science at the University of Chicago, internationally known political and feminist social theorist with strong connections to the Frankfurt Department of Philosophy, argues for the self-determination of indigenous peoples in the context of an as yet visionary global democracy, but against a notion of freedom as complete non-interference, even where human rights are at stake. Alain-G. Gagnon, Professor of Political Science at McGill University and Senior Research Fellow at the Institute for Research on Public Policy in Montreal, is one of the most highly respected experts on the status of Québec within a federal Canada. He challenges the idea of a Canadian multiculturalism as "a denial of Québec's distinct identitive status in Canada" and instead offers a Québec concept of interculturalism that might serve as a model for countries around the globe facing the challenge of an increasing polyethnicity. Juan Bruce-Novoa, Professor of Spanish at the University of California, Irvine and, at the time of his lecture, a Fulbright Visiting Professor in Erlangen, is a leading expert on Chicano and Latino literatures and a well-known writer. In a highly personal contribution he rejects ethnic nationalism, cultural fragmentation and essentialist resistance patterns in favor of a model of a 1960s' ideal of tolerance and love. Werner Sollors, Professor of English and Afro-American Studies at Harvard, German-born author of many books on African American and other ethnic literatures and chief exponent of the new studies in the multilingual literature of the United States, reviews the American debate on multiculturalism and compares it to European positions, but then goes on to focus on the necessity of looking "beyond multiculturalism" in order to do justice to the growing number of ethnically mixed identifications. Rüdiger Kunow, who is Professor of American Studies at the University of Potsdam and a specialist in American fiction, multicultural literatures, and the theory of stereotypes, explores contemporary ethnic fiction "in the larger social and cultural manifold of an increasingly post-national United States," focusing on the politics and poetics of space. One of the authors discussed in his paper is Gerald Vizenor, the celebrated postmodern Native American novelist, poet and essayist and Professor of Native American Studies at the University of California, Berkeley. Vizenor concludes the present volume with a scathing critique of photographic and other images of native cultures which he exposes as "*interimage* simulations," as tools of dominance which he contrasts with the creative and elusive play of presence and absence in native ceremonies.

Vizenor has coined the term "postindian" to indicate a dynamic situation of cultural hybridity and personal interraciality beyond traditional ethnic classifications. While his position is particularly radical inasmuch as it points out the insufficiency of multicultural essentialisms even with regard to the descendants of the original population of the Americas, others also indicate the necessity to move "beyond ethnicity" (the title of one of Sollors' books) to a recognition of the demands made by multiple affiliations characterizing the identity constructions of present-day cultural groups as well as individuals. In their introduction, Helmbrecht Breinig and Klaus Lösch try to sketch a theory of *transdifference* on the basis of a dynamic concept of culture as it applies to contemporary multicultural societies.

    The bulk of the organizational work for the lecture series was shouldered by the staff of the *Lehrstuhl für Amerikanistik* and of the *Institut für Politische Wissenschaft* as well as Annemarie Börnke of the *Deutsch-Amerikanisches Institut Nürnberg* and was coordinated by Klaus Lösch. The *Amerikanistik* staff also prepared the publication of this volume. The editors wish to thank Dr. Hans-Otto Keunecke and the editors of the *Erlanger Forschungen* for accepting the book for their series and the *Universitätsbund Erlangen-Nürnberg* for providing the necessary financial support. Edward Reif polished the English of the introduction. Ute Eckstein and Jens Klenner deserve gratitude and admiration for preparing the manuscript, checking countless sources and lending other editorial assistance.

Helmbrecht Breinig, Jürgen Gebhardt, Klaus Lösch

Introduction: Difference and Transdifference

Helmbrecht Breinig and Klaus Lösch

In the summer of 1999, *Boston Globe* reporter Wil Haygood undertook a "journey into poor white America" to talk to people about racism, white-black relations, the roots of prejudice and the chances of change. Haygood is black. Most of his interview partners were in their twenties; women were more responsive than men. What he encountered, apart from instances of sheer rejection and hatred, was an array of slowly changing attitudes, a thin layer of tolerance with memories of the radical racism that was virulent among the previous generation or during one's own youth. Such racism or at least suspicion and a tendency to retreat to an attitude of "one's own group first" kept surfacing, even among the well-intentioned.

> I ask Becky about affirmative action.[1] She squinches up her face. "I don't know. I'm not prejudiced, by any means, but I think it's as many whites need help as blacks. [. . .] I think whites should help the whites. Everybody starts out on the ground. Some people make it. Some don't." [. . .] "I don't understand," Lori is saying, "this new thing with blacks and their culture: 'This is our culture.' Well, it's not my fault somebody went over to Africa and captured you!"[2]

Even among people who consider themselves free of the racism of earlier generations, basic elements of a racist society continue to shape their attitudes: a binary thinking along color lines – including the collectivizing "you" for all blacks, past and present; an emphasis on economics as the bedrock of the social order; a competitive individualism bolstered by a sense of belonging to the white majority; an unwillingness to consider the consequences of a majority-minority situation, nay, of a hierarchy of power deriving from historical injustice (for which the speaker doesn't feel any personal responsibility); and finally a distrust of the new claims to a specific culture of their own articulated by African Americans. The last point looks like the reverse-order proof for the correctness of Nathan Glazer's assumption that multiculturalism has its origins in the black civil rights movement and in the expansion of the latter's agenda to include not only the issues of political, social and economic equality, but also a group culture tracing some of its important roots back to Africa.³

Multiculturality and Multiculturalism in the United States

If multiculturalism is defined as a collective term describing efforts in contemporary societies to respond to their diversity, efforts mainly focusing on tolerance and mutual respect as an aim of education, constitutional provisions, state or local measures, it concerns all nations and the world community at large, as the events of September 11, 2001 have abundantly revealed. Multiculturalism is a result of that multiculturality which social scientists and anthropologists have come to see as a pervasive feature of any territorially-defined human society. Let us for the moment regard this term as only referring to ethnic diversity. While ethnic multiculturality or cultural diversity is a global phenomenon, multiculturalism is not. As an active awareness of such diversity, a public debate on the necessary or desirable consequences and, potentially, the educational and social programs associated with the latter, it is by no means a universally accepted way of dealing with problems arising from the heterogeneous composition of national populations.

The term "multiculturalism" was coined by a Canadian Royal Commision in 1965, and has undergone various developments in different parts of the world. Even where the countries in question share some parts of their tradition, as is the case in those "eight national contexts with historical links in British colonialism" studied in David Bennett's *Multicultural States,* countries united by English as a national or at least one of the dominant languages, there is an enormous variety of social orders.⁴ Major differences exist between old and new immigrant states; between nations built across a plurality of existing ethnic boundaries in the wake of colonialism and those long considered monocultural; between those where multiculturalism is imposed on from above and those where it is clamored for from below.

Although the term "multiculturalism" originated elsewhere and although other countries have also played leading roles in developing strategies for dealing with questions of diversity and mutual respect and recognition, the United States is an exemplary case, not only because of its magnitude and leading global role but also because of the nature of its diversity and the plurality of approaches dealing with it. While America is the principal source of globalization as a development towards economic and, to a certain extent, social and cultural interconnectedness and hence homogenization of the world population, one of the collateral aspects of globalization, the New Immigration, has made US diversity even more multifaceted, more extreme and at the same time even more of a model for the many changes which all industrial societies are experiencing or will soon have to undergo. Thus, to focus on American multiculturalism, with only one paper devoted to Canadian biculturalism and with only occasional side-glances at conditions in Europe, as we do in the present volume, nonetheless provides a wealth of information and arguments to further the discussion on this side of the Atlantic.

At the same time, it has to be admitted that not only the degree but also the roots of American multiculturality are different from those to be found in Western Europe. This difference derives from the nature of American society as composed of (1) immigrants and their descendants, (2) the offspring of African slaves forcibly brought to the New World, and (3) the slowly recovering but numerically small remnants of the formerly large indigenous population all but wiped out by the European invasion. Even in colonial days, one immigrant group, the English, claimed dominant or even exclusive status. In 1751, Benjamin Franklin expounded the dangers of German immigration in no uncertain terms:

> And since Detachments of English from Britain sent to America, will have their Places at Home so soon supply'd and increase so largely here; why should the Palatine Boors be suffered to swarm into our Settlements, and by herding together establish their Language and Manners, to the Exclusion of ours? Why should Pennsylvania, founded by the English, become a Colony of *Aliens*, who will shortly be so numerous as to Germanize us instead of our Anglifying them, and will never adopt our Language or Customs, any more than they can acquire our Complexion.[5]

Franklin's xenophobia leaves him with the primary option of exclusion, the nativist position that was responsible for the Chinese Exclusion Acts and has remained popular in portions of the American population to this day. Franklin also hints at the other solution which indeed became the dominant model: "Anglifying," in other words, assimilation. "Anglifying" later turned into "Americanization" and won out. Over the decades and, eventually, centuries, untold millions of immigrants were absorbed into "American culture," and those who were initially regarded as not only culturally but also genetically different – first Germans, then Irish, Italians, Polish, Jews and others – were adopted into an American population that may not have been Anglo-Saxon any more, but at least "Caucasian" or, simply, "white." It is a remarkable fact that, for instance, Italians and, much later, Jews, who were first regarded as *racially* different from the majority, gradually became "white" and thus all but invisible as minorities. There are other models of the merging or at least uniting of immigrant groups besides that of assimilation: the "melting pot" as conceptualized in Israel Zangwill's 1908 play by that title, but latent as early as in Crèvecoeur's reflections on "What is an American?"; in Horace M. Kallen's concept of a "Federation of Nationalities," which saw in America a mosaic of peoples separated by their respective ancestry, that is, "blood"; in Randolph Bourne's "Transnational America" and other early twentieth-century versions of cultural pluralism.[6] All of them acknowledged cultural, ethnic, and even racial diversity as a temporary or stable pattern of American society, but none of these theories had an impact like that of the multiculturalist movement. Although the percentage of the American population that did not speak any or hardly any English was several times higher in the 1890s (the last major phase of immigration before the late twentieth century) than in the 1990s, and although back then ethnic and foreign-language newspapers, theaters, community and religious rituals were much more common than they are now, this fact did not lead to a multiculturalist debate as it does today.

Cultural Difference, Race, and Ethnicity

There is no doubt that American multiculturalism, that is the debate on the degree and kind of cultural separateness of particular groups of the population, on group identity and its preservation in society as a whole, as well as on the consequences in the public and private spheres has much to do with race. In a review essay of Glazer's *We Are All Multiculturalists Now* and Michael Walzer's *On Toleration*, K. Anthony Appiah points out the proliferation and imprecision of the term "culture" and the persistence of racial and racist categories behind it. Whereas whiteness in America is still regarded as an unquestioned and undefined norm, as a category that has absorbed numerous peoples from Europe and beyond and is not identified with a specific culture (as are or were the groups that were gradually accepted as belonging to this category), blackness denotes that which has not and cannot be assimilated into whiteness, in spite of all efforts in the wake of the Civil Rights movement.

> White people rarely think of anything in their culture as white: normal, no doubt, middle-class, maybe, and even, sometimes, American; but not white. Black Americans, by contrast, do think of much in their lives in racial terms: they may speak black English (which some respectfully call Ebonics), go to black churches, dance and listen to black music. (And it isn't just how black people think; other people think that way about them.) [. . .] Black people created a culture in the slave quarters from pieces of Africa, pieces of Europe, pieces of North American Indian tradition, and a fair amount of heroic innovation. Africans became blacks here, just as the European immigrants became whites.[7]

There is a scholarly consensus that "race" is a biological fiction, that there is hardly any correlation between a person's genetic material and her/his racial category. Categorization by race offers almost no information about the person's (biological, let alone intellectual or temperamental) characteristics except about such crude phenotypical features as skin color, hair and, potentially, bone structure.[8] But the construction of racial difference, purely discursive though it may be, is extremely important with regard to *cultural* difference. Whiteness and blackness are racial categories whose discursive construction is based on culturally available norms and belief systems,[9] but while both white and black are racial terms, only black is also generally regarded as a cultural term – there is hardly any aspect of contemporary America that is perceived as "white culture." This observation concerning black culture is also true for Native Americans, Asians, and Hispanics, the latter being a particularly interesting case because here the assumption of cultural difference creates a *racial* difference in many people's minds even where the person referred to is of pure European stock. In this context we are in a vicious circle concerning all supposedly "visible" population groups: the observation of cultural difference leads to the assumption of a racial difference. The latter, being considered indelible, results in inequality and segregation, at least among the poorer population. The largest group affected by these conditions in the twentieth century, the blacks, could therefore not rest satisfied even had they achieved not only equal rights but also equal economic opportunities – which they have not, to a satisfactory degree, to this very day –, but felt compelled to claim a strongly distinctive cultural identity.

Other groups followed suit. In addition to the push of discrimination, there was the pull of what Appiah calls the "politics of nostalgia" because of the fading of cultural differences between the older immigrant groups such as Italians, Poles and Scandinavians.[10] When socio-economically defined groups insisted on the *cultural* capital of collective traditions, descendants of such older immigrant portions of the population felt that the process of assimilation had not only provided them with an American identity but had also robbed them of a valuable cultural heritage. More importantly, however: if discrimination was a dominant stimulus for claims of cultural difference, there could be no end to constructions of group "cultures" once not only ethnic but also social groups and regional populations discovered the benefits of cultural specificity. Women, gays, the old, the young, the poor, the Southern – the list of potential groupings of this kind was interminable. Appiah points out the inflation of the term "culture" – "[. . .] everything from anorexia to zydeco is illuminated by being displayed as the product of some group's culture," but he insists on the overwhelming cultural homogeneity of America in spite of its "much-vaunted variety."[11] In other words: the multicultural agenda as a set of claims made by the underprivileged originates not in major and pervasive cultural differences but in discrimination based on social constructions of race, gender, or sexual orientation. It is mainly because the discrimination against individuals from a variety of backgrounds could not be ended that these individuals felt a stronger allegiance to their group or origins than to America. The result is that even American assimilationists like Nathan Glazer grudgingly admit that there is no way around the acceptance of group-cultural identity claims.

Whether multiculturalism is discussed (as in Germany) as mainly an *inter*cultural issue or rather an *intra*cultural problem (as in the United States), it has come under attack from all political corners. As can be seen in the case of Arthur M. Schlesinger, Jr., liberal and conservative positions can merge in the criticism of multiculturalism as a threat to what is seen as American national identity and American culture, a unity resulting from a consensus on sociopolitical and ideological values overarching the ethnic diversity of a population from so many backgrounds.[12] The cultural canon which is supposed to shape educational programs is then either stable and restrictive, following a supposedly universally applicable pattern of American traditions, or liberal in the sense of tolerance and inclusiveness of the productions of cultural groups. Neither school questions the basic structures of the social institutions which are potentially responsible for majority and minority status and other inequalities.[13] A more radical position calling these structures into doubt would therefore be considered as a disruptive, separatist version of multiculturalism.

The main charge of the left is that of "culturalism": the cultural focus of multiculturalism is regarded as being "merely" cultural, ignoring the underlying social inequalities and their origins. However, as Günter Lenz rightly objects,

> [. . .] the critique of multiculturalism as a "culturalist" displacement of the "real" structural inequalities in society often tends to rely on a more or less clean-cut distinction among the various "spheres" of modern societies such as the economy, politics, and culture that is no longer adequate for conceptualizing the complex and heteronomous social processes, interactions, and representations in post-Fordist, postmodern Western societies that force us to redefine the concepts of culture, the boundaries of the political, and the meaning of multicultural identities and communities in crucial ways.[14]

Yet efforts like K. Anthony Appiah's to establish a set of distinctive terms such as "nation," "social identity" and "cultural identity" and finally to separate the shared sphere of national institutions and social behavior on the one hand and that of the plurality of cultural identities on the other may be no more than heuristically successful.[15] As Lenz continues,

> [. . .] a self-reflective critique of the dynamics of contemporary culture must articulate in its discursive strategies a crucial *doubleness* or *ambiguity* in the use of the term "culture." On the one hand, cultural critics today are asked to see the various "realms" of a society in a common focus or, better, address their interrelations and their differences as a network of complex and often conflicting interactions and not limit their analysis to the traditional sphere of "culture" in a narrower sense. On the other hand, it is exactly the seeming "omnipresence" of these processes of cultural mediation and the increasing economic, social, political, and public role "cultural processes" have acquired in American and other Western and non-Western societies over the last decades in the context of the post-Fordist economy of postindustrialism and of postmodernity that challenge cultural critics to reassert distinctions and differences and carefully analyze the *specific* historical modes of representation at work in the public sphere.[16]

Definitions of "culture" will be necessarily fuzzy, but in the context of multiculturalism they will have to meet certain minimum requirements. They must originate in the distinction of ethnic groups rather than, for instance, the differentiation between "culture" and "civilization" which used to be popular in Germany. But they must transcend the ethnic level in order to be applicable to transnational as well as microsocietal phenomena. They must be flexible enough to define essential value systems, forms of behavior, social organizations and forms of symbolic expression, interaction and self-definition not only for groups following the ethnicity model (Bavarians, Sinti and Roma, Germans, Caucasians) but also other social group formations: the genders, gays and lesbians, working class people, subsistence farmers, and big city populations. In other words, the term "culture" will mean different things when, in the current American debate on multiculturalism, it is applied to (1) the non- or not-yet-assimilable, (2) the assimilated but nostalgic, and (3) the underprivileged of any variety, but there must be a definitional core to keep the term functionable.

Concepts of Culture and Differentiation

"Ethnicity" as a term defining membership in a given group – a people, a nation or even a "race" – is a differential concept denoting forms of in-group vs. out-group identification.[17] It is no less fuzzy than "culture," but as a term referring to the interface of race and culture, it is essential for the recognition of the ethnic origins of the concept of culture as it is used in the multiculturalism debate. The multiethnicity of nations such as the United States forms the core of their multiculturality. For this reason it is useful to start a discussion of the term "culture" with traditional ethnographic concepts derived from tribal societies, even though these concepts have long been superseded and are not adequate for complex modern societies,[18] and although to speak of *the* ethnographic definition of culture is an abstraction[19] and means supporting what some have called a scholarly fiction.[20] Edward B. Tylor's classic definition is still valid in the range of phenomena considered cultural (though it does not consider the fields of economy and material culture): "Culture or Civilization, taken in its wide ethnographic sense, is that complex whole which includes knowledge, belief, art, morals, law, custom, and any other capabilities and habits acquired by man as a member of a society."[21] Tylor's holistic concept implies that culture comprises every aspect of the life of a circumscribed human population that is not biologically given and that, for the individual member of this group, it is a complex of knowledge and behavior acquired by socialization defined as enculturation.

This notion of a homogeneous shared culture has been criticized as insufficient mainly in the following six respects: (1) The assumption of cultural homogeneity ignores intracultural variation such as that existing between the genders within a social community.[22] (2) It also denies the range of personal choice options for individuals even within strictly organized traditional societies.[23] Culture is never completely standardized or even conventionalized, and although the "cultural imaginary"[24] will set certain patterns even in the realm of imagination and reflection, such deterministic shaping of individual thought and action can never be complete. (3) Even tribal cultures undergo endogenic change; there is no "people without history."[25] To ascribe alteration only to influences from outside reduces major portions of humanity to the status of victims and makes change in their societies appear as exclusively destructive. (4) The classic definition excludes the aspect of intracultural power relations: there is no culture which is not characterized by asymmetrical power distribution, by open or hidden contests for definitional authority between genders, generations or classes. (5) Even traditional cultures are in a constant process of change because of their interaction with other cultures: adaptations, syncretist or hybrid mergings of traditions, or replacements of whole components of the cultural spectrum have characterized intercultural contact for thousands of years. (6) When we extend the meaning of "culture" to refer not only to ethnic but to a wide range of social groups as is the case in contemporary multiculturalist thinking, it has to be accepted that individuals belong to more than one cultural group at the same time and that their identities are shaped by such pluri-affiliations.

If we take the modifications derived from these six points into account, we arrive at a concept of culture as non-holistic group culture, with a range of applicability from the tribal through sociocultural to national and transnational group formations. It serves as a flexible frame of coherence and communication, where the central ideas and ideals of human behavior and interaction are negotiated by individuals and social (sub-)groups, although most of this happens anonymously in the manner of Foucauldian discourse formations. The range of reference for the term can and has to be extended to cover even subcultures:

> Subcultures are the meaning systems and modes of expression developed by groups in particular parts of the social structure in the course of their collective attempt to come to terms with the contradictions in their shared social situation. More particularly, subcultures represent the accumulated meanings and means of expression through which groups in subordinate structural positions have attempted to negotiate or oppose the dominant meaning system. They therefore provide a pool of available symbolic resources which particular individuals or groups can draw on in their own specific situation and construct a viable identity.[26]

Obviously, such *intracultural* differentiation can also become (or be experienced as) *intercultural*, when the set of cultural patterns selected for its demarcation is regarded as sufficiently distinctive. The term "culture" can also refer to different levels within a cultural system, from the overarching whole to partial or microcultures comprising only portions of the population. All of these levels constantly exchange cultural capital in a fluctuation that comprises not only vertical (not necessarily hierarchical) levels such as elite culture and everyday culture, but also horizontal overlappings.[27] It is possible not only for individuals but also for whole groups to belong to several "cultures" at the same time. Ideally, such a system would allow a great measure of self-regulation of social groups no matter at which level, but in practice such pluralism is often a battlefield of conflicting interests, notably not only over economic capital but also over what Pierre Bourdieu has called "social" and "symbolic capital."[28] Since communicational relations are also always relations of power, such pluralism is the contested diversity of multicultural societies.

In their effort to acquire or defend cultural capital, members of certain societies and social subgroups may posit "their" culture as authentic and continuous, however biased this perception may be, but descriptions from the outside, in the interest of a political or even a scholarly demarcation of the cultural Other, have no advantage in terms of objectivity. Acknowledging this epistemological limitation, James Clifford has drawn the most drastically constructivist conclusions:

> Cultures are not scientific "objects" (assuming such things exist, even in the natural sciences). Culture, and our views of "it," are produced historically, and are actively contested. There is no whole picture that can be "filled in" since the perception and filling of a gap lead to the awareness of other gaps.

Extending this notion from the level of observation to that of the evasive "object" itself, he continues:

> If "culture" is not an object to be described, neither is it a unified corpus of symbols and meanings that can be definitively interpreted. Culture is contested, temporal, and emergent. Representation and explanation – both by insiders and outsiders – is implicated in this emergence.[29]

To conceive of cultures as open, dynamic systems raises the question of what holds them together and what differentiates them from others. A descriptive analogy might be found in Charles Olson's adoption of the concept of the field as it is used in physics when he tried to delineate his new, postmodern "open field" poetics: the poem has an open rather than a closed form and is held together not by an outer structure but by its own dynamic field of energy.[30] What is needed, then, are core elements (such as gender relations) serving as a gravitational force recognized by the members of the group as well as by outsiders and sufficiently specific in their combination of components to mark difference from other cultures. It is essential, however, to regard cultural identity not as autochtonous, self-perpetuating, and autogenous, but as relational, produced by interaction and negotiation, by a differentiation which, in itself, takes place as an interplay of articulated self-perception and perception by the socio-cultural Other. "'Cultural' difference is no longer a stable, exotic otherness; self-other relations are matters of power and rhetoric rather than of essence. A whole structure of expectations about authenticity in culture and art is thrown in doubt."[31]

The emerging cultural diversity on the horizontal plane of transnational, national and local or subgroup formations in their intersection with the vertical levels of everyday, popular and elite culture, i.e. multiculturality as it has become an accepted albeit not consensually defined fact in contemporary nations calls for intercultural tolerance, recognition, and respect. This is what some of the papers in this volume propose. But the authors also point to difficulties arising from the heterogeneity of need: economic, political and cultural (in a narrower sense) demands cannot be met in the same way, and the specifics of each group require a wide range of possible answers. It has to be accepted that in some power contests, as in the case of land claims made by indigenous people, essentialist positions are necessary; they will be presented and defended.

There is another aspect that has to be addressed. Difference, whether defined in constructivist or in essentialist terms, can never be adequate for defining the identity positions of individuals and groups in the face of multiple affiliations, and these are particularly pressing in multicultural contexts. Beyond the differences between communities, there are those within the communities down to the level of the individual.

> At times the concept [of culture] was purely differential: cultural integrity involved recognized boundaries; it required merely an acceptance by the group and its neighbors of a meaningful difference, a we-they distinction. But what if the difference was accepted at certain times and denied at others? And what if every element in the cultural melange were combined with or borrowed from external sources?[32]

Writers have outlined the contingencies of biracial or bicultural existence.[33] Critics have responded with concepts of hybridity (mainly in postcolonial migratory contexts), *mestizaje*, transculturation. We propose another, comprehensive term, *transdifference*, which also implies a shift of emphasis away from notions of a melange in the direction of a simultaneity of – often conflicting – positions, loyalties, affiliations and participations.

Our presentation of the term transdifference proceeds in four steps. In the first section, we try to position it in the field of the current investigation of nonlinear processes and give a working definition by describing some of its core features. Next we focus on the intrasystemic level and show that phenomena of transdifference are a by-product of any construction of meaning, and that the very production and reproduction of meaning and – by extension – of a symbolic order engenders transdifference. The third section deals with intersystemic negotiations of difference, which is to say, the construction of identity and otherness along and across cultural boundaries; then we tackle the question of how cultural boundaries could be best conceived of; and finally we contrast transdifference with related concepts which address contact, conflict, exchange, translation, and borrowing between cultures and the consequences these processes entail for the conceptualization of self/other relations beyond models of cultural purity – such as hybridity, *mestizaje*, creolization, or transculturality. The concluding section seeks to delineate the term's relevance and significance for the study of intergroup relations in the contemporary American discursive space, mainly drawing on the uses transdifference can be put to by individuals with multiple affiliations and/or more than one cultural heritage in their endeavor to liberate themselves from rigid regulations of inclusion and exclusion by claiming transdifferent positionalities.

Positioning Transdifference

Heuristically speaking, transdifference is an umbrella concept that allows us to inspect phenomena that do not neatly fit models of clear-cut difference, thus defying – at least to a certain extent – explanation on the basis of binary logic. Highlighting the moments of uncertainty, indecidability, and contradiction that difference adumbrates, it enables us to discern what eludes the cognitive grasp of thinking in terms of difference. Transdifference can be seen as part of the wide range of phenomena of non-linearity that has come increasingly under investigation in recent times. In his review of Gilles Deleuze's *Différence et répétition*, Michel Foucault credits Deleuze with opening a "theater" of non-linear thinking where identity has become questionable, where analogy and identity do not serve clarity but are exposed in their function of covering up difference and the difference of differences, where repetition can be thought of as being without origin, of not referring to the return of the same. In Foucault's rewriting of the myth of Theseus and Ariadne, the latter has hanged herself, her line is broken and Theseus is free to give himself up to the non-linearity (in a double sense) of the labyrinth, to lose himself in chaos.[34] The concept of transdifference is related to such non-linearity because it interrogates categorical distinctions and either/or attributions, the difference of differences, as it were; it focuses on what lies beyond both identity and alterity. In this respect, it is relevant not only for nonlinear models of art and culture but also for theories that try to close the gap between the natural sciences and cultural studies by applying originally scientific conceptualizations such as rhizomatic networks, dissipative structures, or quantum mechanics to the cultural sphere, notably the cultural materialist approach of Gilles Deleuze and Félix Guattari and their followers.[35]

There is a specific difference between transdifference and other concepts of nonlinearity, however. While most recently developed models of networks tend to downplay or to ignore difference in their more or less wholesale rejection of structuralist thinking and their emphasis on perpetual flux, the concept of transdifference does not do away with binary logic but assumes that the construction of difference is an indispensable, yet intrinsically problematic tool for human constructions of order. This should not come as a surprise, since transdifference has to be seen as complementary to, and therefore not simply "beyond" difference. Thinking in terms of transdifference may be motivated by a deeply felt dissatisfaction with the reductiveness of binarisms coupled with a longing for the overcoming of binary thinking; it is, however, inevitably redirected towards difference.

Transdifference, as we define it, denotes all that which resists the construction of meaning based on an exclusionary and conclusional binary model.[36] While there can be no transdifference without difference – transdifference does not mean indifference –, the term refers to whatever runs "through" the line of demarcation drawn by binary difference. It does not do away with the originary binary inscription of difference, but rather causes it to oscillate. Thus, the concept of transdifference interrogates the validity of binary constructions of difference without completely deconstructing them. This means that difference is simultaneously bracketed and yet retained as a point of reference. The term transdifference refers to such areas of language, thought, and experience that are excluded by the either/or while retaining difference both in its logical and experiential aspects.

Transdifference can be seen as present in basic processes of language and thought. Thus, we regard the non-propositional reality projections engendered by "creative metaphors"[37] as instances of transdifference both on the level of experience and of expression. Just as the more extreme forms of metaphor produce "cognitive dissonance" in Leon Festinger's sense of the term ("dissonance" being defined as "nonfitting relations among cognitions"[38]) and hence psychological and rational discomfort, so do situations of transdifference in general. They require what John Keats has called "*Negative Capability*," that quality "when a man is capable of being in uncertainties, mysteries, doubts, without any irritable reaching after fact and reason."[39]

Intrasystemic Level: Transdifference and the Construction of Meaning

The concept of transdifference can not only be applied to "differences between," that is to negotiations of identities on the *intersystemic* level between cultural systems (cultures of particular groups) or psychic systems (individuals), but also to the *intrasystemic* level, that is to questions of "difference within."[40] We will refrain from commenting on phenomena of transdifference within psychic systems here and concentrate on intrasystemic phenomena of transdifference on the level of systems of meaning, which we usually refer to as "cultures."

With regard to the fundamental plane of the construction of reality, the concept of transdifference may be crucial to analyzing the precariousness of symbolic orders in general, because it enables us to describe the production and reproduction of symbolic order as a process which is dominated by pervasive attempts to "exorcize" alternative possibilities in order to fix meaning, attempts that are bound to fail, as will be shown below. The concept can thereby be helpful in unveiling the violent nature of binary logic on which symbolic order, language and identities rest. In this respect, transdifference is related to Jacques Derrida's concept of *différance*, and Gilles Deleuze's work on difference and repetition;[41] it is essential to note, however, that it differs from these approaches by not following their move towards radical deconstruction.

If meaning, according to Niklas Luhmann, serves "the reduction of world complexity" insofar as it is a selection from a vastly greater repertoire of possibilities, and if meaning thus always carries an implicit "reference to other possibilities,"[42] these other possibilities can never be completely controlled in any system of meaning. The main function of systems of meaning may thus be seen in coping with the problem of contingency. While the symbolic order of a given society may appear as natural, consistent and historically continuous from an ingroup perspective, from a second order perspective it is a historically contingent construction that owes its seemingly undisputable validity to the continuous repression of alternatives and "difference within difference." Since systems of meanings are not simply given but must constantly be reproduced through social interaction, this process of "purification," as it were, never comes to an end. A large amount of cultural energy is necessarily invested in the on-going exclusion of other possibilities for the sake of naturalizing the symbolic order, thereby reiterating incessantly what is being repressed. From a diachronic perspective, systems of meaning can therefore be aptly described as palimpsests: what has been excluded can never be erased, but only overwritten by what has been selected. The traces of the repressed are therefore present and the repressed alternatives can be recovered. Expanding the metaphor of the palimpsest in dynamic terms, we propose to call the reproduction of systems of meaning a palimpsestic *process*: in the cycles of reproduction the excluded has to be re-inscribed and overwritten again and again in order to neutralize its destabilizing threat. One could argue that this iterative moment produces transdifference, since it reintroduces world complexity by necessarily referring to other possibilities to validate its selection. To a degree, systems of meanings, or cultures, then, do not only carry suppressed seeds of transdifference within them but permanently reproduce moments of transdifference. This means that transdifference can never be completely controlled; even repressed transdifferences can be recovered from the palimpsestic cultural text in progress and can be used by individuals and/or subgroups as a starting point for interrogating the consistency and the truth claims of the symbolic order, thus serving as seeds of resistance, as it were, against rigid patterns of inclusion and exclusion and the concomitant normative pressures.

Intersystemic Level: Transdifference and the Negotiation of Identities Across Cultural Boundaries

In the context of cultural, ethnic, and territorial identity construction, transdifference refers to a wide range of phenomena arising from the multiple overlappings and mutual crosscuttings of boundaries between cultures and collective identities, no matter whether these are conceptualized in essentialist or constructivist terms. Transdifference thus refers to moments of contradiction, tension and indecidability that run counter to the logic of inclusion/exclusion. All processes of constructing and marking difference necessarily produce transdifference insofar as they, on the one hand, highlight individual aspects of the self/other relation at the expense of others and, on the other hand, stand in contradiction to various other differences along alternative lines of inclusion/exclusion. Not surprisingly, transdifference, understood as a by-product of any process of identity formation, is usually suppressed in the articulation of identities, since the function of identity and alterity must be seen precisely in the reduction of complexity for the sake of an – albeit illusionary – ontological safety of groups (and individuals) in a fundamentally contingent world. Investigating the various processes of identity formations on the levels ranging from the personal to communities to societies (or, in spatial terms, from the local to the regional, the national and the global) in light of transdifference aims at recovering the intricate interwovenness, the interrelatedness and interdependence of self and other that is being obfuscated or even obliterated in the discourses that engage in identity politics.

If we accept Fredric Jameson's dictum that culture "is not a 'substance' or a phenomenon in its own right, [but] an objective mirage that arises out of the relationship between at least two groups," "the constitutive role of the boundary"[43] becomes evident. Cultural boundaries may be conceived of in different ways: as lines of demarcation, as unbridgeable gaps, as contact zones, or as spaces in between. While the first two conceptualizations focus on cultural opposition, separation, and closure, the latter two regard boundaries as zones of interaction and interrelation in which the negotiation of identity and alterity between groups take place. In this view, a boundary is not simply the line where the inner sphere of one culture ends but also a threshold where the cultural other appears as potential interlocutor. In short, the boundary can be seen as a space of intercultural dialogue, where the images of self and other as elaborated by one group and addressed to the other meet and interact with those created by the other group. The outcome of this confrontation and contestation is very likely a "contamination" of self-produced constructs of identity and alterity with hetero-produced ones. What is reflected to the original sender from this liminal space of intercultural dialogue is not quite the same as what had been articulated in the first place, for it contains at least echoes of the other's voice. This, once again, can be seen in terms of transdifference: the originally inscribed binary difference between self and other begins to oscillate. In the space between cultures, the binary construction of self, construed as presence, and other, construed as absence, one group has elaborated meets with that of the other group, resulting in a juxtaposition of two presences and two absences, which one might call a chiastic quaternary constellation that destabilizes the respective binarisms. Let us hasten to add that to speak of two cultures interacting is a simplifying abstraction, for in reality, this negotiation of identities is even more complicated in a multicultural context, in which we have to reckon with numerous cultural articulations of cultural difference, constituting a multiple cultural dialogue.

From these considerations follows that in light of transdifference, texts of cultural identity must be seen as interdependent and interwoven texts, each bearing the mark of others, that is as intertexts. The very notion of exclusive self-representation is thrown into doubt by the realization that narrations of group identity have a dialogic quality – no matter how hard some groups try to present a bounded, authentic cultural tradition of their own in sharp contradistinction to other groups. Simply put, there can be no such thing as "pure" self-representation, no autonomous (counter-)discourse, since all narrations of identity are somehow intertwined with the narrations of other groups – in the case of a counter-discourse this will be the hegemonic discourse. Thus, the term transdifference opens up an awareness of the fact that within the US and other multicultural societies, the negotiations of cultural difference take place within a multilayered, complex frame of reference, where each attempt to establish a sharp delimitation meets with different ways of drawing the line. In being exposed to and having to respond to alternative constructions, notions of fixed cultural differences and the binary logic of "inclusion vs. exclusion," "us vs. them," "sameness and otherness," which informs these notions, get (temporarily) destabilized. Transdifference denotes this more or less fleeting moment of destabilization in the interstitial space. We call it fleeting, since transdifference is subject to being quickly subdued by the discourses of identity and power for its questioning the validity of the symbolic order on which the idea of being a distinct group as well as the established patterns of internal and external relations rest.

In what follows, we try to contrast transdifference with related concepts. In the field of contemporary Cultural Studies, a number of descriptive/interpretive terms and concepts compete in the effort to characterize the outcome of cultural interaction in the contact zones of national, ethnic, regional and local or tribal cultures: terms such as syncretism, creolization, hybridization, transculturality, *mestizaje,* or border culture foreground the dynamic aspects of exchange and change produced by the continuous circulation of people, goods, information and ideas across long established borders and boundaries. While these concepts certainly differ with regard to the questions whether (1) massive interaction and exchange between cultural traditions and currents of meaning is a fairly recent or a (trans-)historical phenomenon and whether (2) the result of this process is (or will be) the emergence of new cultural systems distinct from their two (or more) "root" cultures (and from one another), or (3) a dissolution of cultural differences and boundaries, that is, in the long run, homogenization on a global scale, they all share the basic assumption that cultures are not bounded and crystallized structures but fuzzy systems that are in a constant process of change. They all reveal that older models of culture and cultural interaction are insufficient to analyze the complex field of cultural contact and translation insofar as these models tend to foster notions of relatively stable differences between meaning systems and "culture bearing" units. While the term transdifference quite obviously shares most of these findings, it nevertheless differs in two main respects: it means neither synthesis nor radical deconstruction. It bears a strong temporal index: it refers to moments in which difference becomes temporarily unstable, or to put it metaphorically, loses its grip without vanishing into thin air. This is a far cry on the one hand from the various forms of cultural synthesis, which the terms *mestizaje*, transculturality, and creolization refer to, and on the other hand from a "complete" deconstruction of difference, which the strong concept of hybridity implies. Transdifference opens new ways of theorizing and describing from a metadiscursive perspective moments of historical rupture in narratives of identity, suppressed or camouflaged internal contradictions in systems of meaning, the heterogeneous composition of groups, the arbitrary nature of cultural boundaries and barriers as well as the impurity of putatively authentic traditions. At the same time, thinking in terms of transdifference implies that the construction of difference is indispensable not only on the empirical level of intergroup interaction. The concept enables us to study situations in which constructions of difference are interrogated but not necessarily overcome or done away with. Thus, the term may not only refer to changes induced by cultural interaction and concomitant reconfigurations of difference but also to (fleeting) constellations that either suspend established differences temporarily or bring the incompatibility of cross-cutting demarcations of difference to light. To reiterate a central feature of transdifference, there is no transdifference without difference.

Let us illustrate this general description by pointing to a few selected aspects that distinguish transdifference from other related concepts. In models of cultural melange that focus on the waning of historical cultural differences in the process of an ever increasing circulation of people, goods and ideas, the distinction between intercultural variation and intercultural difference is often dissolved in a more or less complete cultural synthesis. While this holds true for syncretism as well as for *mestizaje*, a particularly relevant case in point is Wolfgang Welsch's concept of transculturality. Referring to the overwhelming speed, that the global exchange of cultural forms and practices has recently gained, Welsch – in his fervor to repudiate all forms of cultural closure as regressive and harmful – does not stop short of claiming that intercultural difference has been transformed into intracultural diversity (which emerges by way of arranging specific elements of a supposedly globally accessible, *transcultural* repertoire of cultural forms) and concludes that there is nothing intrinsically foreign today.[44] Against such a sweeping dismissal of the intercultural, the concept of transdifference, while acknowledging that the distinction between the intracultural and the intercultural is more of a gradual than a categorical one, requires to hold to this distinction for two reasons, namely the different degrees of incommensurability involved and the problem of epistemic violence. Even if we accept that all cultures are (1) being produced and reproduced through interaction and exchange with other cultures and are (2) subject to internal differentiation and power struggles, it would be shortsighted to ignore the fact that subcultures (such as youth, gay and lesbian cultures) share the cultural register of the dominant culture to a considerably larger extent than colonized indigenous or "transplanted" cultures (such as Native American and African American cultures), which have been able to retain or to reconstruct at least some elements of their "autochthonous" cultural register against all pressures to assimilate. This difference constitutes, quite obviously, different degrees of mutual otherness and incommensurability between the respective minority culture and the dominant one. The second reason why it is imperative to keep the distinction is the problem of epistemic violence that is present both in empirical intergroup relations and in scholarly discourse on these relations. To treat groups which regard themselves as individual cultures simply as *subcultures* would obviously be an outright neocolonial act that violates their right to self-determination.

As to hybridity in its strong version, transdifference differs in that it (1) does not definitively deconstruct difference and (2) is not restricted to a specific historical-political context. Homi Bhabha's widely received theory of hybridity focuses on the impossibility of self-presence, pointing to a "third space," a "split-space" in the enunciation of identity that blocks the attempted self-identification and does away with the binary logic of Self versus Other.[45] In this respect, Bhabha's concept of hybridity, which relies heavily on Derrida's notion of *différance*, can be taken as a kind of radical deconstruction.[46] As has been said before, transdifference, depending (as it does) on difference as its complementary, cannot entail radical deconstruction. While the concept implies that pure self-representation is impossible, it does not deny the possibility of self-presence. Furthermore, it shifts the focus from the enunciation or articulation of identity to the interference of articulated identities in the space between cultures. Bhabha's theory is not universalist in a strict sense, for it arose from and is linked to the particular historical and political constellation of postcolonialism with its highly specific conditions. Transdifference, in contrast, is not restricted to such specific constellations in any comparable way, but may be applied to all situations of intercultural contact and interaction.

The Contemporary American Discursive Space and Transdifferent Positionalities

With these considerations in mind, let us now turn to the contemporary situation in the US. The entanglement of cultures yields a picture of blurred cultural boundaries. A theoretical reflection on contemporary cultural narrations of identity and alterity within the palimpsestic discursive space of America suggests that cultural interaction and exchange, different grades of mixing, partial fusions, linking and de-linking of cultural traditions are the norm. This observation does not mean, however, that cultural differences are waning in a process of homogenization, leading to a consolidation of a common national culture. Quite to the contrary, the national cultural space has to be seen as a field that is (a) itself only fuzzily delimited as it opens to various transnational connections (as can be seen in border culture, diasporic cultures, cultures of origin of immigrant groups, or the Black Atlantic), and (b) internally marked by a very complex overlaying of fuzzy cultural boundaries between ethnic groups (African Americans, Native Americans, Chicano/as, Asian Americans, or Latino/as) and sociocultural groups constituted according to gender, sexual preference, class, age, religion. This heterogeneous pattern unfolds an abundance of interstitial sites – at times multiply connected –, in which cultural difference is constantly being negotiated. This process of negotiation engenders myriad moments of transdifference – moments when the various constructions of difference that are articulated in(to) the liminal spaces between cultures intersect and mutually destabilize each other. Needless to say, these phenomena of transdifference are anathema to all programs of boundary maintenance. This refers both to the dominant group that is interested in maintaining the status quo of power relations, as well as to those minority groups that base their political claims for empowerment at least strategically on essentialist notions of group identity together with the concomitant ideas of a shared homogeneous culture and a common historical experience. Multiculturalism strengthens this resistance to the realization of transdifference. In its strong or separatist versions which insist on the incommensurability of cultural systems it is a political program that relies somewhat paradoxically on a transcultural conceptual framework, a "metaculture of difference," as Ulf Hannerz has called it,[47] which posits that cultural difference is the indispensable cornerstone of all attempts to manage intergroup relations. Adherence to this notion inevitably results in highlighting intergroup difference at the expense of realizing aspects of transdifference (both on the intercultural and the intracultural level), thus fostering received notions of a pure, bounded, and independent culture that is "possessed" by the group in question, which in turn presupposes a fixed and permanent identification by members.

These claims have recently met with resistance by quite a number of individuals, mainly intellectuals, who are supposed to be members of a minority group. Gerald Vizenor's concept of the "postindian" comes to mind, as does Guillermo Gómez-Peña's transliminal performativity.[48] Against the rigid inclusion/exclusion-binarism of filiation, a concept of primordial ties based on genealogy or "roots" that calls for an either/or decision, they insist on the free choice of (multiple) affiliations. They resist engagement in identity politics in favor of what one could call a "politics of interrogation" by highlighting the transdifferent consequences of the intersection of mutually contradictory filiations and affiliations in their subject position. Such a subject position can be seen as the nodal point in which numerous discursive subjectivations intersect, interlock, and compete. The outcome is a complex situation which is characterized by contradictions and tensions between multiple and mutually exclusive (af)filiations that the individual is unable to resolve. Needless to say, this situation engenders transdifference. The personal experience of transdifference – in the sense of belonging to different groups without feeling at home in any, or, of living in the interstices of belonging – which has long been seen as the tragic fate and the stigma of mixed bloods and marginalized individuals alike, is now being reinterpreted as an asset that bears the potential for individual liberation. Thus, formerly insulting terms such as "breed," "hybrid," or "bastard" are being positively transvalued. Against this background, relatively fixed subject positions may be opened into fluid transdifferent positionalities that allow for at least a temporary suspension of the yoke of collective calls for cultural "fidelity" and solidarity, which limit the mobility of the individual with respect to her/his choice of cultural and political affiliative practices. Articulating experiences of transdifference in the presentation of a multiple and fragmented identity may thus be seen as a striving for emancipation and individuation. Transdifferent positionalities can serve as a starting point for the construction of alliances or even "communities" on the basis of "groundless solidarity," a concept that Diane Elam described as follows:

> Groundless solidarity is the possibility of a community which is not grounded in the truth of a presocial identity. Solidarity forms the basis, although not the foundation, for political action and ethical responsibility. That is to say, groundless solidarity is a stability but not an absolute one; it can be the object of conflict and need not mean consensus. [. . .] This notion of community could not be equated with organic totality, or have a natural foundation any more than it would lay claim to absolute solidarity. The community of groundless solidarity could cross natural borders, just as it might be the meeting place for any number of different ethnicities, religious affiliations, and sexualities, for instance. Groundless solidarity, then, could be understood as a political coalition brought together on the basis of shared ethical commitments, but it would make no claim to inclusiveness.[49]

This is obviously an alluring new model for community building beyond essentialist notions, a model that does seem quite utopian – at least for the majority of our contemporaries. Given the various forms and degrees of dependence on social others one has not chosen freely, it seems reasonable to assume that the chances to articulate transdifferent positionalities are distributed in a highly asymmetrical way. The opportunity to use personal experiences of transdifference as cultural capital and to convert it into symbolic capital seems very much restricted to the fields of artistical and academic discourses, as the examples of minority intellectuals show who proclaim fluctuating positionalities in diasporic situations, border cultures, and in-between spaces as an antidote to the personally limiting and violence-engendering essentialisms that loom large in empirical interactions.

A number of the essays in this volume refer to phenomena which we would subsume under the term transdifference – phenomena belonging both to empirical group interactions and their artistic expression. However, the concept of transdifference can be applied to contexts other than those discussed in this volume. Since it is now widely understood that theorizing is always embedded in particular cultural contexts, it seems appropriate to formulate a few caveats. To the extent that all national societies are multicultural, they must obviously deal with diversity and consequently internal cultural differences to a certain degree, but the particular mechanisms of incorporation may vary in significant ways, depending both on the distinct historical experiences and on the salience of cultural diversity in contemporary public and political discourses. While our considerations may be developed into an apt analytical tool for the study of intergroup relations in the US – and their reflection in literature and other media – the application of the concept of transdifference to other societies and their respective discourses of cultural expression will demand careful differentiations and qualifications in order to avoid an uneasy scholarly universalism. We should be aware that this concept can only provide a theoretical starting point for detailed investigations into specific cultural, historical, and political contexts.

Notes

[1] A set of legal measures to create positive discrimination in the job market or in the field of educational opportunities for those underprivileged because of ethnicity, gender, etc.

[2] Wil Haygood, "A Black Writer's Journey into Poor White America," *The Boston Globe Magazine* 25 July 1999: 37.

[3] Nathan Glazer, *We Are All Multiculturalists Now* (Cambridge, MA: Harvard University Press, 1997); and Glazer's contribution to this volume under the same title, "We Are All Multiculturalists Now."

[4] David Bennett, ed., *Multicultural States: Rethinking Difference and Identity* (London and New York: Routledge, 1998) 2. The countries under discussion are: the USA, Canada, South Africa, India, Australia, New Zealand, Ireland, and the United Kingdom. "All of them are *de facto* multicultural states, some of them *de jure* multiculturalist or biculturalist."

[5] "Observations concerning the Increase of Mankind, Peopling of Countries, &c.," *The Papers of Benjamin Franklin*, vol. 4, ed. L. W. Labaree et al. (New Haven: Yale University Press) 234.

[6] For a survey of such theories and educational programs cf. Mathias Hildebrandt, *Multikulturalismus und* Political Correctness *in den USA*, forthcoming.

[7] K. Anthony Appiah, "The Multiculturalist Misunderstanding," *New York Review of Books* 9 Oct. 1997: 30.

[8] K. Anthony Appiah, "The Uncompleted Argument: DuBois and the Illusion of Race," *"Race," Writing, and Difference*, ed. Henry Louis Gates, Jr. (Chicago: University of Chicago Press, 1986) 31. Appiah relies heavily on Masatoshi Nei and Arun K. Roychoudhury, "Genetic Relationship and Evolution of Human Races," *Evolutionary Biology* 14 (1983): 1-59.

[9] Only recently has whiteness received attention as a discursive construction. Cf. for example Toni Morrison, *Playing in the Dark: Whiteness and the Literary Imagination* (New York: Random House, 1992); Ruth Frankenberg, ed., *White Women, Race Matters: The Social Construction of Whiteness* (Minneapolis: University of Minnesota Press, 1993); Mike Hill, ed., *Whiteness: A Critical Reader* (New York: New York University Press, 1997); Valerie Babb, *Whiteness Visible: The Meaning of Whiteness in American Literature and Culture* (New York: New York University Press, 1998).

[10] Appiah, "Multiculturalist Misunderstanding" 33.

11   Ibid., 30, 31.

12   Arthur M. Schlesinger, Jr., *The Disuniting of America: Reflections on a Multicultural Society* (New York: Norton, 1992).

13   Cf. Charles Taylor's communitarian critique of "difference-blind liberalism" in "Multiculturalism and the Politics of Recognition," *Multiculturalism: Examining the Politics of Recognition*, ed. Amy Gutmann (Princeton: Princeton University Press, 1994) 62, quoted in Bennett, *Multicultural States*, 8.

14   Günter H. Lenz, "Historians, Histories, and Public Cultures: Multicultural Discourses in the United States and Germany," *Transatlantic Encounters: Multiculturalism, National Identity and the Uses of the Past*, ed. Günter H. Lenz and Peter J. Ling (Amsterdam: VU University Press, 2000) 66.

15   Kwame Anthony Appiah, *Identity Against Culture: Understandings of Multiculturalism* (Berkeley: Doreen B. Center for the Humanities, 1994).

16   Lenz, "Historians, Histories, and Public Cultures," 66 f.

17   Cf. Werner Sollors, "Ethnicity," *Critical Terms for Literary Study*, ed. Frank Lentricchia and Thomas McLaughlin (Chicago: University of Chicago Press, 1990) 288-305.

18   For an extended version of the following outline discussion cf. the chapter "Kulturkonzepte" in Klaus Lösch, *Interkulturalität: Kulturtheoretische Prolegomena zum Studium der neueren indianischen Literatur Nordamerikas*, ZAA Studies (Tübingen: Stauffenburg, 2002).

19   As early as 1952 Alfred L. Kroeber and Clyde Kluckhohn listed more than 160 such definitions. Cf. *Culture: A Critical Review of Concepts and Definitions*, Papers of the Peabody Museum of American Archaeology and Ethnology 47 (Cambridge, MA: Harvard, 1952).

20   Thus Roy Wagner, *The Invention of Culture*, rev. ed. (Chicago: University of Chicago Press, 1980).

21   Edward B. Tylor, *Primitive Culture: Researches into the Development of Mythology, Philosophy, Religion, Art, and Custom*, vol. I (London: J. Murray, 1871) 1.

22   Cf. Sherry B. Ortner, "Gender Hegemonies," *Cultural Critique* 14.4 (1990): 35-80.

23   Marshall Sahlins, *Historical Metaphors and Mythical Realities: Structure in the Early History of the Sandwich Islands Kingdom* (Ann Arbor: University of Michigan Press, 1981).

24   Winfried Fluck, *Das kulturelle Imaginäre: Eine Funktionsgeschichte des amerikanischen Romans 1790-1900* (Frankfurt/M.: Suhrkamp, 1997).

25   Cf. Eric Wolf, *Europe and the People Without History* (Berkeley: University of California Press, 1982).

26   Graham Murdock, "Mass Communication and the Construction of Meaning," *Reconstructing Social Psychology*, ed. Nigel Armistead (Harmondsworth: Penguin, 1974) 213 f.

27 For a model of a heterarchically organized, fluctuating system of "trivial culture," "everyday life culture [Lebenskultur]," "elite culture" and transcultural "world culture" see Walter L. Bühl, "Kultur als System," *Kultur und Gesellschaft: Kölner Zeitschrift für Soziologie und Sozialpsychologie*, Sonderheft 27, ed. Friedrich Neidhardt et al. (Opladen: Westdeutscher Verlag, 1986) 118-44.

28 Cf. Pierre Bourdieu, "The Forms of Capital," *Handbook of Theory and Research for the Sociology of Education,* ed. John G. Richardson (New York: Greenwood Press, 1986) 241-58; and *Distinction: A Social Judgement of Taste*, trans. Richard Nice (Cambridge, MA: Harvard University Press, 1984).

29 James Clifford, "Introduction: Partial Truths," *Writing Culture: The Poetics and Politics of Ethnography*, ed. James Clifford and George E. Marcus (Berkeley: University of California Press, 1986) 18, 19.

30 Charles Olson, "Projective Verse," *Selected Writings*, ed. Robert Creeley (New York: New Directions, 1966) 15-26.

31 James Clifford, *The Predicament of Culture: Twentieth-Century Ethnography, Literature, and Art* (Cambridge, MA: Harvard University Press, 1988) 14.

32 Ibid., 323.

33 Claudine Chiawei O'Hearn, ed., *Half and Half: Writers on Growing Up Biracial and Bicultural* (New York: Pantheon Books, 1998).

34 Michel Foucault, "Ariane s'est pendue," *Le Nouvel Observateur* 229 (1969). The small volume of exchanges between the two French thinkers, Gilles Deleuze/Michel Foucault, *Der Faden ist gerissen*, trans. Walter Seitter and Ulrich Raulf (Berlin: Merve, 1977), contains a German translation of this review and other relevant texts. Further essays referring to the metaphor of the broken line and non-linearity in the arts, literature and science can be found in a special issue of *Kunstforum* 155 (June/July 2001), *Der gerissene Faden: Nichtlineare Techniken in der Kunst*, ed. Thomas Wulffen.

35 The key text is Gilles Deleuze and Félix Guattari, *Mille plateaux: Capitalisme et Schizophrénie*, 1980; English version: *A Thousand Plateaus: Capitalism and Schizophrenia*, trans. Brian Massumi (Minneapolis: University of Minnesota Press, 1987).

36 In this sense, it forms one of the key concepts under investigation in the current multidisciplinary doctoral program (*Graduiertenkolleg*) on "Cultural Hermeneutics: Perspectives of Difference and Transdifference" at Erlangen University.

37 Recent theories of the metaphor provide interesting discussions of such basic schemata; see, for instance, Mark Johnson, *The Body and the Mind: The Bodily Basis of Meaning, Imagination, and Reason* (Chicago: University of Chicago Press, 1987).

38 Leon Festinger, *A Theory of Cognitive Dissonance* (Stanford: Stanford UP, 1957, reissued 1962) 3.

39 John Keats, "Letter to George and Thomas Keats," 28 December 1817, *The Complete Works of John Keats*, ed. H. Buxton Forman, vol. IV (New York: Thomas Y. Crowell & Co., n.d.) 50.

40 Rosi Braidotti uses the terms "difference between" and "difference within" in her discussion of subject positions and feminist alliances; cf. *Nomadic Subjects: Embodiment and Sexual Difference in Contemporary Feminist Theory* (New York: Columbia University Press, 1994), 158-67, 177-9.

41 See Jacques Derrida, "La différance," *Margins of Philosophy*, trans. Alan Bass (Chicago: University of Chicago Press, 1982) 1-27; and Gilles Deleuze, *Différence et répétition*, 1968; English version: *Difference and Repetition*, trans. Paul Patton (London: Athlone Press, 1994).

42 Cf. Niklas Luhmann, *Soziologische Aufklärung: Aufsätze zur Theorie sozialer Systeme*, vol. 1 (Opladen: Westdeutscher Verlag, 1970) 116, our translation.

43 Fredric Jameson, "On 'Cultural Studies,'" *Social Text* 34.1 (1993): 17-52, here 33.

44 Wolfgang Welsch, "Transkulturalität: Zur veränderten Verfassung heutiger Kulturen," *Hybridkultur: Medien, Netze, Künste*, ed. I. Schneider and C.W. Thompson (Köln: Wienand, 1997) 67-90; a version of this essay appeared in English under the title "Transculturality: The Puzzling Form of Cultures Today," *California Sociologist* 17/18 (1994/95): 19-39.

45 Cf. Homi K. Bhabha, *The Location of Culture* (London and New York: Routledge, 1994) 219: "What is at issue is the performative nature of differential identities: the regulation and negotiation of those spaces that are continually, *contingently*, 'opening out,' remaking boundaries, exposing the limits of any claim to a singular or autonomous sign of difference."

46 See Harald Zapf, *Dekonstruktion des Reinen: Hybridität und ihre Manifestationen im Werk von Ishmael Reed* (Würzburg: Königshausen & Neumann, 2002).

47 Ulf Hannerz, *Transnational Connections: Culture, People, Places* (London and New York: Routledge, 1996) 50.

48 Cf. Gerald Vizenor, *Manifest Manners: Postindian Warriors of Survivance* (Hanover: Wesleyan University Press, 1994) and Guillermo Gómez-Peña, *The New World Border: Prophecies, Poems and Loqueras for the End of the Century* (San Francisco: City Lights, 1996).

49 Diane Elam, *Feminism and Deconstruction* (London and New York: Routledge, 1994) 109.

We Are All Multiculturalists Now

Nathan Glazer

A few years ago I published a book with the title, *We Are All Multiculturalists Now*.[1] This paper is not a reprise of the book and its contents, but a further discussion of some of the puzzles that the word "multiculturalism" and the various realities it refers to present to us. The title of that book was an ironic one, and in the epigraph to the book I referred to two well-known uses of the formulation, "we are all [something] now." In late 19th century England, a Chancellor of the Exchequer, who had been fighting for a small duty on estates at death, against the fierce opposition of the landed classes and the gentry, is said to have remarked, responding to those who were denouncing him for undermining British society, "we are all socialists now." And Richard Nixon, President of the United States in the early 1970's, is said to have remarked, when he was forced in an economic downturn to accept Keynesian measures, "we are all Keynesians now." The formulation bears a complex triple meaning. It tells us first that the person using this locution is announcing that something has indeed changed, and that we have adopted a policy or position that we opposed in the past. Then there is a second meaning communicated by the rather resigned tone of this expression: We are not very happy about the new policy or position but we have no alternative. But then there is a third implication. something like a wink, which says, we are not *really* socialists or Keynesians – or multiculturalists. At least, we have not whole-heartedly adopted the new position.

That was my message in using this title. The formulation I used gave hostile reviewers an easy opening for a response: "Not me," some said, or "not yet." Most of the reviewers were indeed hostile, because most of those who write about multiculturalism are critical of it. Most of the books dealing with multiculturalism in the United States have been hostile to its development. The best known book on multiculturalism in the United States is probably the work of the distinguished American historian, Arthur Schlesinger, Jr., titled the *Disuniting of America*.[2] This theme –

"America is coming apart because of multiculturalism" – has been repeated in many other book titles. Robert Hughes has written *The Fraying of America*.[3] John Miller has written *The Unmaking of Americans*.[4] Todd Gitlin has written *The Twilight of Common Dreams*.[5] Peter Salins has written *Assimilation: American Style*.[6] All argue against multiculturalism. Lawrence Levine's *The Opening of the American Mind* is the only significant book by a leading American historian or intellectual supporting it.[7] Journalists, historians, sociologists, are all concerned, as these book titles indicate, that one of America's great successes – the molding of a common and united nation out of many ethnic strands – is being undermined by the rise of multiculturalism.

The term, and the reality, is everywhere. A new term, "diversity," has in the past few years arisen to replace in many contexts the somewhat too provocative "multiculturalism," but it refers to very much the same thing. I will say something later about the implications of the milder term "diversity." But the use of the new term has not changed the ever-present reality of the widespread sense that there has been a big change in the United States. We have always had groups of different race, ethnicity, culture, but these were all expected to merge into a common American people. The various ethnic groups and nonwhite races were subordinate socially, for a long time politically too, and accepted their subordination. Today each demands respect and the acknowledgment of its presence as a fully-accepted part of the American people, American society, American polity. They demand this acceptance even if their culture, which may be different in some respects from the majority culture, is retained. The assumption behind the claim to multicultural equality is not that differences will merge and disappear, but that they will continue, and continue with some degree of public support.

The argument is not over political acceptance as Americans, that is, formal political equality – as immigrants, as citizens, as a full part of the American people – of persons of any ethnic group or race. The argument is over what that full acceptance implies on the part of the new entrant into American society. It is clear there is a widespread feeling among many – as the titles of the books I have referred to indicate – that the terms of the bargain involved in becoming an American have changed, and changed for the worse from the point of view of American unity. The contrast is sharpest with the America of the 1950's and before when it was taken for granted that the aim of all the sub-groups of the United States was to become American like the Americans who had preceded them, with their distinctiveness, if any remained, to be reduced to a matter of merely private interest that deserved no public acknowledgement. That arrangement can be illustrated by some remarks of former President Theodore Roosevelt, who – like almost all American Presidents – was a friend of immigration. During World War I, and before American entry, he was alarmed by strong national sentiments among immigrants, favoring their home countries. He insisted that the immigrants should assimilate, in language and in loyalty. "We believe," he wrote, "that English and no other language is that in which all school exercises should be conducted [. . .]. We have no room in a healthy American community for a German-American vote or an Irish-American vote [. . .]."[8]

No American President or statesman would speak that forcefully today. He would at the least recognize the contribution of all groups to the making of America, though he might remain silent on the continuity of language, culture, and loyalty. Today in many states children have a right to be educated in a foreign language, if that is the language of their home, for a few years. In many cases this education in a non-English language is extended far beyond the time it would be necessary to learn English. Education in one's home language in public schools commonly includes instruction in the culture and history of the country from which the children came, designed to maintain pride in that cultural background. The idea that background should simply be ignored – as it was in the education for Americanization of immigrants that prevailed until the 1960's – would be unacceptable to teachers and administrators. The cultural background of immigrant children is today acknowledged, and praised.

Multiculturalism or diversity crops up everywhere in the United States today. Every corporate training program includes something on "diversity," every entering college class will be instructed in "diversity," every college has a director of multiculturalism or diversity, every political campaign tries to appeal to various diverse groups, every public program has to take "diversity" into account. The difficult point about both multiculturalism and diversity is that they go beyond any simple concern with discrimination and prejudice. They do not imply simple fairness or nondiscrimination for the individual. What makes them provocative is first an emphasis on celebration of the various cultures and diverse groups: They are a benefit to America, they add to its strength, and thus they must be positively acknowledged or embraced. And second, which is the most provocative aspect, they imply necessarily a sharp criticism of the America of the past and its practices, the America which assumed, as in the quotation from Theodore Roosevelt, the necessity or desirability of the abandonment of culture and language and loyalty.

I will take up three questions about multiculturalism in this discussion. The first is, why has this change occurred? The second: Why is it so successful in one of the key areas of American society for assimilation and acculturation, the public schools, despite the sharp criticism of multiculturalism by the greater part of the American intellectual elite? The third is, what does multiculturalism portend for the America of the future? Must we expect the disuniting, the unravelling, the fraying, the twilight of common dreams, that so many book titles alarmingly announce? I will also add some remarks on why we see something like multiculturalism begin to take hold and become an issue in the rather different circumstances of Europe. All of these are large and difficult questions, and it is clear my answers will be tentative. We will undoubtedly be learning much more about these questions in the next few years.

To the first: Why multiculturalism now? The 1990's have been the big decade of multiculturalism. If one reviews books, articles, references in newspapers, as one can with contemporary electronic sources, one will be surprised to find almost no references to the term before the 1990's. Then there was a remarkable upsurge in the use of the term "multiculturalism," and in conflicts, primarily in public schools and colleges, over "multiculturalism." There has been a recent lull in conflicts, and concurrent decline in the use of the term, as "diversity" has replaced it. There is one simple and widespread answer to the question why this change has occurred, but I think it is wrong. The simple answer is that the expansion of immigration to the United States, an expansion which has been steady since the end of World War II, and the broadening of the sources of immigration from Europe to Asia and Latin America, has caused this change. America has in fact become more diverse. Because it has become more diverse, we have seen the rise of multiculturalism.

What has happened in immigration – the increase in volume, and the shift in sources – is indeed terribly important. To describe what has happened in American immigration briefly: For forty years, from the passage of immigration restriction legislation in the mid 1920's, to the passage of new legislation eliminating ethnic and racial restrictions in immigration in 1965, the United States was not a country of major immigration. During this forty-year period, majority public sentiment was against any substantial reduction in the barriers to immigration. So for 40 years, one can say, the mantra that the United States is a country of immigration was not true. Immigration resumed modestly after World War II, and increased substantially after the change in immigration law in 1965. But more important than the increase in numbers – which in the nineties has reached a million immigrants a year – has been the change in the sources of immigration. Until the 1970's, immigration was overwhelmingly European; since the 1970's, it has been overwhelmingly Latin American or Latino, Asian, and Caribbean. With this shift of sources, immigration has changed from overwhelmingly white to overwhelmingly nonwhite.

Because America has changed in its ethnic and racial composition, and the number of non-Europeans has increased substantially, it is believed, we have multiculturalism as a response. This is too easy an answer: There was a much greater volume of immigration in the early part of the century of groups that were considered as foreign and distant to most Americans then as the immigrants of today appear now. But that led to no multiculturalism. On the contrary it led to an increased emphasis on the need to assimilate and Americanize the new immigrants. Something else has happened to make Americanization or assimilation unfashionable.

I believe two changes have been crucial, one easily visible and whose significance is undoubted, the second murkier. The first change is the rise in the public sphere of the significance of the race issue, that is, the condition of American blacks, African Americans. Blacks – they were then called the colored or Negroes – played almost no role in the argument over immigration in the first two decades of this century, though we know they were severely affected by immigrant competition. Indeed, they played no role in any major public issue. They could not vote in the South, and in the North they were few. Basically blacks were disfranchised and were ignored in public policy. Their leaders demanded equal rights with all other Americans, but those equal rights they demanded were primarily political and social, and did not extend to equal rights for black culture. Indeed, the leaders of the civil rights movement did not think much about black culture until the 1970's. In the heat of the struggle for equal rights, they could not think much about what would happen after, and insofar as they did think about it, they were assimilationist: Blacks with equal rights would be Americans like all other Americans. One can find in the history of the black struggle for equal rights little emphasis on, or any reference to, black culture or black distinctiveness. The references were all to equal rights, the same rights white Americans possessed.

But no great struggle takes the shape that its leaders and proponents expect. As the struggle for equal rights grew and expanded to become a major American domestic issue in the 1960's, other issues came up to reshape that struggle. First and most markedly there was the demand for "black power" – the right of blacks to run their own communities, including most prominently, their schools – and then the emphasis on black cultural distinctiveness, epitomized in the slogan "black pride."

Changes in the character and goals of America's largest minority have often been marked by a change of name. The "colored" people of the earlier part of the century became the Negro in the 1930's. In the 1960's, under the impact of the "black power" movement, they became "blacks." Today, under the impact of the demand for group pride and vigor accentuation of group cultural distinctiveness and achievement, they have become "African Americans," which is now perhaps the favored term for a group which has borne so many names.

I believe one cannot overestimate the role of the civil rights movement and the rise to a substantial degree of political and social influence of the black population in creating the present favoring atmosphere for multiculturalism and diversity in the United States. It was under the impact of the success of the civil rights movement in the 1960's and 1970's that social science textbooks began to include more and more about blacks, and that hundreds of colleges and universities introduced "black studies" centers and departments. This development spread to include other groups. Hispanic Americans or Latinos, various Asian groups, American Indians or native Americans, became in various degrees the beneficiaries (if benefit it is) of such developments emphasizing group pride and group culture too. But it is not among these groups, and for these groups, that the change from assimilation to multiculturalism began. Nor were they the strongest advocates of this change. It was paradoxically a group that has been part of the American population and society since its origins that became the leading force in introducing multiculturalism into American school curricula, not the new immigrants of the 1970's and 1980's.

The advocates of multiculturalism claim that all these groups are different from the dominant culture of the United States, which they characterize as Anglo-American, and deserve recognition and respect. But the differences among these groups are profound, and they are by no means uniform in their advocacy of multiculturalism. Asians, it is clear, would be quite happy with the traditional arrangement, in which newcomers were expected to assimilate and to reserve their distinctive cultural interests and concerns for the private, non-governmental sphere. Hispanics are so diverse in their national backgrounds that there is no common stand on these issues, and in each group there is also divergence between ethnic militants and nationalists and assimilationists. Mexican-Americans and Puerto Ricans come closest to African Americans in the vigor of their demands for multiculturalism, but even among these there is substantial divergence. American Indians are in a class by themselves, not only because they are by far the smallest of the so-called "minorities," but because of their very distinctive history as the aboriginal people of the United States. They have territories of their own, which they control, and institutions receiving public support, which they control too. They now have the odd benefit of being able, legally, to open gambling casinos on their reservation lands, which has made some tribes rich.

The fact is the first multicultural demands came from, and for, African Americans. There were then imitative developments among other minority ethnic groups. But their grievances were not as deep, their culture not as deeply rooted in American life, their history not as significant for the development of the United States. One could make black culture and history central for a curriculum in literature or the social studies. One could not do the same for other minorities. (It would take me too far afield to explain why certain groups in the United States are considered "minorities," and others not, and why some groups change their status, so that Jews, for example, are no longer considered a "minority.")

But this great change in how Americans were to be educated and view themselves required the acquiescence of the majority population, and it is this that must also be explained. What had happened to the point of view of Theodore Roosevelt and other American nationalists? Why did so many waver in their commitment to the Americanizing or assimilating project?

Here one must add to the equation the great cultural change that took place in the United States in the course of the 1960's and 1970's. The reasons for this change would be impossible to specify to general satisfaction, but change there was, and its overall consequence was that self-confidence about American values, American strength, American justice and rightness, weakened. Whether it was the assassination of national leaders, or the difficulties and eventual loss of the war in Vietnam, or the rise of Japanese and European economic competitiveness, or the increasingly successful challenge to Puritan values, or the growing awareness of the indignities to which the black population had been subjected throughout American history, for many reasons the brash self-confidence that America was the best as well as the strongest society wavered. There was a great increase in tolerance generally, for other points of view, other kinds of behavior, other values, but this increase was not based only on generosity, but on uncertainty about the goodness and justice of American culture and power. The uncertainty affected judgment as to how America had behaved, at home and abroad, and spread to how we understood the American past too. Questions were raised that had been discussed in the past but had not gotten great attention. Had America successfully incorporated other groups or simply suppressed them? Had its founding principles been hypocritical? Were we an ever-improving and ever-inclusive society, as the official understanding had it, or a society that in its arrogance had not recognized the cultural rights of others?

The sharp entry into American public life of our (until then) largest minority, which had so long been in so many respects invisible, combined with the weakening of American self-confidence, seem to me the best explanation of the explosion of multiculturalism. One may ask why multiculturalism became much more of an issue in the nineties than it had been in the seventies and eighties, and ask what was special about the nineties? I would make two comments in response to this point. First, multiculturalism was indeed spreading in the seventies and eighties – one could see it most markedly in the curricula of the public schools, and in the colleges and universities. There was simply less public notice of it, and less public conflict over it. Second, there was a steady increase in black frustration during the eighties, as the economic and educational progress of the earlier two decades stalled. This gave additional force to their multiculturalist demands: If blacks could not make it in the existing system, black leaders and educationists asserted, it was because their culture was not recognized, and one route to greater advance was a wider recognition of the importance and distinctiveness of black history, black literature, black culture, and the incorporation of black themes into the American mainstream.

From the point of view of culture, this has been the major change introduced by multiculturalism. Black culture is now mainstream culture. This is not true for the culture of the other minorities, even though they now receive a much greater degree of attention in higher education. But the products of Hispanic or Latino or Asian-American culture remain marginal for American culture generally. There are no canonical works, as there are for black culture, where the autobiography of Frederick Douglass is as important possibly as the autobiography of Benjamin Franklin, where W. E. B. DuBois' *The Souls of Black Folk* is an American Classic, where Ralph Ellison's *Invisible Man* stands as high as any novel of the time, and where all are read as widely in American colleges as any equivalent achievements of white America. The programs and achievements of other minority groups are anemic compared to what we have seen in black culture – in music, the novel, drama, poetry.

Our second question: The greatest success of multiculturalism has been in the public schools and in the colleges and universities. In the former, the teaching of social studies and history and literature has been transformed, despite the best efforts of the critics, and multiculturalism is fully established. In the colleges and universities, we find many programs in African American studies, special orientations for entering students on multiculturalism and diversity, special officers in charge of multiculturalism and diversity, required courses in many institutions that every student must take that introduce students to multiculturalism and diversity, and physically there are theme houses and centers on many campuses for African American and other minority students. How do we explain this distinctive success, particularly in the light of the fact that the American intellectual elite, if judged by writings and positions taken, is skeptical or opposed to this development?

Multiculturalism has been denounced regularly all through the nineties. It is hard to see much evidence that this denunciation has affected its strong presence in public school curricula and in colleges and universities, though there may be some reversal. (One of the red flags to critics of multiculturalism was the assertion, in the social studies curriculum for New York State, that the American Indian Iroquois confederation influenced the framers of the American constitution. This has been dropped in a revision proposed in 1998; but in other respects there is no weakening of the elements in the curriculum that arouse the anger of the critics of multiculturalism.[9])

One of the most surprising examples of stubborn multicultural advance in the face of dominant elite opposition has been the case of the "national history standards," standards for teaching in elementary and high schools in history that were created by a national group of historians and educators set up by government grant. The chief Federal official in charge of giving out this grant, Lynne Cheney, director of the National Endowment for the Humanities, is a conservative, and one would have expected she would have taken every caution to control multicultural excesses. Yet when the standards were published, they pushed multiculturalism further, and were denounced by Lynne Cheney, by the United States Senate, and by many leading historians. So they were revised. But even as revised, they were not very different, and the director of the National Endowment for the Humanities wrote a book denouncing the standards that her organization had helped create.[10]

The great success of multiculturalism in the public schools and colleges and universities is an anomaly, since it is there that one would expect the strong intellectual and elite opposition to multiculturalism would be most effective. But it is not. I believe what has happened in the public schools and the colleges and the universities requires somewhat different explanations. In the public schools, the most powerful forces for multiculturalism are the schools of education, the state departments of education, and the professionals who run the local school systems. State legislators are not for the most part advocates of multiculturalism, parents are for the most part no great advocates, the major newspapers and media have been critics of multiculturalism, and as I have indicated elite opinion is not friendly. But as against all these, the culture of the schools of education, affecting state and local school administrators has been more powerful. It may not have skillful and brilliant public advocates, and it has no one who can stand for example against Arthur Schlesinger, but it has the possession of the institutions in which the high professionals of education are shaped.

But why has multiculturalism established itself so solidly in the graduate schools of education? The main reason is that these are linked to a failing institution, the public schools, and thus they seek everywhere for the new approaches that will overcome its failures. The failure is most marked in the big city schools, where the majority of students are black or Hispanic. It seems reasonable to conclude, in view of the strong politically liberal orientation of educators and school of education professors, that some form of education appealing distinctively to these students may be more effective than what has been attempted in the past. Multiculturalism in the public schools is the product of this middle stratum of professionals, state education departments and local school system administrators. It is not the product of the elected boards of citizens, who are supposed to have the ultimate authority in running school systems. They go along with the professionals. It does not come from the judgment of teachers, though many may agree that multicultural emphases may be more effective with their minority students. This professional judgment then affects the national textbook producers, who introduce the new multicultural emphases in their texts, it makes its appearance in the tests that states create for students to judge their achievement, in effect the new emphasis becomes thoroughly established, and militants from the minority communities – not necessarily the majority in these communities – fight to defend and expand these emphases.

In the colleges and universities, something similar has happened. The main supporters of multiculturalism and diversity are the administrators, the college presidents and their staffs. They are uniformly supporters of multiculturalism and diversity. One will find no voice of dissent among 3000 college presidents. The alumni, who are important in raising money and getting political support for colleges and universities, are no friends of multiculturalism. The trustees, who formally have the ultimate power in running colleges and universities, are no great advocates of multiculturalism, but will accept the judgment of their appointed president. The faculties go along with the actions of their presidents and administrators rather than support them. There are many dissidents among them, but they tend to keep their doubts to themselves. After all, many fields – such as the sciences and engineering, business administration, economics – are not affected by multiculturalism. Among the students, one finds strong support among militant students among the minorities. The militant students may not represent the majority, but the majority will not oppose them.

But then why do the administrators generally support multiculturalism? One explanation is their fear of disruption from militant students, and there have been many disruptions, as these occupy administrative offices and demand more multicultural programs and courses. (Generally their major demand is for more minority students.) One may add a more generous interpretation: Leaders of institutions such as universities have an important national role, they have to look to more than the interests of their current faculty and the current fields of teaching and research. They see the country changing, and they feel they should change in response, particularly if they are given a push. But one must also add the effects of the change overall in the culture: The loss of self-confidence generally among Americans about their country and its culture spreads to the leaders of specific institutions, and they become less firm in their commitment to an established and traditional curriculum. So administrators may be more willing for example to consider a required course that will teach the students about America's diversity than faculty. But in the end it is faculty who will have to agree to give such courses, so one should perhaps not make too much of the differences between administrators and faculty when it comes to multiculturalism.

Here it is necessary to say something about administrators' support for diversity, which is stronger and firmer than their support for multiculturalism. When it comes to the latter, administrators are pushed; when it comes to the former, they lead. But just what is the distinction between multiculturalism and diversity? I have said earlier that the term diversity increasingly replaces muiticulturalism because it is a milder and less provocative term, but its implications are also somewhat different. There is an overlap: Commitment to diversity as well as to multiculturalism will take the form of appreciation for and advocacy of a larger role for the culture of minorities. But there are two other elements in diversity that do not play as large a role in multiculturalism. One is concern for good relations among the various groups. Multiculturalism suggests that these relations may improve as the majority learns more about the minorities, develops some appreciation for their achievement and culture. But the advocate of multiculturalism is as likely to expect that emphasis on minority culture will occasion conflict rather than understanding. Diversity is softer: It does not direct us to expect conflict but rather appreciation, understanding, better relations. Diversity programs, as in colleges and in corporations, will seek for this directly, using various approaches designed to increase understanding and rapport among groups. The difference in nuance is that multiculturalism implies appreciation for minorities because their culture is worthy; diversity implies appreciation because they are human, just like everyone else.

And yet a second difference in the nuances suggested by the two terms: Diversity becomes a euphemism for preferential admissions and racial selectivity in admissions and in faculty appointments. Multiculturalism directs us more to culture and less to representation, more to justice and less to good relations.

Perhaps I make too much of the difference, but I think not. And in a national mood of self-doubt and unwillingness to judge, the America described in Alan Wolfe's *One Nation, After All*,[11] diversity makes a stronger appeal than multiculturalism. It is a kinder term. It suggests to us that America has become more and more inclusive, rather than reminding us of the exclusivities that we took for granted in the past.

We come to the third question: And what does it mean for America? What does it mean for the undoubted success in forging a common nation of many strands? I believe that process continues, but by other means than in the past. The alarm over multiculturalism raises the specters of Lebanon, Yugoslavia, Canada. These are, as most recognize, inappropriate parallels and extreme scenarios for the United States. Minorities in the United States have no territorial base, despite the concentration of African Americans in the South, Mexican Americans in the Southwest, Cubans in Florida, etc. Their demands are less for the conditions that will permit a vibrant and whole culture to thrive than for recognition of the modest symbols of difference they wish to maintain. There is no language base for a separate culture for minority groups in the United States. The argument over whether the Latinos should retain Spanish and whether the schools should help them to do so is conducted in English, on both sides. The dominance of English is unchallenged. The only effect of the bilingual programs that maintain Spanish beyond its natural life in children living in an English environment is probably to hamper their incorporation into the economy and their involvement in other sectors of American society. But it cannot create a separate people.

Clearly multiculturalism has created a stronger sense among African Americans of difference, and the legitimacy of difference. But the content of that difference consists of preferences in music and in forms of social intercourse, a pride in blacks who achieve in various spheres, and a fierce and deep concern – I cannot call it obsessive, though others will think it so – with the details of their history and all they have suffered in America. I do not think multiculturalism will do anything near as much in maintaining a sense of different identity, divorced from the mainstream, among Latinos or Asian Americans. Their sense of difference is more closely related to what the European ethnic groups feel than what African Americans feel: And it is inevitable it should be so. For them, America is still, for the most part, a land of greater opportunity, a chance for a better life, voluntarily chosen. For blacks, the matter is quite different. I need not rehearse the differences – slavery, the Civil War, segregation, civil rights – but they have created a history that we simply cannot yet put behind us and which raises every day questions as to whether we can fully incorporate blacks into American society. For blacks, multiculturalism, whether they embrace it or reject it, has to be an issue of much greater magnitude than for other groups, and it is.

The forms of becoming American are changing, and the forms that define the good American are changing. They are less exclusive than they were in the past, not only in how we understand what is American in culture, but in other respects too. Consider that we are more tolerant of dual citizenship than we were in the past. The whole sense of nationality is becoming looser. I cannot regret the change: Consider the change in rhetoric from the days of Theodore Roosevelt to Ronald Reagan; or from John F. Kennedy to Bill Clinton. I cannot consider it all loss.

How does all this connect with Europe? Europe does not have the history of a permanent, subordinated minority that we have in the United States. It also does not have a history of a displaced aboriginal people. There are in European countries regional differences, language differences, and now, after the postwar immigration from Turkey and North Africa, Europe has new non-European minorities of religion and culture far from those native to Europe. Thus the issue of "multiculturalism" comes up in Europe too. I know there are difficult problems that arise here in schooling, in public acknowledgement of religion, in citizenship. But there is nothing here like the situation of African Americans in the United States, with a near-400 year history of slavery and subordination, followed by a great national effort to achieve equality. This has to make multiculturalism a more serious matter for the United States than for Europe.

On both sides of the Atlantic one senses the decline of a self-confident exclusiveness in identity, and one sees the weakening of strong national identities and commitments in the face of the rise of a federated Europe. But another force also is weakening old identities and commitments, that is, classic nationalism, and this is the ever-broader acknowledgement of the claim of all peoples and individuals to equal respect. Assimilation goes on, but less by means of directed public action than by the powerful undirected forces of the culture and the mass media. The forces of equality have been in the saddle for 200 years, ever broadening in scope and implications. Equality within nations now spreads to demand some degree of equality among nations, and equality among those who live within common borders, whatever their differences in race, religion, language, ethnicity.

The powerful march of equality now demands respect and acknowledgement of minority cultures and the people who bear them. We cannot any longer assume the superiority, in Europe or the United States, of the dominant ethnic groups that have defined our nations, and we will both have to live with the consequences this new diversity entails.

Notes

[1] Nathan Glazer, *We Are All Multiculturalists Now* (Cambridge, MA: Harvard University Press, 1997).

[2] Arthur Schlesinger, Jr., *The Disuniting of America: Reflections on a Multicultural Society* (New York: Norton, 1992).

[3] Robert Hughes, *Culture of Complaint: The Fraying of America* (Oxford: Oxford University Press, 1993).

[4] John J. Miller, *The Unmaking of Americans: How Multiculturalism Has Undermined the Assimilation Ethic* (New York: Simon & Schuster, 1998).

[5] Todd Gitlin, *The Twilight of Common Dreams: Why America is Wracked by Culture Wars* (New York: Owl Paperback/Henry Holt, 1996).

[6] Peter Salins, *Assimilation: American Style* (New York: Basic Books, 1997).

[7] Lawrence Levine, *The Opening of the American Mind* (Boston: Beacon Press 1996).

[8] Quoted in David Brooks,"Bully for America," *The Weekly Standard* 23 June 1997: 16-7.

[9] See *Wall Street Journal* 17 Nov. 1998: editorial page.

[10] I discuss this story in more detail in *We Are All Multiculturalists Now* 67-9.

[11] Alan Wolfe, *One Nation, After All: What Middle-Class Americans Really Think About God, Country, Family, Racism, Welfare, Immigration, Homosexuality, Work, The Right, The Left, and Each Other* (New York: Viking Press, 1998).

On Cultural Respect*

Homi K. Bhabha

One of the most common self-descriptions of the contemporary world is to say that we are part of the "global" condition. Advances in digital technologies, the creations of cyberspace, and the international division of labor go some way towards suggesting that we are members of a brave new global world. But the global world still seems full of anxious apprehensions from the local communities that we inhabit. For as we reach out to touch the new geo-political surfaces and cultural circumferences that are offered to us through the rhetoric of the "global" we often lose a tangible connection, and are thrown back, willy-nilly, on cultivating a national perspective in the most effective areas of our lives. This does not mean that we should be luddites, and fail to see what is opening up before us – a world of more complex boundaries, where we are forced to stretch our social and historical imaginations beyond what we can readily visualize or experience. As we make our global leap – a leap in technology as well as human faith – we must be aware of that early form of globalization that we have known for the last two hundred and fifty years as the history of imperialism and neo-colonialism. Can the inequalities of power and wealth between First and Third Worlds, the North and the South within the "west" itself, allow us to celebrate the global *as if we are all participants in the same local festival?* The human family still has its poor relatives, its stepchildren, its orphans. What these ambiguities in the global condition produce are profound anxieties about the way in which we see ourselves as part of a "shared" history of human civilization and barbarism – now, sometimes, called multiculturalism. Can there ever be "one" of us, when the "Other" stands, *beside* one-self, as the (un)acknowledged double – the living shadow of the stereotype – in a "proximity, beyond intentionality, [which] is the relationship with the neighbor in the moral sense of the term."[1]

It is *of* the proximity of the neighbor "in the moral sense of the term" that I want to speak today. Who is one of us, in the midst of that jurisdictional unsettlement that accompanies the condition of migration, the existence of minoritization, the clamor of multiculturalism? Let me begin, anachronistically, in a time-lag, by returning to Joseph Conrad's *Lord Jim* where the colonial and postcolonial worlds become neighbors to each other, in a profound questioning of the ethicality and the narrativity of "home."

It could have been you or me – any one of us – caught in the failures of fellowship, the fragility of friendship, the betrayal of a code, or the shadow of shame and seduction. Any one of us caught, as was Jim, in that moment when, as Joseph Conrad describes it, choice "was not a lie – but it wasn't the truth all the same [. . .]. There was not the thickness of a sheet of paper between the right and wrong of this affair."[2] What does it mean, in such straitened circumstances, to be "one of us?" This is a question that Conrad asks repeatedly across the range of his fiction, tracking the lives of those – like ourselves, almost a hundred years later – who inhabit the shadows of those places where, as Marlow speaks, "light (and even electric light) had been carried [. . .] for the sake of better morality and – and – well – the greater profit too."[3] To ask who is one of us, of whom or what can we now speak as "one," is to enter something infinitely more complex and crepuscular than the "heart of darkness"; it is to emerge in a kind of "jurisdictional unsettlement" at the very threshold of "home." Listen to Conrad:

> I was going home, and he had come to me from there, with his miserable trouble and his shadowy claim, like a man panting under a burden in a mist. I cannot say I had ever seen him distinctly – not even to this day [. . .] but it seemed to me that the less I understood the more I was bound to him in the name of that doubt which is the inseparable part of our knowledge. I did not know so much more about myself. And then I repeat, I was going home – to that home distant enough for all its hearthstones to be like one hearthstone, by which the humblest of us has the right to sit. We wander in our thousands over the face of the earth, the illustrious and the obscure, earning beyond the seas our fame, our money, or only a crust of bread; but it seems to me that for each of us going home must be like going to render an account. [. . .] *I only knew he was one of us.* [. . .] I am telling you so much about my own instinctive feelings and bemused reflections because there remains so little to be told of him. He existed for me, and after all it is only through me that he exists for you. [. . .] Were my commonplace fears unjust? [. . .] You may be able to tell better since the proverb has it that the onlookers see most of the game. [. . .] And besides, the last word is not said – probably shall never be said. Are not our lives too short for that full utterance which through all our stammerings is of course our only and abiding intention? I have given up expecting those last words [. . .].[4]

It is in the name of historical and ethical doubt that Conrad asks us to consider what it may mean to be "one of us," in global or post-colonial conditions where singularity of identification is at once supplementary or split – Jim and Marlow are bound to each other in an uncertainty of knowledge – and hence, the "us" or "we" of commonality or community is both contingent and situational: "*I only knew he was one of us.* [. . .] [You have] [. . .] my own instinctive feelings and bemused reflections because there remains so little to be told of him." In the doubleness of such colonial and post-colonial "doubt" we are summoned to imagine not so much a "return" home as a retroactive revision of dwelling at "home," a coming-to home, in that haunting temporality, *future's past*. Home, then, "for all its hearthstones [. . .] one hearthstone," *e pluribus Unum,* is no longer the singular or sovereign dwelling of a "jurisdictional" authority, because the very distance that produces its "picturesque manifestations" – in Conrad's phrases, its saving power, the grace of its secular right to our fidelity – also produces the ethical/historical distantiation, the unsettlement, that creates the straggling, errant desire to return; but to return to what? It is this jurisdictional "doubting" of home – *not its failure or obsolescence* – that makes me want to move the question of who is "one of us" away from an ontology of "being," and, for want of a better phrase, locate it in the spatial and temporal narrative of what Conrad articulates as the "uneasy anchorage of life" that becomes the law of living in "post-colonial" modernity.

It is in the wandering interstices of Marlow's home-coming, his return to render an account, and Jim's miserable trouble that comes mistily from "home" that "home" and the "world" are caught in a lateral proximity of desire. A form of coexistence that throws into doubt – even when it is violently asserted – the very jurisdiction of what it is that binds and bounds our sense of a form of being "one of Us." It is here, then, that in the lateral proximity between home-coming and its unsettled jurisdiction the "global" or the transnational emerge not as the horizon of some new inclusive conceptual category or expansionist pedagogy, nor even as a resistant singular locality, but as an anxious, liminal "edge" of the lifeworld of late modern experience. Home, now, becomes the object of another jurisdiction, another inquiry. Jurisdiction – *Juris/dictio* – loses a measure of its constative and spatial grounding in *place person and police*, and – with Jim's leap into the unknown – enters into a proleptic performance of having to constitute, in the act of adjudication, what it means to be-come "one of us" by making oneself "accountable," as Derrida describes it in the context of the New International, "by a decision that begins by getting caught up, like a responsibility, in the snares of an injunction that is already multiple, heterogeneous, contradictory, divided [. . .]."[5] *Who, then, is one of us?*

In the discourse of cultural rights – provoked in large part by the presence of minorities, multiculturalism, immigration, communities of interest – the question of the "right" to a culture – *as the representation and regulation of who is one of us* – turns on the ethical and political freedom of "choice": the freedom to choose a cultural affiliation, the right to be free to constitute or preserve a culture, or indeed to oppose it by exercising the moral "right of exit." There are of course many social limitations to cultural choice – poverty, illiteracy, homophobia, economic hardship, unemployment. At this stage, however, I will only say that terms like "choice" and "respect" – alluding to enablement or empowerment – have an immediate and ready applicability across discourses of difference. It is that general or common sense that I want to examine as much for its power of translation, as for its sedimented resonances in the shared syntax of the "good life."

What, then, is the nature of cultural choice in the transnational contexts of migration, in the societal conditions of multicultural translation, where cultures are passing through "continua of transformation, not abstract areas of identity and similarity," to cite Walter Benjamin?[6] For instance, take the recent peace agreement in Northern Ireland, a society in a state of transition. There is a widespread feeling in Ireland itself – one that I encountered repeatedly on a recent visit – that what the accord demonstrates, as Fintan O'Toole writes, is a sense in which "people at the end of the twentieth century [can] live without knowing that they belong once and for all, to a well-defined nation."[7] In a section of his essay entitled "US," of which the first line consists of two words, "Not Them," O'Toole asks why, despite the widely shared and diffuse support for the I.R.A. in the Republic of Ireland, the Sinn Fein repeatedly failed to poll more than 3% of the vote. His answer is salient from the perspectives of both the shifting grounds of home and the beckoning shores of "abroad": O'Toole writes the affective history of the republic with one eye turned to the Northern Troubles and another turned towards the West – the migratory desire for America is factored into the very existence of the historical nation. "Having grown up in a culture that was very sure of itself [. . .] we imagined that an unfinished, messy, contradictory nation, might after all, have a lot to offer us [. . .]. Was a civil war, even if it made our political identity perfectly clear, going to get us what we felt we needed."[8]

What do cultural options look like, then, from the optics of exile or a form of cultural, even national, displacement?

> What does it mean to be a good immigrant? [. . .] For example, is the good immigrant the one who shares his material success with his comrades at home, or the one who invests in her new country? [. . .] Is the good immigrant the one who brings up assimilated children, or the one who preserves a bit of the culture of the homeland?[9]

Posing these questions in "Immigration and the Ethics of Choice," Teresa Sullivan suggests that there are no clear answers or guidelines because "the social role of immigrant does not carry with it a lot of [the accepted and accredited] normative expectations."[10] It is a feature of multicultural societies that there is, around the issue of cultural choice, an intensification of normative underspecificity or indeterminacy. At the judicial level this translates frequently into arbitrary decision making. Jurisprudence within the European Court of Human Rights in respect of second generation immigrants attempting to resist deportation following criminal convictions exemplifies this process. Long settled lawful residents within E.U. states are deported to a fictive "home" to North Africa or South Asia at the end of their criminal sentences, thus being subjected to double jeopardy or punishment, on the basis of "fictive nationalities." In the world of public policy, in a reworking of Charles Taylor's argument, Rainer Bauböck suggests that the "politics of recognition" has to contend with "objects of choice [that] include the additional options of multiple membership and toleration of syncretic and hybrid practices."[11]

An ethical ethnography of such hybridization is at the divided heart of Clifford Geertz's Tanner Lecture, "The Uses of Diversity." The traditional concept of culture-as-self-containedness becomes estranged in the ethical responsibility of encountering "diversity." "Our duty is to make us visible to ourselves," Geertz writes, "by representing us and everyone else as cast into the midst of a world full of irremovable strangenesses we can't keep clear of"[12] that produce moral asymmetries within the boundary of a *we*. "*Foreignness does not start at the water's edge but at the skin's.*"[13]

It is, I believe, the *amniotic* structure of cultural spacing — a watery skin if ever there was one, a "difference" that is at once liminal and fluid — that Geertz does not fully grasp as the *temporal movement that crosses between* the boundaries of cultural containment. The moral dilemmas arising from the communication and coexistence of cultural diversity are, within his brilliant argument, insistently represented in *spatial metaphors*. The temporal disjuncture *within the moral asymmetry of multicultural society,* where we are interstitially inscribed, between the foreignness of the skin and the nation's boundary — citizens and migrants, gendered and raced, historical subjects of "unremembered" oppression and affective subjects of the repressed unthought. Instead of dancing in the "entre" of his ethnography of diversity, Geertz does a soft shoe shuffle and finally lands on his foundational feet: "[T]he world is coming at each of its local points to look more like a Kuwaiti bazaar than like an English gentlemen's club (to instance what, to my mind – perhaps because I have never been in either of them – are the polar cases)."[14] How do we choose?

It is a belief held by many interesting "left" liberal legal philosophers of multicultural ethics, that situations of "subcultural anomie" cannot be adequately assuaged by revising "toleration" within civic relations (Parekh) or applying the remedy of "non-discrimination rights" to the moral asymmetries within the boundary of a multicultural "we." This leads Joseph Raz to his alternative: a "multiculturalism without territorial separation."[15] "The core options that give meanings to our lives," Raz suggests, are "dense webs of complex actions and interactions [. . .] conglomerations of interlocking practices" that "make it impossible for the subject or the individual to consider and decide deliberately. A lot has to be done, so to speak automatically."[16] What Raz describes as "automatic behavior" is close to what Judith Butler sees as the citationality of "excitable speech" in multicultural contexts: "*the operation [. . .] by which the subject who 'cites' the performative is temporarily produced as the belated and fictive origin of the performative itself.*"[17] We now have the spectacle of the attenuation of the free liberal subject; not unfree because of the restrictions on choice or the plurality of choice as "objects," but a "dependent," mediated subject of enunciation, caught in the performative, contingent logic of cultural "representation," in the very enactment of the discourse of multicultural "value plurality."

At this moment of utterance, the "autonomic" so-called sovereign individual becomes uncannily confronted with its agonistic "automatic" double. What occurs, within the body of Raz's discussion of value pluralism, is a kind of discursive or enunciative split, a double inscription in relation to choice. One form of the conflict of choice, Raz argues, is endemic to value pluralism and consensual in nature. It maintains the moral mastery and the autonomy of the self and conforms to the mundane reality that "two values are incompatible if they cannot be realized or pursued to the fullest degree in the same life [. . .]. What one loses is of a different kind from what one gains [. . .] faced with valuable options [. . .] one simply chooses one way of life rather than another, both being good and not susceptible to comparison of degree."[18] But "affirmative multiculturalism" can bring no such closure to incommensurable values and choices. Its enunciation is perfomatively constituted in the very tension that makes knowledges of cultural difference dense, conglomerative, and non-deliberative. What emerges spectrally is the agonistic and ambivalent subject of a double, displaced multicultural choice:

> Tension is an inevitable concomitant of accepting the truth of value-pluralism (in the context of affirmative multiculturalism). And it is a tension without stability, without a definite resting point of reconciliation of the two perspectives, the one recognizing the validity of competing values and the other hostile to them. There is no point of equilibrium, no single balance which is correct and could prevail to bring the two perspectives together. One is forever moving from one to the other, from time to time.[19]

Raz tries to rescue this split, ambivalent moment of choice that vacillates between values – moving from one to the other – struggling between cultural norms, in-between interpellation and agency, the automatic and the autonomic; a mode of enunciation "sowing confusion between them and standing between at the same time." He attempts to reinstate the "singular balance" of the individualist subject through the moral rhetoric of "respect." But "respect" finally becomes a way of "standing back or apart" from the most radical proposal of "value pluralism" which is *to place the subject of ethical and political choice* at the anxious, agonistic point of "no equilibrium," no single balance – only the movement from the one to the other, time to time. Respect struggles to still the movement of iteration in which the agent comes to be inscribed, now a double-agent, constituted in the "tension" between the agonistic and the deliberative, the autonomic and the automatic.

    The ungovernability of "home rule," the un-mastering of the metropolis and its "unitary" neo-liberal hearthstone in rendering an account of who is "one of us" is part of the political passion of our time, that is "constantly aroused by the need for the aspirations of minorities [. . .] to be socially recognized."[20] Minorities represent a range of interests and claims – class, employment, welfare benefits, sexual discrimination, racism, AIDS, environmentalism – through a shared mode of recognition and representation that *paradoxically* combines, as Claude Lefort describes it, "the idea of legitimacy and the representation of a particularity."[21] It is this paradox that I want to explore both for its symbolic constitution of the "rights" of minoritization, and its unsettled jurisdictional utterance: What, and where, is the "us" of which, and from which, one speaks? The relation between the ethical/symbolic discourse of minority rights and the institutionalized language of state power is constituted in a "transitional" relation that Lefort names "separation":

> [. . .] faced with the demand for or defence of a right, [the state] has to respond [. . .] according to the criteria of the just and the unjust and not only of the per-

mitted and the forbidden [...] the right affirmed against the claims of state power to decide, according to its own imperatives and its own expansion, does not attack it head on, but obliquely; by circumventing it, as it were, it touches the centre from which it draws the justification of its own right to demand the allegiance and obedience of all.[22]

The oblique authority of "rights," derived through the act of "separation" – "drawing justification [for rights] by touching the centre only by circumventing it" – is a mode of agonistic agency that reveals a "third space," an internal boundary, the ambivalent liminality of state power. If this "rights"-strategy of symbolic deterritorialization is read in the spirit of Jacques Lacan's notion of "separation," then minoritarian "agency" is not condemned to be insistently reactive or "marginal." Separation, for Jacques Lacan, is the subject's attempt to free itself – or "to free something," to enter the function of freedom. The oblique, "symbolic" authority of minoritarian "rights" – confrontation through circumvention, drawing authority by moving beyond and then tangentially touching it, elliptically evacuating the "center" – shares a movement with the jurisdiction of desire: separation is the process by which the subject maps a space that goes beyond or falls short of the binary representation of antagonisms, bringing to being what is unknown, uncharted territory, and instating its desire for freedom in the interstices, in that interval in-between two moments of the signification of "authority." Lacan elaborates the notion of "separation" through the example of the relation of master-and-slave showing how the essence of the master is "manifested at the moment of terror," revealing "how much radical alienation there is in the master himself."[23] Likewise, what I have called the "symbolic" space of thirdness opened up by an *opposition de droit*

> tests out rights that have not yet been incorporated in [the democratic state], it is the theatre of contestation, whose object cannot be reduced to the preservation of a tacitly established pact but which takes form in centres that power cannot entirely master. [...] there has developed on the basis of the rights of man a whole history that transgressed the boundaries within which the state claimed to define itself, a history that remains open.[24]

However, here political philosophy must learn the lesson of psychoanalysis and its lagged, repetitious temporality – repression, retroactivity, sublimation. For transgression is a *negotiated unsettlement* with no guarantee of its sustained progressivity: a history that remains open also comes to be occupied; closure is only another form of the contingent. The failure of mastery by the symbolic oppositions of rights – significant as they are – must not obscure the fact that rights can be freely granted without needs being met; or indeed to blunt "interests" and co-opt them into the universal, utopic language of man.

What the minoritarian perspective emphasizes in the "culture of rights" is an enabling, even empowering sense of the "transitionality" of the "subject" of cultural difference. For Stuart Hall such transitionality emerges as the temporality that constitutes dialogical transformation: "within every moment of reversal, there is always the surreptitious return of the trace of the past; within any rupture are the surprising effects of reduplication, repetition, and ambivalence [. . .] [and] incomplete displacement."[25] It is there, in what Mouffe/Laclau and Bonnie Honig see as the "spaces of dilemma" within agonistic democracy, "the unending, never quite mastered struggles of resistance, adjustment, negotiation."[26] Transitionality – the on-going history of "unresolved differences" – defines the "culture of rights" tenuously preserved by the secular Indian left, caught between Hindu nationalism and its Muslim response. As Rajeev Bhargava wrote recently in his defense of the "right to culture":

> A culture of rights presupposes the existence of difference. Also a commitment to settle these differences peacefully and through reason [. . .]. However it insists that the cost of an enforced settlement is greater in the long run, than the cost of accepting unresolved differences. The notion of rights is therefore cultural-laden.[27]

In what sense can we be obligated to a "culture of rights" in the midst of "repetition, ambivalence, incomplete displacement" (Hall)? Or as Conrad put it, how can we be one of us in the midst of the "uneasy anchorage of life?" The sense of the "transitionality" of cultural difference that I want to propose as a mode of minoritarian agency is suggested by Gramsci on grammar. Gramsci's brief comments on "grammar" as a normative practice of the "syntax" of society and community go beyond the disciplinary study of language, for as he writes, "Language also means culture and philosophy" and "does not presuppose any single thing existing in time and space."[28] In this sense then, his notion of grammar, in this essay, is more about the ethical and authoritative act of enunciation in conditions of cultural difference and social disjunction. Gramsci's emphasis on grammar is an attempt to understand the contested construction of cultural norms from the on-going, performative process by which choice and judgment become part of the hegemonic or subaltern "elaboration" of the public sphere.

To turn Gramsci's discussion of grammar to a consideration of the "transitionality" of difference in a "culture of rights," I want to emphasize a statement in his essay that is placed in parenthesis, a minor moment that barely impacts directly on the argument. Gramsci asks, "Who can control the linguistic innovations introduced by returning emigrants, travellers, readers of foreign newspapers and languages, translators, etc.?"[29]

Taking my lead, then, from migrants, travelers, foreigners and translators – where the ungovernability and unsettled jurisdiction of home is profoundly in question – I want to restage Gramsci's argument as an act of "separation"; not a full frontal attack but a "confrontation-by-circumvention." "Written normative grammars," Gramsci writes, "tend to embrace the entire territory of a nation and its 'total linguistic volume,' to create a unitary national linguistic conformism."[30] The antagonistic agency of "separation" is initiated in the "spontaneous" discourse of cultural and grammatical normativity, speaking in the voice of the popular public sphere. "What do you mean?" "What are you trying to say?" it repeatedly iterates in a performative speech act that Gramsci calls "reciprocal monitoring" and "reciprocal teaching." Such interlocution is at the very heart of the "right to language and the freedom of expression," for "by virtue of the establishment of these relations, a situation is constituted [. . .] in which the duality of speaking and hearing in the public sphere is multiplied instead of being frozen in the relation of authority, or being confined in privileged places."[31] Located in the popular life world of minorities, caught up in the "heterogeneity of the forms of protest and demand"[32] – the discourse of spontaneous grammar is engaged in the negotiation of unresolved, ongoing difference: its commitment to "a culture of rights" is inscribed in its very conditions of enunciation – the dialogism of "spontaneous grammar" produces a speech community, Gramsci writes, that is "necessarily disconnected, discontinuous and limited to the local social strata or to local ['subaltern'] centres."[33] The fragmented spontaneous grammars – of which there are many – do not directly confront the power of the totalitarian normative-national discourse; a binary or polar signification of cultural difference and its contestation is not the method of subaltern "separation." Spontaneous grammar, whose authority emerges in a dialogical articulation of disjunctive or disconnected "local" sites subverts the national by circumventing its centralized power through an appeal to the disseminated site of an international context. It is this (unworked out) mode of articulating the regional or local with the international while, at the same time, "confronting-by-circumventing" the limits of the national, that is the productive moment of "transitionality" that inheres in the differential "culture of rights." For cultural discontinuity and disjuncture that activate spontaneity of popular dialogic discourse, its "inorganic and incoherent forces" are repositories of what Gramsci calls "the variable combination of old and new."[34] The alterity represented by minorities, the "uncontrollable innovations" and identification signified by emigrants, translators, and foreigners who bring to the "spontaneous," subaltern public sphere, a deep seated awareness that, to quote Gramsci,

> the linguistic fact, like any other historical fact, cannot have strictly defined national boundaries, but that history is always "world history" and that particular histories exist only within the frame of world history [. . .] [just as] the national language cannot be imagined outside the frame of other languages that exert an influence on it through innumerable channels which are often difficult to control.[35]

It is indeed the "uncontrollable" jurisdiction of the spontaneous popular "grammar" that enables the disjunctive or "regional" link between the "local" and the "international" not as a repudiation of "home" but as its separation; the opening up of an interstitial moment and movement between the national and the international by working through the transitionality of the ongoing difference of minority cultures in the transnational community of rights.

As we gather in the terrain of our times, where the "face to face" social encounter is veiled by distance or difference, and any desire for "transparency" is trammeled in the continua of translation or transition, we are often left, as I leave you, in the place of the questioner: what does it require for the subject to be at once inside and outside the encompassing group; how can we survive, caught as we are, un-balanced or recovering our posture, somewhere between "self-respect and the criticism of the other"? We have returned, as you are no doubt aware, to the ethical grounds of the stereotypical encounter, which is as much a Conradian question of the "doubt" that afflicts home-truths, as it is a Gramscian problem of popular, spontaneous "grammars." Let us turn the minoritarian question of living within "unresolved" differences, to that peculiar jurisdiction of the Freudian joke, where the ambiguity of person and place – stereotype and syntax – play a major role.

It could be argued that the Freud's tendentious, self-critical joke – "a rebellion against [. . .] authority, a liberation from its pressure"[36] – may be a strategy of cultural resistance and agency committed to a community's survival. Read as a minority speech-act, the cultural *choice* to tell the joke, circulates around a doubly-articulated subject: the negatively marked subject, singled out, at first, as a figure of fun or abuse, is turned through the joke-act into an inclusive, yet agonistic, form of self-critical identification for which the community takes responsibility.

> [. . .] the intended rebellious criticism is directed against the subject himself, or to put it more cautiously, against someone in whom the subject has a share – a collective person, that is (the subject's own nation for instance). The occurrence of self-

> criticism as a determinant may explain how it is that a number of the most apt jokes [. . .] have grown up on the soil of Jewish popular life [. . .]. The jokes made about Jews by foreigners are for the most part brutal comic stories in which a joke is made unnecessary by the fact that Jews are regarded by foreigners as comic figures. The Jewish jokes which originate from Jews admit this too; but they know their real faults as well as the connection between them and their good qualities, and the share which the subject has in the person found fault with creates the subjective determinant [. . .] of the joke-work.³⁷

Self-irony as a minority gesture does not consist in "balancing" the extrinsic and intrinsic view in some proposed zero-sum game of cultural equity played out between universalism and relativism; nor does it lie in the binary confrontation of cultural insiders and outsiders – Self and Other – each straining to achieve a more holistic or authentic identity at the expense of the other. Through the very performance of the self-critical joke-work there *emerges* a structure of identification – what Freud calls "the subjective determination of the joke-work" – that provides a way for minority communities to confront and regulate the abuse that comes from "outside" or the criticisms that emerge inwardly, from within the community itself. These negative perceptions are different both in kind and quality, but the "self-critical" posture allows them to be represented without a defensive drawing of the boundaries around "ethnicity," "customary experience," "social victimage," or other forms of cultural essentialism or historical exceptionalism. In fact, the performative act of "sharing in" – "the *share* which the subject has *in* the person found fault with," "someone *in whom the subject has a share* – a collective person, that is (the subject's own nation for instance)" (my emphasis) – is a mode of communal identification where cultural affiliation results from an ambivalence that afflicts the authority, and authorization, of those "limits" that establish the location and locution of cultural boundaries. *To share in* is to participate communally, to associate in fellowship; *to have a share in* assumes, at the same time, a contradictory process of division, partialization, separation. The affect of the joke-work, its structure of feeling and phrasing, arises from the interleaved dissemblings of the joke-work, caught in the interstices between these double subjects of "sharing."

There can, therefore, be no *synchronous entry* of social difference into the communal habitus. To represent one's interests as a group or a community, to have a *share within* the wider social circle, demands the iterative practice of the self-critical joke-work. Its affiliative articulation – making connections between the community's real faults and its good qualities – is a highly mediated, tendentious process that emerges from the ambivalence generated by the double "subject" of the jest, and remains unavailable to a transcendent, archimedian perspective. For the formation of the self-critical community is predicated on the repetition of the instance of cultural alterity that is neither disavowed nor suppressed but worked-around – just like the starting point of the self-critical joke which is, at first, a play without a person as its object. Such a process of re-articulation or transvaluation makes the self-critical community the ground for a complex and productive "cultural confrontation" (no simplification, warns Fanon). The value in belonging to a community, or signifying a sense of collective solidarity, does not lie in cultivating some deep structure of cultural authenticity conserved in the homogeneous empty time of Tradition. A productive cultural confrontation lies in the ability to negotiate the ambivalent liminalities of a culture, its perceptual and experiential boundaries. A community's "real fault," its internal contradictions, or a "singled out" subject of difference, becomes the passageway through which a "negation" turns into the basis for a negotiated share in a collective person. Such a passageway must be kept open for a range of border-crossings and cross-border identifications so that, in that iterative process, the community may be re-membered – both in the sense of the revision of memory and the re-location of its agents.

As is well known, for Freud, the action of the joke is its relentless drive towards the "third person" – a person who is neither the joker nor the person who is the object of the joke, but an "outside person" whose reaction makes evident the pleasure or success of the joke "as though the self did not feel certain in its judgment on the point."[38] The uncertainty or indeterminacy of modern knowledge becomes an *act* of cultural survival and historical renewal. To take the hearer into account is to share *in* the making of a "collective person" – nation, community, group – from the ambivalent movement that circulates in-between first and third persons. To be the first person is to be the witness, the victim, the actor, bound to the event and perhaps blinded by it; to be the third person – the "outside person," the supplementary *you* – is to be the hearer, the overseer, the assessor, in an interstitial yet evidentiary position. But the first person who shares the experience feels a deep uncertainty in its judgment, and the third person who has a share *in* the experience has the freedom to speculate with what is only partial, piecemeal, fragmented. To invoke the double-sharing of the joke in the context of the tense, incommensurable choices of multiculturalism or cultural difference is to hope that the memory-work of our shared future, no doubt unbalanced and ethically asymmetrical, will be carried out somewhere between tears and laughter.

Notes

* Parts of the text have been published in *The Turn to Ethics*, ed. Marjorie Garber, Beatrice Hanssen, Rebecca L. Walkowitz (New York and London: Routledge, 2000) as Homi K. Bhabha, "On Cultural Choice," 181-200.

1. Emmanuel Lévinas, *Collected Philosophical Papers*, trans. Alphonso Lingis (Dordrecht and Boston: Martinus Nijhoff Publishers, 1987) 119.

2. Joseph Conrad, *Lord Jim* (New York: Norton, 1968) 79.

3. Ibid., 134.

4. Ibid., 135-7, my emphasis.

5. Jacques Derrida, *Specters of Marx: The State of the Debt, the Work of Mourning, and the New International*, trans. Peggy Kamuf (New York: Routledge, 1994) 93.

6. Walter Benjamin, "On Language as Such and on the Language of Man," *One-Way Street and Other Writings*, trans. Edmund Jephcott and Kingsley Shorter (New York: Verso, 1985) 117.

7. Fintan O'Toole, "The Meanings of Union: Taking the Trouble Out of the Troubles," *The New Yorker* 27 April 1998: 54.

8. Ibid., 62.

9. Teresa Sullivan, "Immigration and the Ethics of Choice," *International Migration Review* 30.1 (1996): 98.

10. Ibid., 98.

11. Rainer Bauböck, "Cultural Minority Rights for Immigration," *International Migration Review* 30.1 (1996): 209.

12. Clifford Geertz, "The Uses of Diversity," *Michigan Quarterly Review* 25.1 (1986): 121.

13. Ibid., 112.

14. Ibid., 121.

15. Joseph Raz, "Multiculturalism: A Liberal Perspective," *Ethics in the Public Domain: Essays in the Morality of Law and Politics* (Oxford: Clarendon Press, 1994) 174.

16. Ibid., 176-7.

17. Judith Butler, *Excitable Speech: A Politics of the Performative* (New York: Routledge, 1997) 49.

18. Raz, "Multiculturalism" 180.

19. Ibid., 179.

20. Claude Lefort, *The Political Forms of Modern Society: Bureaucracy, Democracy, Totalitarianism*, ed. John B. Thompson (Cambridge, MA: Polity Press, 1986) 264.

21. Ibid.

22. Ibid., 265.

23 Jacques Lacan, *The Four Fundamental Concepts of Psycho-Analysis*, ed. Jacques-Alain Miller, trans. Alan Sheridan (Harmondsworth: Penguin, 1986) 220.

24 Lefort, *Political Forms* 258.

25 Stuart Hall, "For Allon White: Metaphors of Transformation," *Stuart Hall: Critical Dialogues in Cultural Studies*, ed. David Morley and Kuan-Hsing Chen (London: Routledge, 1996) 300.

26 Lefort, *Political Forms* 259.

27 Rajeev Bhargava, unpublished essay.

28 Antonio Gramsci, *A Gramsci Reader: Selected Writings 1916-1935*, ed. David Forgacs (London: Lawrence and Wishart, 1988) 347.

29 Ibid., 355.

30 Ibid., 354.

31 Lefort, *Political Forms* 257.

32 Ibid., 264.

33 Gramsci, *Reader* 354.

34 Ibid., 353.

35 Ibid., 355.

36 Sigmund Freud, *Jokes and Their Relation to the Unconscious*, trans. and ed. James Strachey, ed. Angela Richards (New York: Pelican, 1976) 149.

37 Ibid., 156-7.

38 Ibid., 196.

Redistribution, Recognition, and Participation: Toward an Integrated Conception of Justice

Nancy Fraser

In today's world, claims for social justice seem increasingly to divide into two types. First, and most familiar, are redistributive claims, which seek a more just distribution of resources and goods. Examples include claims for redistribution from the North to the South, from the rich to the poor, and (not so long ago) from the owners to the workers. To be sure, the recent resurgence of free-market thinking has put proponents of redistribution on the defensive. Nevertheless, egalitarian redistributive claims have supplied the paradigm case for most theorizing about social justice for the past 150 years.[1]

Today, however, we increasingly encounter a second type of social-justice claim in what has been called the "politics of recognition." Here the goal, in its most plausible form, is a difference-friendly world, where assimilation to majority or dominant cultural norms is no longer the price of equal respect. Examples include claims for the recognition of the distinctive perspectives of ethnic, "racial," and sexual minorities, as well as of gender difference. This type of claim has recently attracted the interest of political philosophers, moreover, some of whom are seeking to develop a new paradigm of justice that puts recognition at its center.

In general, then, we are confronted with a new constellation. The discourse of social justice, once centered on distribution, is now increasingly divided between claims for redistribution, on the one hand, and claims for recognition, on the other. Increasingly, too, recognition claims tend to predominate. The demise of communism, the surge of free-market ideology, the rise of "identity politics" in both its fundamentalist and progressive forms – all these developments have conspired to decenter, if not to extinguish, the politics of redistribution.

In this new constellation, the two kinds of justice claims are often dissociated from one another – both practically and intellectually. Within social movements such as feminism, for example, activist tendencies that look to redistribution as the remedy for male domination are increasingly dissociated from tendencies that look instead to recognition of gender difference. And the same is true of their counterparts in the academy, where feminist social theorizing and feminist cultural theorizing maintain an uneasy arms-length coexistence. The feminist case exemplifies a more general tendency to decouple the cultural politics of difference from the social politics of equality.

In some cases, moreover, the dissociation has become a polarization. Some proponents of redistribution reject the politics of recognition outright, casting claims for the recognition of difference as "false consciousness," a hindrance to the pursuit of social justice. Conversely, some proponents of recognition applaud the relative eclipse of the politics of redistribution, which for them smacks of an outmoded materialism that can neither articulate nor challenge key experiences of injustice. In such cases, we are effectively presented with what is constructed as an either/or choice: redistribution or recognition? class politics or identity politics? multiculturalism or social democracy?

These, I maintain, are false antitheses. It is my general thesis that justice today requires *both* redistribution *and* recognition. Neither alone is sufficient. As soon as one embraces this thesis, however, the question of how to combine them becomes paramount. I shall argue that the emancipatory aspects of the two paradigms should be integrated in a single, comprehensive framework. Theoretically, the task is to devise a two-dimensional conception of justice that can accommodate both defensible claims for social equality and defensible claims for the recognition of difference. Practically, the task is to devise a programmatic political orientation that integrates the best of the politics of redistribution with the best of the politics of recognition.

My argument proceeds in four steps. In section one, I shall outline the key points of contrast between the two political paradigms, as they are presently understood. Then, in section two, I shall problematize their current dissociation from one another by introducing a case of injustice that cannot be redressed by either one of them alone, but that requires their integration. Finally, I shall consider some normative philosophical questions (section three) and some social-theoretical questions (section four) that arise when we contemplate integrating redistribution and recognition in a single comprehensive framework.

1. Anatomy of a False Antithesis

I begin with some denotative definitions. The politics of redistribution, as I shall understand it, encompasses not only class-centered orientations, such as New Deal liberalism, social-democracy, and socialism, but also those forms of feminism and anti-racism that look to socioeconomic transformation or reform as the remedy for gender and racial-ethnic injustice. Thus, it is broader than class politics in the conventional sense. The politics of recognition, in contrast, encompasses not only movements aiming to revalue unjustly devalued identities, for example, cultural feminism, black cultural nationalism, and gay identity politics, but also deconstructive tendencies, such as queer politics, critical "race" politics, and deconstructive feminism, which reject the "essentialism" of traditional identity politics. Thus, it is broader than identity politics in the conventional sense.

In general, then, I reject the familiar assumption that the politics of redistribution focuses exclusively on injustices of class, whereas "identity politics" focuses instead on injustices of gender, sexuality, and "race." Rather, I treat redistribution and recognition as *dimensions of justice that can cut across all social movements*.

Thus understood, the politics of redistribution and the politics of recognition can be contrasted in three key respects. First, the two approaches assume different conceptions of injustice. The politics of redistribution focuses on injustices it defines as socioeconomic and presumes to be rooted in the political-economy. Examples include exploitation, economic marginalization, and deprivation. The politics of recognition, in contrast, targets injustices it understands as cultural, which it presumes to be rooted in social patterns of representation, interpretation, and communication. Examples include cultural domination, nonrecognition, and disrespect.

Second, the two approaches propose different sorts of remedies for injustice. For the politics of redistribution, the remedy for injustice is political-economic restructuring. This might involve redistributing income, reorganizing the division of labor, or transforming other basic economic structures. (Although these various remedies differ importantly from one another, I mean to refer to the whole group of them by the generic term "redistribution.") For the politics of recognition, in contrast, the remedy for injustice is cultural or symbolic change. This could involve upwardly revaluing disrespected identities, positively valorizing cultural diversity, or the wholesale transformation of societal patterns of representation, interpretation and communication in ways that would change everybody's identity. (Although these remedies, too, differ importantly from one another, I refer once again to the whole group of them by the generic term "recognition.")

Third, the two political orientations assume different conceptions of the collectivities who suffer injustice. For the politics of redistribution, the collective subjects of injustice are classes or class-like collectivities, which are defined economically by a distinctive relation to the market or the means of production. The classic case in the Marxian paradigm is the exploited working class. But the conception can cover other cases as well. Also included are racialized groups of immigrants or ethnic minorities that can be economically defined, whether as a pool of low paid menial laborers or as an "underclass" largely excluded from regular waged work, deemed "superfluous" and unworthy of exploitation. When the notion of the economy is broadened to encompass unwaged labor, moreover, women too become visible as a collective subject of economic injustice, as the gender burdened with the lion's share of unwaged carework and consequently disadvantaged in employment. Also included, finally, are the complexly defined groupings that result when we theorize the political economy in terms of the intersection of class, "race," and gender.

For the politics of recognition, in contrast, the victims of injustice are more like Weberian status groups than Marxian classes. Defined not by the relations of production, but rather by the relations of recognition, they are distinguished by the lesser esteem, honor, and prestige they enjoy relative to other groups in society. The classic case in the Weberian paradigm is the low-status ethnic group, whom dominant patterns of cultural value mark as different and less worthy. But the conception can cover other cases as well. In today's politics of recognition, it has been extended to gays and lesbians, whose sexuality is interpreted as deviant and devalued in the dominant culture; to racialized groups, who are marked as different and lesser; and to women, who are trivialized, sexually objectified, and disrespected in myriad ways. It is also being extended, finally, to encompass the complexly defined groupings that result when we theorize the relations of recognition in terms of "race," gender, and sexuality simultaneously as intersecting cultural codes.

Increasingly, as I noted at the outset, the politics of redistribution and the politics of recognition are posed as mutually exclusive alternatives. Some proponents of the former reject "identity politics" as a counterproductive diversion from the real economic issues, claiming, in effect, that "it's the economy, stupid." Conversely, some proponents of recognition reject difference-blind redistributive politics as assimilationist, claiming in effect that "it's the culture, stupid."

This, however, is a false antithesis.

2. Exploited Classes, Despised Sexualities, and Bivalent Collectivities: A Critique of Justice Truncated

To see why, let us imagine a conceptual spectrum of different kinds of social collectivities. At one extreme are modes of collectivity that fit the politics of redistribution. At the other extreme are modes of collectivity that fit the politics of recognition. In between are cases that prove difficult because they fit both political orientations simultaneously.[2]

Consider, first, the redistribution end of the spectrum. At this end let us posit an ideal-typical mode of collectivity whose existence is rooted in the economic structure of society, as opposed to the status order. By definition, then, any structural injustices its members suffer will be traceable to the political economy. The core of the injustice will be socio-economic maldistribution, while any attendant cultural injustices will derive ultimately from the economic structure. At bottom, therefore, the remedy required to redress the injustice will be redistribution, as opposed to recognition.

An example that appears to approximate the ideal type is the exploited working class, as understood in orthodox, economistic Marxism. In this conception class differentiation is an artifact of an unjust political economy. The injustice is at bottom a matter of distribution, as the proletariat shoulders an undue share of the system's burdens, while being denied its fair share of the system's rewards. To be sure, its members also suffer serious cultural injustices, the "hidden injuries of class."[3] But far from being rooted directly in an autonomously unjust status order, these derive from the economic structure, as ideologies of class inferiority proliferate to justify exploitation. The remedy for the injustice, consequently, is redistribution, not recognition. The last thing the proletariat needs is recognition of its difference. On the contrary, the only way to remedy the injustice is to restructure the political economy in such a way as to put the proletariat out of business as a distinctive group.

Now consider the other end of the conceptual spectrum. At this end let us posit an ideal-typical mode of collectivity that fits the politics of recognition. A collectivity of this type is rooted wholly in the status order, as opposed to the economic structure, of society. Thus, any structural injustices its members suffer will be traceable ultimately to the society's institutionalized patterns of cultural value. The core of the injustice will be misrecognition, while any attendant economic injustices will derive ultimately from the status order. The remedy required to redress the injustice will be recognition, as opposed to redistribution.

An example that appears to approximate this ideal type is a *despised sexuality*, understood through the prism of the Weberian conception of status. In this conception, the social differentiation between heterosexuals and homosexuals is grounded in the status order of society, as institutionalized patterns of cultural value constitute heterosexuality as natural and normative, homosexuality as perverse and despised. The result is to construct gays and lesbians as despised others who lack not only the standing to participate fully in social life but even the right to exist. Pervasively institutionalized, such heteronormative value patterns generate sexually specific forms of *status subordination*, including ritual shaming, imprisonment, psychiatric "treatment," assault, and murder; exclusion from the rights and privileges of intimacy, marriage, and parenthood, and from all the entitlements that flow from them; impaired rights of privacy, expression, and association; diminished access to employment, health care, military service, and education; impaired rights of immigration, naturalization, and asylum; exclusion from or marginalization in civil society and political life; and invisibility and/or stigmatization in the media. These harms are injustices of misrecognition. To be sure, gays and lesbians also suffer serious economic injustices; they can be summarily dismissed from work and are denied family-based social-welfare benefits. But far from being rooted directly in the economic structure, these derive instead from an unjust pattern of cultural value. The remedy for the injustice, consequently, is recognition, not redistribution. Overcoming homophobia and heterosexism requires changing the sexual status order, deinstitutionalizing the heteronormative value patterns and replacing them with patterns that express equal respect for gays and lesbians.

Matters are thus fairly straightforward at the two extremes of our conceptual spectrum. When we deal with collectivities that approach the ideal type of the exploited working class, we face distributive injustices requiring redistributive remedies. What is needed is the politics of redistribution. When we deal with collectivities that approach the ideal type of the despised sexuality, in contrast, we face injustices of misrecognition requiring remedies of recognition. What is needed *here* is the politics of recognition.

Matters become murkier, however, once we move away from these extremes. When we posit a type of collectivity located in the middle of the conceptual spectrum, we encounter a hybrid form that combines features of the exploited class with features of the despised sexuality. I will call such a collectivity "bivalent." Rooted at once in the economic structure and the status order of society, they suffer injustices that are traceable to political economy and culture simultaneously. Bivalently subordinated groups suffer both maldistribution and misrecognition *in forms where neither of these injustices is an indirect effect of the other, but where both are primary and co-original.* In their case, accordingly, neither a politics of redistribution alone nor a politics of recognition alone will suffice. Bivalently subordinated groups need both.

Gender, I contend, is a bivalent collectivity. Neither simply a class nor simply a status group, gender is a hybrid category rooted simultaneously in political economy and in culture. From the distributive perspective, gender structures the fundamental division between paid "productive" labor and unpaid "reproductive" and domestic labor, as well as the division within paid labor between higher-paid, male-dominated, manufacturing and professional occupations and lower-paid, female-dominated "pink collar" and domestic service occupations. The result is an economic structure that generates gender-specific modes of exploitation, economic marginalization, and deprivation. Here, gender appears as a class-like differentiation. And gender injustice appears as a species of economic injustice that cries out for redistributive redress.

From the perspective of the status order, however, gender encompasses elements that are more like sexuality than class and that bring it squarely within the problematic of recognition. Gender codes pervasive patterns of cultural value, which are central to the status order as a whole. As a result, not just women, but all low-status groups, risk being feminized, and thereby demeaned. Thus, a major feature of gender injustice is androcentrism: an institutionalized pattern of cultural value that privileges traits associated with masculinity, while devaluing everything coded as "feminine." The result is to construct women and girls as subordinate and deficient others who cannot participate as peers in social life. Pervasively institutionalized, this androcentric value pattern generates gender-specific forms of *status subordination*, including sexual assault, domestic violence, lifelong tutelage, arranged marriages, dowry deaths, mass rape as a weapon of war, genital mutilation, and sexual enslavement; hence, denial of bodily integrity, reproductive freedom, and sexual self-determination; but also diminished access to housing, food, land, health care, and education; impaired immigration, naturalization, and asylum rights; exclusion from or marginalization in civil society and political life; media stereotyping and objectification; and harassment and disparagement in everyday life. These harms are injustices of recognition. They are relatively independent of political economy and are not merely "superstructural." Thus, they cannot be overcome by redistribution alone but require additional, independent remedies of recognition.

Gender, in sum, is a "bivalent" mode of collectivity. It combines a class-like dimension, which brings it within the ambit of redistribution, with a status dimension, which brings it simultaneously within the ambit of recognition. It is an open question whether the two dimensions are of equal weight. But redressing gender injustice, in any case, requires changing both the economic structure and the status order of society.

The bivalent character of gender wreaks havoc on the idea of an either/or choice between the politics of redistribution and the politics of recognition. That construction assumed that the collective subjects of injustice are either classes or status groups, but not both; that the injustice they suffer is either maldistribution or misrecognition, but not both; that the group differences at issue are either unjust differentials or unjustly devalued cultural variations, but not both; that the remedy for injustice is either redistribution or recognition, but not both.

Gender, we can now see, explodes this whole series of false antitheses. Here we have a collective subject that is a compound of both status and class, that suffers injustices of both maldistribution and misrecognition, whose distinctiveness is compounded of both economic differentials and culturally constructed distinctions. Gender injustice can only be remedied, therefore, by an approach that encompasses both a politics of redistribution and a politics of recognition.

Gender is not unusual in this regard. "Race," too, is a bivalent mode of collectivity, a compound of status and class. Rooted simultaneously in the economic structure and the status order of society, racism's injustices include both maldistribution and misrecognition. In the economy, "race" organizes structural divisions between menial and non-menial paid jobs, on the one hand, and between exploitable and "superfluous" labor power, on the other. As a result, the economic structure generates racially specific forms of maldistribution. Racialized immigrants and/or ethnic minorities suffer disproportionately high rates of unemployment and poverty and over-representation in low-paying menial work. These distributive injustices can only be remedied by a politics of redistribution.

In the status order, meanwhile, Eurocentric patterns of culture value privilege traits associated with "whiteness," while stigmatizing everything coded as "black," "brown," and "yellow," paradigmatically – but not only – people of color. The effect is to construct ethnic minorities, racialized immigrants, indigenous peoples, and/or métis as inferior and degraded others who cannot be full members of society. Pervasively institutionalized, Eurocentric norms generate racially specific forms of status subordination, including stigmatization, assault, police brutality, enslavement, "ethnic cleansing," and genocide; discrimination in housing, health care, and welfare provision; diminished rights of immigration, naturalization, and asylum; media stereotyping; devaluation of immigrant and/or minority culture; exclusion or marginalization in public spheres and political institutions; harassment and disparagement in everyday life; and denial of the full rights and equal protections of citizenship. Quintessential harms of misrecognition, these injustices can only be remedied by a politics of recognition.

Neither dimension of racism is wholly an indirect effect of the other, moreover. To be sure, the distributive and recognition dimensions interact with one another. But racist maldistribution is not simply a byproduct of status hierarchy; nor is racist misrecognition wholly a byproduct of economic structure. Rather, each dimension has some relative independence from the other. Neither can be redressed indirectly, therefore, through remedies addressed exclusively to the other. Overcoming the injustices of racism, in sum, requires both redistribution and recognition. Neither alone will suffice.

Class, too, is probably best understood as bivalent for practical purposes. To be sure, the ultimate cause of class injustice is the economic structure of capitalist society. But the resulting harms include misrecognition as well as maldistribution. And cultural harms that originated as byproducts of economic structure may have since developed a life of their own. Left unattended, moreover, class misrecognition may impede the capacity to mobilize against maldistribution. Thus, a politics of class recognition may be needed to get a politics of redistribution off the ground.[4]

Sexuality, too, may be treated as bivalent for practical purposes. To be sure, the ultimate cause of heterosexist injustice is the heteronormative value pattern that is institutionalized in the status order of contemporary society.[5] But the resulting harms include maldistribution as well as misrecognition. And economic harms that originate as byproducts of the status order have an undeniable weight of their own. Left unattended, moreover, they may impede the capacity to mobilize against misrecognition. Thus, a politics of sexual redistribution may be needed to get a politics of recognition off the ground.

For practical purposes, then, virtually all real-world axes of subordination may be treated as bivalent. Virtually all implicate both maldistribution and misrecognition in forms where each of those injustices has some independent weight, whatever its ultimate roots. To be sure, not all axes of subordination are bivalent in the same way, nor to the same degree. Some, such as class, tilt more heavily toward the distribution end of the spectrum; others, such as sexuality, incline more to the recognition end; while still others, such as gender and "race," cluster closer to the center. Nevertheless, in virtually every case, the harms at issue comprise both maldistribution and misrecognition in forms where neither of those injustices can be redressed entirely indirectly but where each requires some practical attention. As a practical matter, therefore, overcoming injustice in virtually every case requires both redistribution and recognition.

The need for this sort of two-pronged approach becomes more pressing, moreover, as soon as we cease considering such axes of injustice singly and begin instead to consider them together as mutually intersecting. After all, gender, "race," sexuality, and class are not neatly cordoned off from one another. Rather, all these axes of injustice intersect one another in ways that affect everyone's interests and identities. Thus, anyone who is both gay and working-class will need both redistribution and recognition. Seen this way, moreover, virtually every individual who suffers injustice needs to integrate both those two kinds of claims. And so, furthermore, will anyone who cares about social justice, regardless of their own personal social location.

In general, then, one should roundly reject the construction of redistribution and recognition as mutually exclusive alternatives. The goal should be, rather, to develop an integrated approach that can encompass, and harmonize, both dimensions of social justice.

3. Normative-Philosophical Issues: Justice as Participatory Parity

How, then, can we develop such a two-pronged approach? How can we integrate redistribution and recognition in a single framework so as to overcome their current dissociation? In the remainder of this essay I want to consider two sets of issues, normative-philosophical issues, which concern the relation between recognition and distributive justice as categories in moral theory; and social-theoretical issues, which concern the relation between economy and culture.

The project of integrating redistribution and recognition in a single framework impinges on ongoing debates over three normative philosophical questions. First, is recognition really a matter of justice, or is it a matter of self-realization? Second, do distributive justice and recognition constitute two distinct, *sui generis*, normative paradigms, or can either of them be subsumed within the other? And third, does justice require the recognition of what is distinctive about individuals or groups, or is recognition of our common humanity sufficient?

With respect to the first question, I propose to understand recognition as an issue of justice, not of self-realization. Thus, one should not answer the question "what's wrong with misrecognition?" by saying that it impedes self-realization by distorting the subject's "practical relation-to-self."[6] One should say, rather, that it is unjust that some individuals and groups are denied the status of full partners in social interaction simply as a consequence of institutionalized patterns of cultural value in whose construction they have not equally participated and which disparage their distinctive characteristics or the distinctive characteristics assigned to them.

Let me explain. To view recognition as a matter of justice is to treat it as an issue of *status*. This in turn means examining institutionalized patterns of cultural value for their effects on the *relative standing* of social actors. If and when such patterns constitute actors as *peers*, capable of participating on a par with one another in social life, then we can speak of *reciprocal recognition* and *status equality*. When, in contrast, institutionalized patterns of cultural value constitute some actors as inferior, excluded, wholly other, or simply invisible, hence as less than full partners in social interaction, then we can speak of *misrecognition* and *status subordination*.

This account has a number of advantages. First, it permits us to sidestep unresolvable disagreements about self-realization and the good. Second, it explains why misrecognition is not simply a matter of prejudicial attitudes resulting in psychological harms but a matter of institutionalized patterns of cultural value that impede equal participation in social life. Finally, it avoids the patently dubious view that everyone has an equal right to social esteem. What it *does* entail is that everyone has an equal right to pursue social esteem under fair conditions of equal opportunity. And such conditions do not obtain when, for example, the institutionalized patterns of cultural value pervasively downgrade femininity, "non-whiteness," homosexuality, and everything culturally associated with them. When that is the case, women and/or people of color and/or gays and lesbians face obstacles in the quest for esteem that are not encountered by others. And everyone, including straight white men, faces further obstacles if they opt to pursue projects and cultivate traits that are culturally coded as feminine, homosexual, or "nonwhite."

Does it follow, turning now to the second question, that distributive justice and recognition constitute two distinct, *sui generis*, normative paradigms? Or can either of them be reduced to the other?

In my view the answer is no. As we saw, recognition cannot be reduced to distribution, as one's status in society is not simply a function of one's class position. Witness the case of the African-American Wall Street banker who cannot get a taxi to pick him up. In this case, the injustice of misrecognition has little to do with maldistribution. It is rather a consequence of institutionalized patterns of cultural value that constitute people of color as comparatively unworthy of respect and esteem. To handle such cases, a theory of justice must reach beyond the distribution of resources and goods to examine patterns of cultural value. It must consider whether institutionalized patterns of cultural value constitute some social actors as less than full partners in social interaction.

Conversely, likewise, distribution cannot be reduced to recognition, as one's access to resources is not simply a function of one's status. Witness the case of the skilled white male industrial worker who becomes unemployed due to a factory closing resulting from a speculative corporate merger. In that case, the injustice of maldistribution has little to do with misrecognition. It is rather a consequence of imperatives intrinsic to an order of specialized economic relations whose raison d'être is the accumulation of profits. To handle such cases, a theory of justice must reach beyond cultural value patterns to examine the economic structure of society. It must consider whether economic mechanisms that are relatively decoupled from cultural value patterns and that operate in a relatively impersonal way deprive some social actors of the resources they need to participate fully in social life.

In general then, neither distribution nor recognition can be reduced to the other. Rather than endorsing either one of these paradigms to the exclusion of the other, I propose to develop what I shall call a "two-dimensional" conception of justice. A two-dimensional conception treats distribution and recognition as distinct perspectives on, and dimensions of, justice. Without reducing either dimension to the other, it encompasses both of them within a broader, overarching framework.

As already noted, the normative core of my conception is the notion of *parity of participation*. According to this norm, justice requires social arrangements that permit all adult members of society to interact with one another as peers. For participatory parity to be possible, I claim, at least two social conditions must be satisfied. First, the distribution of material resources must be such as to ensure participants' independence and "voice." This I call the "objective" condition of participatory parity. It precludes arrangements that institutionalize deprivation, exploitation, and gross disparities in wealth, income, labor and leisure time.

In contrast, the second condition for participatory parity I call "intersubjective." It requires that institutionalized patterns of cultural value express equal respect for all participants and ensure equal opportunity for achieving social esteem. This condition precludes cultural patterns that systematically depreciate some categories of people and the qualities associated with them, whether by burdening them with excessive ascribed "difference" from others or by failing to acknowledge their distinctiveness.

Both the objective condition and the intersubjective condition are necessary for participatory parity. Neither alone is sufficient. The objective condition brings into focus concerns traditionally associated with the theory of distributive justice, especially concerns pertaining to the economic structure of society and to economically defined class differentials. The intersubjective condition brings into focus concerns recently highlighted in the philosophy of recognition, especially concerns pertaining to the status order of society and to culturally defined hierarchies of status. Thus, a two-dimensional conception of justice oriented to the norm of participatory parity encompasses both redistribution and recognition, without reducing either one to the other.

This brings us to the third question: Does justice require the recognition of what is distinctive about individuals or groups, over and above the recognition of our common humanity? Here it is important to note that participatory parity is a universalist norm in two senses. First, it encompasses all adult partners to interaction. And second, it presupposes the equal moral worth of human beings. But moral universalism in these senses still leaves open the question whether recognition of individual or group distinctiveness could be required by justice as one element among others of the intersubjective condition for participatory parity.

This question cannot be answered, however, by abstract conceptual analysis alone. It needs rather to be approached in the spirit of pragmatism as informed by the insights of critical social theory. Everything depends on precisely what currently misrecognized people need in order to be able to participate as peers in social life. And there is no reason to assume that all of them need the same thing in every context. In some cases, they may need to be unburdened of excessive ascribed or constructed distinctiveness in order to be able to participate as full partners in interaction. In other cases, they may need to have hitherto underacknowledged distinctiveness taken into account. In still other cases, they may need to shift the focus onto dominant or advantaged groups, outing the latter's distinctiveness, which has been falsely parading as universality. Alternatively, they may need to deconstruct the very terms in which attributed differences are currently elaborated. Finally, they may need all of the above, or several of the above, in combination with one another and in combination with redistribution. Which people need which kind(s) of recognition in which contexts depends on the nature of the obstacles they face with regard to participatory parity.

4. Social-Theoretical Issues: An Argument for "Perspectival Dualism"

This brings us to the social-theoretical issues that arise when we try to encompass redistribution and recognition in a single framework. Here, the principal task is to understand the relations between class and status, and between maldistribution and misrecognition, in contemporary society. An adequate approach must allow for the full complexity of these relations. It must account *both for the differentiation of class from status and for the causal interactions between them.* It must accommodate, as well, *both the mutual irreducibility of maldistribution and misrecognition and their practical entwinement with one another.*

To this end, I propose a thought experiment. Consider an ideal-typical pre-state society of the sort described in the classical anthropological literature, while bracketing the question of ethnographic accuracy. In such a society, the master idiom of social relations is kinship. Kinship organizes not only marriage and sexual relations, but also the labor process and the distribution of goods; relations of authority, reciprocity, and obligation; and symbolic hierarchies of status and prestige. In such a society, class structure and status order are effectively fused. Because kinship constitutes the overarching principle of distribution, kinship status dictates class position. Status subordination translates immediately into (what *we* would consider to be) distributive injustices. Misrecognition directly entails maldistribution.

Now consider the opposite extreme of a fully marketized society, in which economic structure dictates cultural value. In such a society, the master determining instance is the market. Markets organize not only the labor process and the distribution of goods, but also marriage and sexual relations; political relations of authority, reciprocity, and obligation; and symbolic hierarchies of status and prestige. In this society, too, class structure and status order are effectively fused. But the determinations run in the opposite direction. Because the market constitutes the sole and all-pervasive mechanism of valuation, market position dictates social status. In the absence of any quasi-autonomous cultural value patterns, distributive injustices translate immediately into status subordination. Maldistribution directly entails misrecognition.

In both of these societies, accordingly, (what *we* would call) class and status map perfectly onto each other. So, as well, do (what *we* would call) maldistribution and misrecognition, which convert fully and without remainder into one another. As a result, one can understand both these societies reasonably well by attending exclusively to a single dimension of social life. For the fully kin-governed society, one can read off the economic dimension of domination directly from the cultural; one can infer class directly from status and maldistribution directly from misrecognition. For the fully marketized society, conversely, one can read off the cultural dimension of domination directly from the economic; one can infer status directly from class and misrecognition directly from maldistribution. For understanding the forms of domination proper to the fully kin-governed society, therefore, culturalism is a perfectly appropriate social theory.[7] If, in contrast, one is seeking to understand the fully marketized society, one could hardly improve on economism.[8]

When we turn to other types of societies, however, such simple and elegant approaches no longer suffice. They are patently inappropriate for contemporary societies, which contain both marketized arenas, in which strategic action predominates, and non-marketized arenas, in which value-oriented interaction predominates. The result is a partial uncoupling of economic distribution from structures of prestige and thus a gap between status and class. In contemporary societies, then, the class structure ceases perfectly to mirror the status order, even though each of them influences the other. Because the market does not constitute the sole and all-pervasive mechanism of valuation, market position does not dictate social status. Partially market-resistant cultural value patterns prevent distributive injustices from converting fully and without remainder into status subordination. Maldistribution does not directly entail misrecognition, although it certainly contributes to the latter. Conversely, because no single status principle such as kinship constitutes the sole and all-pervasive principle of distribution, status does not dictate class position. Relatively autonomous economic institutions prevent status subordination from converting fully and without remainder into distributive injustices. Misrecognition does not directly entail maldistribution, although it, too, surely contributes to the latter. As a result, one cannot understand contemporary societies by attending exclusively to a single dimension of social life. One cannot read off the economic dimension of domination directly from the cultural, not the cultural directly from the economic. Likewise, one cannot infer class directly from status, nor status directly from class. Finally, one cannot deduce maldistribution directly from misrecognition, nor misrecognition directly from maldistribution. It follows that neither culturalism nor economism suffices for understanding contemporary societies. Instead, one needs an approach that can accommodate differentiation, divergence, and interaction at every level.

What sort of social theory can handle this task? If neither economism nor culturalism is up to the task, a dualism of some sort is required. But everything depends on what sort. Two possibilities present themselves.[9] The first I call "substantive dualism." It treats redistribution and recognition as two different "spheres of justice," pertaining to two different societal domains. The former pertains to the economic domain of society, the latter to the cultural domain. When we consider economic matters, such as the structure of labor markets, we should assume the standpoint of distributive justice, attending to the impact of economic structures on the relative economic position of social actors. When, in contrast, we consider cultural matters, such as the representation of female sexuality on MTV, we should assume the standpoint of recognition, attending to the impact of institutionalized patterns of cultural value on the status and relative standing of social actors.

Substantive dualism may be preferable to economism and culturalism, but it is nevertheless inadequate. Treating economy and culture as two separate spheres, it mistakes social differentiations for impermeable and sharply bounded divisions. In fact, the economy is not a culture-free zone, but a culture-instrumentalizing and -resignifying one. Thus, what presents itself as "the economy" is always already permeated with cultural interpretations and norms – witness the distinctions between "working" and "caregiving," "men's jobs" and "women's jobs," which are so fundamental to historical capitalism. In these cases, gender meanings and norms have been appropriated from pre-existing cultures and bent to economic purposes, with major consequences for both distribution and recognition. Likewise, what presents itself as "the cultural sphere" is deeply permeated by "the bottom line"– witness global mass entertainment, the art market, and transnational advertising, all fundamental to contemporary culture. *Contra* substantive dualism, then, nominally economic matters usually affect not only the economic position but also the status and identities of social actors. Likewise, nominally cultural matters affect not only status but also economic position. In neither case, therefore, are we dealing with separate spheres.

Substantive dualism is not a solution to, but a symptom of, the current uncoupling of redistribution and recognition. A critical perspective, in contrast, must probe the connections between them. It must make visible, and *criticizable*, both the cultural subtexts of nominally economic processes and the economic subtexts of nominally cultural practices. Treating *every* practice as simultaneously economic and cultural, albeit not necessarily in equal proportions, it must assess each of them from two different perspectives. It must assume both the standpoint of distribution and the standpoint of recognition, without reducing either one of these perspectives to the other.

Such an approach I call "perspectival dualism." Here redistribution and recognition do not correspond to two substantive societal domains, economy and culture. Rather, they constitute two analytical perspectives that can be assumed with respect to any domain. These perspectives can be deployed critically, moreover, against the ideological grain. One can use the recognition perspective to identify the cultural dimensions of what are usually viewed as redistributive economic policies. By focusing on the production and circulation of interpretations and norms in welfare programs, for example, one can assess the effects of institutionalized maldistribution on the identities and social status of beneficiaries.[10] Conversely, one can use the redistribution perspective to bring into focus the economic dimensions of what are usually viewed as issues of recognition. By focusing on the high "transaction costs" of living in the closet, for example, one can assess the effects of heterosexist misrecognition on the economic position of gays and lesbians.[11] With perspectival dualism, then, one can assess the justice of any social practice from two analytically distinct normative vantage points, asking: Does the practice in question work to ensure both the economic conditions and the cultural conditions of participatory parity? Or does it, rather, undermine them?

Moreover, perspectival dualism offers a major practical advantage. It allows us to conceptualize some practical difficulties that can arise in the course of political struggles for redistribution and recognition. It appreciates that neither claims for redistribution nor claims for recognition can be contained within a separate sphere. On the contrary, they impinge on one another in ways that may give rise to unintended effects.

Consider, first, that redistribution impinges on recognition. Virtually any claim for redistribution will have some recognition effects, whether intended or unintended. Redistributive policies aimed at mitigating poverty, for example, have status implications, which can harm the intended beneficiaries. For example, public assistance programs aimed specifically at the poor often function to mark them as "deviants" and "scroungers." In such cases, the net effect is to add the insult of misrecognition to the injury of deprivation. In general, then, redistributive claims often affect the status and social identities of social actors. These effects must be thematized and scrutinized, lest one end up fueling misrecognition in the course of remedying maldistribution.

Conversely, however, recognition impinges on distribution. Virtually any claim for recognition will have some distributive effects, whether intended or unintended. Proposals to redress androcentric evaluative patterns, for example, have economic implications, which work sometimes to the detriment of the intended beneficiaries. For example, top-down campaigns to suppress female genital mutilation aimed at remedying status subordination may have negative effects on the economic position of the affected women, rendering them "unmarriageable" while failing to ensure alternative means of support. Thus, recognition claims can affect class position, above and beyond their effects on status. These effects, too, must be scrutinized, lest one end up fueling maldistribution in the course of trying to remedy misrecognition.

The moral is that one must assess the merits of any claim from both perspectives. One must ask: Does the proposal in question work to challenge both misrecognition and maldistribution? Or does it, rather, mitigate one of those harms at the cost of exacerbating the other? In this way, one can anticipate, and hopefully avoid, unintended effects.

The need, in all cases, is to think integratively, as in the example of comparable worth. Here a claim to redistribute income between men and women is expressly integrated with a claim to change gender-coded patterns of cultural value. The underlying premise is that gender injustices of distribution and recognition are so complexly intertwined that neither can be redressed entirely independently of the other. Thus, efforts to reduce the gender wage gap cannot fully succeed if, remaining wholly "economic," they fail to challenge the gender meanings that code low-paying service occupations as "women's work," largely devoid of intelligence and skill. Likewise, efforts to revalue female-coded traits such as interpersonal sensitivity and nurturance cannot succeed if, remaining wholly "cultural," they fail to challenge the structural economic conditions that connect those traits with dependency and powerlessness. Only an approach that redresses the cultural devaluation of the "feminine" precisely *within* the economy (and elsewhere) can deliver serious redistribution and genuine recognition.

Conclusion

Let me conclude by recapitulating my overall argument. I have argued that to pose an either/or choice between the politics of redistribution and the politics of recognition is to posit a false antithesis. On the contrary, justice today requires both. Thus, I have argued for a comprehensive framework that encompasses both redistribution and recognition so as to challenge injustice on both fronts.

I then examined two sets of issues that arise once we contemplate devising such a framework. On the plane of moral theory, I argued for a single, two-dimensional conception of justice that encompasses both redistribution and recognition, without reducing either one of them to the other. And I proposed the notion of *parity of participation* as its normative core. On the plane of social theory, I argued for a *perspectival dualism* of redistribution and recognition. This approach alone, I contended, can alert us to potential practical tensions between claims for redistribution and claims for recognition.

Perspectival dualism in social theory complements participatory parity in moral theory. Taken together, these two notions constitute a portion of the conceptual resources one needs to begin answering what I take to be the key political question of our day: How can we develop a coherent programmatic perspective that integrates redistribution and recognition? How can we develop a framework that integrates what remains cogent and unsurpassable in the socialist vision with what is defensible and compelling in the apparently "postsocialist" vision of multiculturalism?

If we fail to ask this question, if we cling instead to false antitheses and misleading either/or dichotomies, we will miss the chance to envision social arrangements that can redress both economic and cultural injustices.

Only by looking to integrative approaches that unite redistribution and recognition can we meet the requirements of justice for all.

Notes

1. Research for this paper was supported by the Tanner Foundation for Human Values, Stanford University, and UNESCO. I am grateful for helpful comments from Elizabeth Anderson, Richard J. Bernstein, Judith Butler, Rainer Forst, Axel Honneth, Theodore Koditschek, Steven Lukes, Jane Mansbridge, Linda Nicholson, Anne Phillips, Erik Olin Wright, and Eli Zaretsky.

2. The following discussion substantially revises a section of my essay, "From Redistribution to Recognition? Dilemmas of Justice in a 'Postsocialist' Age," *New Left Review* 212 (July/August 1995): 68-93; reprinted in Nancy Fraser, *Justice Interruptus: Critical Reflections on the "Postsocialist" Condition* (New York: Routledge, 1997).

3. Richard Sennett and Jonathan Cobb, *The Hidden Injuries of Class* (New York: Knopf, 1973).

4. I am grateful to Erik Olin Wright (personal communication 1997) for help in formulating several of these points.

5. In capitalist societies, the regulation of sexuality is relatively decoupled from the economic structure, which comprises an order of economic relations that is differentiated from kinship and oriented to the expansion of surplus value. In the current "post-fordist" globalizing phase of capitalism, moreover, sexuality increasingly finds its locus in the relatively new, late-modern sphere of "personal life," where intimate relations that can no longer be identified with the family are lived as disconnected from the imperatives of production and reproduction. Today, accordingly, the heteronormative regulation of sexuality is increasingly removed from, and not necessarily functional for, the capitalist economic order. As a result, the economic harms of heterosexism do not derive in any straightforward way from the economic structure. They are rooted, rather, in the heterosexist status order, which is increasingly out of phase with the economy. For a fuller argument, see Nancy Fraser, "Heterosexism, Misrecognition, and Capitalism: A Response to Judith Butler," *Social Text* 52/53 (Fall/Winter 1997). For the counterargument, see Judith Butler, "Merely Cultural," *Social Text* 52/53 (Fall/Winter 1997).

6. This formulation represents the alternative approach of Axel Honneth, as developed in his *The Struggle for Recognition: The Moral Grammar of Social Conflicts*, trans. Joel Anderson (Cambridge, MA: Polity Press, 1995).

7. By culturalism, I mean a monistic social theory that holds that political economy is reducible to culture and that class is reducible to status. As I read him, Axel Honneth subscribes to such a theory. See Honneth, *The Struggle for Recognition*, op. cit.

8. By economism, I mean a monistic social theory that holds that culture is reducible to political economy and that status is reducible to class. Karl Marx is often (mis)read as subscribing to such a theory.

[9] In what follows, I leave aside a third possibility, which I call "deconstructive anti-dualism." Rejecting the economy/culture distinction as "dichotomizing," this approach seeks to deconstruct it altogether. The claim is that culture and economy are so deeply interconnected that it doesn't make sense to distinguish them. A related claim is that contemporary capitalist society is so monolithically systematic that a struggle against one aspect of it necessarily threatens the whole; hence, it is illegitimate, unnecessary, and counterproductive to distinguish maldistribution from misrecognition. In my view, deconstructive anti-dualism is deeply misguided. For one thing, simply to stipulate that all injustices, and all claims to remedy them, are simultaneously economic and cultural, evacuates the actually existing divergence of status from class. For another, treating capitalism as a monolithic system of perfectly interlocking oppressions evacuates its actual complexity and differentiation. For two rather different version of deconstructive anti-dualism, see Iris Marion Young, "Unruly Categories: A Critique of Nancy Fraser's Dual Systems Theory," *New Left Review* 222 (March/April 1997): 147-60; and Judith Butler, "Merely Cultural," op. cit. For detailed rebuttals, see Fraser, "A Rejoinder to Iris Young," *New Left Review* 223 (May/June 1997): 126-9; and Fraser, "Heterosexism, Misrecognition, and Capitalism: A Response to Judith Butler," op. cit.

[10] See Nancy Fraser, "Women, Welfare, and the Politics of Need Interpretation" and "Struggle Over Needs," both in Fraser, *Unruly Practices: Power, Discourse and Gender in Contemporary Social Theory* (Minneapolis: University of Minnesota Press, 1989). Also, Nancy Fraser and Linda Gordon, "A Genealogy of 'Dependency': Tracing A Keyword of the US Welfare State," *Signs* 19.2 (Winter 1994): 309-36; reprinted in Fraser, *Justice Interruptus* op. cit.

[11] Jeffrey Escoffier has discussed these issues insightfully in "The Political Economy of the Closet: Toward an Economic History of Gay and Lesbian Life before Stonewall," in Escoffier, *American Homo: Community and Perversity* (Berkeley: University of California Press, 1998): 65-78.

Self-determination and Global Democracy: A Critique of Liberal Nationalism*

Iris Marion Young

Like most eras, ours contains apparently opposing tendencies. On the one hand, processes of globalization challenge the ability of the nation-state to govern the affairs that most affect its citizens. On the other hand, nationalist ideas and movements have lately received renewed popular support.

Recent political theory has responded to and reflected on each of these apparently opposing sociohistorical trends. Some theorists construct moral criticisms of assumptions of state sovereignty and nationalist commitment, and argue for a more cosmopolitan conception of political community. Others argue for the moral value and legitimacy of nationalism in a form compatible with liberal democratic principles and institutions.

"Nationalism and cosmopolitanism have always gotten along well together, as paradoxical as this may seem." So says Jacques Derrida, in *The Other Heading*, his meditation on European identity and responsibility in an imploding world.[1] Derrida himself suggests one interpretation of this enigmatic sentence. European nationalisms have the peculiar form of justifying themselves as cosmopolitan. "Our Frenchness consists in that we gave to the world The Rights of Man."[2] Another interpretation he does not suggest but which is consistent with the spirit of his remark is that the logic of both nationalism and cosmopolitanism gives primacy to sameness over difference. Cosmopolitanism often expresses an abstract individualism that doubts that cultural difference does or should matter politically. Nationalism is sometimes an understandable reaction to a cosmopolitan assertion that we are all simply human, with the same basic human rights and needs. Nationalism, however, even in the liberal versions I will analyze in this essay, asserts the unity of a people over a territory in ways that often suppress dfferences within and wrongfully exclude and oppose differences without.

In this essay I aim to sort out some of what is right and wrong about both cosmopolitanism and nationalism, in order to develop a vision of politics for the contemporary world that includes the proper insights of each while criticizing and rejecting their problematic aspects. This account envisions global political institutions that recognize local and regional cultural and historical differentiation and self-determination. With some reconstructed concepts and arguments, I hope to make the motivations of both cosmopolitanism and nationalism get along well together.[3]

The essay has the following critical and positive elements. First, I criticize the arguments of some political theorists for a liberal version of nationalism. Thinkers such as Yael Tamir, David Miller, and Will Kymlicka are right to affirm the moral value of cultural membership as a source of the self. Efforts to distinguish a distinct kind of cultural group, nation, from other cultural groups, however, presuppose what they aim to justify. Arguments that national members have special obligations of justice they do not have to others, moreover, are problematic. In a world of global interdependence, obligations of justice extend globally. Such moral arguments challenge the legitimacy of a world order composed of independent sovereign states, a world order that economic powers and interactions are challenging practically. Assumption of the norm of independent and unified state sovereignty is also being challenged from within by groups inside states claiming special rights and autonomy. Giving adequate recognition to such group-differentiated movements against the oppression of states, I argue, requires abandoning the concept of nation and replacing it with a concept of distinct people. The idea of a people should be conceptualized in relational rather than substantive terms. Those who theorize the importance of recognizing the distinctness of peoples in politics are right to emphasize a principle of self-determination for peoples. This principle of self-determination still tends to be understood today, however, as the claim for a right to an independent state. This interpretation coheres neither with a challenge to the states system nor with the claim that all peoples should be able to exercise self-determination. Thus the idea of self-determination should also be reconceived in relational terms that cohere with openness and interdependence. The claim of global governance coupled with a principle of self-determination for peoples yields an image of federalism as a global governance principle. I end by articulating some elements of such global democracy.

I. Problems With Liberal Nationalism

Some political theorists are minting a new brand of nationalism, a liberal nationalism. Liberal nationalism endorses values of liberty, formal equality, constitutional law, nondiscrimination, and democratic procedures, and argues that a plausible conception of particular affiliations and obligations of national members can be compatible with these liberal values. For some years Michael Walzer has championed a position like this, though he has not called it liberal nationalism. More recently Charles Taylor, Will Kymlicka, Yael Tamir, David Miller, and Margaret Canovan have formulated versions of a liberal nationalist political theory.

Liberal nationalism would seem to sit comfortably within a more general politics of difference that argues that public discussion and policies should attend to and sometimes affirm social-group differences. In this section I will argue, however, that it is possible and necessary to distinguish a recognition of the difference and autonomy of distinct peoples from the affirmation of nationalism.

I read liberal nationalism as a response to the cosmopolitan individualism that implicitly underlies most contemporary moral and political theory. Such cosmopolitanism considers illiberal and reactionary the inclination of many people to identify with a national group and wish special ties of affiliation with it. Affirmation of nationalist sentiments and sense of obligation, some suggest, wrongly limits the freedom of those persons who do not feel the national identification or identity with a minority group.[4] The idea that nations may elevate the good of their own members above that of any and all outsiders, moreover, conflicts with a moral norm that presumes that all human beings have equal moral worth. Both liberty and good character, then, require of citizens a stance of cosmopolitan individualism. Nation ought not to define the bounds of either moral or political community.[5] A liberal constitution should affirm the rights of individuals as individuals, and states ought to be culturally neutral.

Liberal nationalism responds appropriately to the abstraction and bloodlessness of such cosmopolitan individualism. This position fails to recognize that each of us is born into a community with a given history, set of traditions, and meaning. The particular relations in this community give texture to our social affiliation, and in particular condition the value frameworks within which we develop our ability to make particular decisions, including decisions to change some of the community's practices or to leave the community. We grow up learning a particular language, or sometimes particular languages, and our linguistic particularity gives us an oral and literary history, as well as particular ways of expressing ourselves to particular others who speak the language. Because cultural group membership nurtures us and gives us many meaningful social relationships, we can be obliged to help preserve the group and ensure its well-being for the sake of those whose identities do or will partly depend on it. The depth of languages and cultural flexibility toward the future can live only if many people are deeply immersed in and love them. Human spirits must take particular form; they cannot survive with universal principles and technical formulae alone.[6]

Liberal nationalists go further than affirming the moral value of affinity with particular historical and cultural groups as a source of the self. Some believe that the existence and value of each such distinct people implies special rights and obligations. Some argue that a nation is a particular kind of cultural grouping with a unique claim to statehood. Some also argue that obligations of social justice in the form of redistributive welfare policies hold only between conationals. While I accept the liberal nationalist affirmation of the value of particular membership, I will criticize these second two widely accepted claims, which have received philosophical justification in the literature arguing for liberal nationalism. My critique will focus on David Miller's book *On Nationality*, but I will refer to texts by Kymlicka and Tamir as well.

A. The Concept of Nation

If a nation has special claims to statehood, then not just any cultural grouping can be a nation. Possibly tens of thousands of cultural groupings exist in the world, and most people would agree that we cannot have so many independent states. Thus the political theory of liberal nationalism takes as one of its tasks distinguishing nations from other sorts of cultural groups, often called ethnic groups. This task turns out to be difficult, however. I submit that these accounts attempting to distinguish a nation from an ethnic group tend to be circular. The criteria for distinguishing nations from other cultural groups turn out to presume an idea of independent statehood.

David Miller argues that a nation is the sort of social entity that should have its own set of political institutions and that the best way to ensure this is to advance independent statehood for the nation. A nation is best protected and nurtured if it coincides with a state, and a state is strongest and most stable it if coincides with a single nation. Where history, the geographic dispersion of nations, or scale make multinational states either necessary or more practical, this is a less desirable and less stable organization than a nation-state.[7] Will Kymlicka, on the other hand, believes that multinational states must be the norm in today's world because many nations have become intertwined territorially, historically, and economically. Yet Kymlicka also defines a nation as a special kind of group with inherent rights of self-government that other kinds of groups do not have.[8]

What is supposed to distinguish a nation, which has moral claims to self-government, from an ethnic group, which does not? Miller admits that there is no sharp dividing line between nation and ethnic group. Both are collectives of people with certain shared cultural characteristics such as language, music, a history of visual art, territorial contiguity, and so on. In both cases part of what makes the members of the group a group is the fact that its members recognize one another as members of the same group. Miller admits that nations may evolve from ethnicities.

A nation must be distinct from an ethnic group, however, according to Miller, because many nation-states today have several ethnicities within them. He offers the United States and Switzerland as two key examples.[9] More contentiously, perhaps, Miller invokes the difference between the British nation and its component groups of English, Scots, Welsh, and Northern Irish as evidence that a nation is something distinctive over and above ethnicity or cultural membership.[10] But what is this something?

Miller is careful to say that what national members share that distinguishes them from other groups ought not be thought of as biological or racial, nor is it even essential that members of a nation were all born in the same land. A key difference between *liberal* nationalism and more traditionalist and illiberal nationalisms is this insistence that a nation is not a "natural kind" but, rather, a particular social construction. Thus for Miller, what distinguishes a nation from other kinds of groups is that its members see themselves as belonging together to a community that is extended in history and active in character. The same can be said, however, about many of the groups Miller clearly thinks of as ethnicities or subnational groups, such as African Americans or French Nova Scotians or Fijians of Indian descent. A nation is further characterized, he says, by a connection to a particular territory. This trait, too, while perhaps necessary to the concept of a nation for Miller, cannot be sufficient because it is true of many groups he wants to classify as ethnicities or subnational groups, such as Welsh, Walloons, or Chicanos. There is only one characteristic left that in Miller's concept of nation seems decisively to distinguish a nation from these other kinds of cultural groups with which the idea of nation is closely aligned. A nation is marked off from other communities, he says, by its distinct *public culture*. A public culture is different from private culture. Private culture consists in the tastes, preferences, and specific practices of a group – its recipes, its love of particular sports, the way members of the group typically spend their Sundays. A public culture is a collective's sense of rights and citizen responsibilities as defined by political rules that are the product of a long history of public debate.[11] The one characteristic that most distinguishes the concept of nation from ethnicity, that is, presupposes the existence of distinct and common political institutions within which public discourse takes place among a broad community of strangers and is extended over generations.

Will Kymlicka also distinguishes a nation conceptually from an ethnic group, and for similar reasons. On his account, a nation is a special kind of cultural group with inherent rights of self-government that no other sort of cultural group has. For him a nation is "a historical community, more or less institutionally complete, occupying a given territory or homeland, sharing a distinct language or culture."[12] Because a nation is institutionally complete, and has resided in its own territory for generations, it has a right to self-government. Many nations, such as indigenous nations in North America, have been conquered by other groups who unjustly rule over them and do not recognize their right to self-government. To the extent that the self-governing rights of historic nations are not recognized, they ought to be. Because the history of so many nations has become intertwined or overlapping in territories, state institutions, and economic interdependence, most states today are or should become multinational states whose constitutions grant specific autonomy to their component nations. While this is usually the most just and practical way to recognize the claims of nations, multinational states are inherently unstable because each of the component nations has a tendency to separate from the others.

As it is for Miller, for Kymlicka, the reason to draw a clear distinction between a nation and an ethnic group is to determine which groups have rights of self-government and which do not. For him the concept of nation is an either-or concept. Either a group is a historical community, living in its historic homeland, sharing a distinct language and culture, or it is a cultural group whose members have left their homeland voluntarily to make a new life within another nation. The concept of nation thus dominates the logic of the distinction between nation and ethnic group, as the hegemonic unity of a society that justifies both separate government and the expectation that newcomers will integrate.

This either-or concept of nation, however, does not accommodate well to the actual diversity of peoples. Many people of African descent in the United States, or many of Indian descent in Africa, were forced to migrate, and due to a history of exclusion they maintain a certain degree of distinctness as peoples today. Many other groups worldwide do not fit well into Kymlicka's two-part division of nation versus ethnic groups. Where, for example, are Gypsies? What about Hutus and Tutsies or Khlosa and Swaze? I will argue shortly that in order to accommodate such realities, the distinctness of peoples should be conceptualized in terms of degree rather than kind.

Kymlicka's use of the concept of nation also tends to be circular, I suggest. A distinction among kinds of groups is supposed to give moral foundation to a right of self-government. Implicit in Kymlicka's definition of a nation as a "historical community, more or less institutionally complete, occupying a given territory or homeland" is the assumption that this particular kind of group either is today or once was an independent polity. Like Miller, I suggest, Kymlicka tends to presuppose political community as part of the concept of nation but then uses this concept of nation to justify judging that some groups but not others have legitimate claim to be distinct polities.

Such circularity is unavoidable, I think, because the idea of nation cannot name a distinct kind of cultural group. All efforts to distinguish a nation from an ethnic group seem to presuppose that a nation is a political community and that an ethnic group is not. The idea of a nation entails the idea of a group of people who not only share cultural characteristics and recognize each other as a group but also have, once had, or aspire to have distinct, unified, and independent institutions of political governance. As a number of writers have pointed out, the idea of a nation emerged with the building of modern state forms in Europe.[13] This means, as I have been suggesting, that the concept of nation actually presupposes the concept of sovereign state. For this reason, it cannot be used as an independent criterion to justify claims to sovereign independence.

Such use, however, is the primary political function of the idea of nation. A nation is supposed to be a kind of cultural group distinct in character from other kinds of groups that share language, location, history, and artistic and everyday life traditions. That special character is supposed to justify a unique moral claim to political self-determination. There is no way to distinguish a nation from other kinds of cultural groups, however, without smuggling political self-organization into the idea of nation. Since most people in the world would rather be able to think of themselves as self-governing than governed by others, and since being taken as a nation gives a group a stronger claim to self-government, most groups want recognition as nations. Much energy, negotiation time, and blood is spent on struggle over the boundary between the merely ethnic and the national. This boundary, I have been arguing, is entirely a *political construct* that does not correspond to the cultural character of the contesting groups, their longevity, or degree of cohesion. I will argue below that recognizing the mystifying or ideology character of the idea of nation entails rethinking the meaning, justification, and implications of claims for political self-determination. Before turning to that positive argument, I will examine another common argument for liberal nationalism, the welfare argument.

B. The Welfare Argument

Several philosophers argue that nationalism has positive value because it promotes social justice. The argument, as I understand it, goes as follows. In large, industrial, capitalist societies, promoting social justice requires strong welfare-state policies that meet needs and provide services. Such welfare state policies require redistributive measures whereby some citizens contribute more than others for the sake of the less advantaged. The sense of justice according to which citizens are willing to contribute to and support such welfare state policies, however, depends on particularist affiliations of common culture and a sense of belonging. Yael Tamir puts it this way:

> The "others" whose welfare we ought to consider are those we care about, those who are relevant to our associative identity. Communal solidarity creates a feeling, or an illusion, of closeness and shared fate, which is the precondition of distributive justice. It endows particularistic relations with moral power, supporting the claim that "charity begins at home."[14]

If we look at the history of the formation of welfare states, it is claimed, we find this condition confirmed. Welfare states emerged and remain strong in those societies that had or were able to build a single strong national identity. Nationalism provides the political "engine" that makes the state strong enough to mobilize political resources to enact welfare policies and to enforce them.[15] The achievement of the modern state is universalist in the sense that nationalist movements and commitments motivate individuals to expand their sense of obligation beyond the members of their family, clan, or village to strangers with whom they identify as belonging to the same cultural and historical community. The appeal of nation as "imagined community," then, enables the sense of justice to extend to relatively distant strangers.[16]

I find the welfare argument for liberal nationalism problematic in two respects. Because it endorses the claim that citizens have obligations of justice only to those whom they identify as conationals, this argument can be used to endorse the preservation of privilege and exclusion from benefits that many people find unjust. In making that obligation contingent upon sentiment, moreover, this line of reasoning makes for bad moral argument.

The liberal nationalist construction of national obligation explicitly endorses external exclusions. It does not claim that citizens in a particular nation have no obligations at all to people outside their borders; they have obligations of respect, hospitality, and the defense of human rights. Obligations specifically of distributive justice and attention to the welfare and capabilities of others to live satisfying, productive lives, however, do not extend beyond borders. Each nation is obliged to take care of its own, and to the extent that the leaders of a nation-state fail in discharging those obligations, outsiders have no obligation to take them up, though they may of course decide to help out of a sense of beneficence.

Not only does the welfare argument of liberal nationalism explicitly allow for external exclusion, it opens the door to internal inclusion. The argument that obligations of justice extend only to those with whom citizens identify as belonging to a common national culture and history can legitimate rejection of redistributive policies perceived to benefit groups with whom many citizens do not identify. White Anglo Americans appear increasingly reluctant to support redistributive policies, partly because many of them wrongly believe that these policies primarily benefit African Americans and Latinos, with whom they do not feel such strong ties of common culture and shared history. The feelings of redistributive solidarity for which many Europeans have long been admired are coming under significant strain today in those societies with significant numbers of non-European immigrants, such as those of Turkish, North African, or South Asian origin.[17] This resistance to redistribution seems especially strong when some of those who would benefit from redistributive policies not only are culturally different from others in the society but refuse to assimilate to a dominant national culture, and even claim self-determination for their people. Some New Zealanders of European descent question redistributive welfare policies to Maori, who themselves assert a right of self-determination in the context of New Zealand society. The position that obligations of justice extend only to conationals justifies anti-immigration politics and policies. On this argument, restrictions on immigration are justified not only to preserve a national culture[18] but also to preserve or enlarge redistributive policies from which citizens withdraw support when they perceive immigrants benefiting from them.[19]

The argument that nationalism is a positive value because it motivates citizens to support redistributive policies, moreover, is philosophically problematic. It makes obligation contingent on sentiment. It might be true today that the willingness of citizens to be taxed to pay for public services and redistribution depends on nationalist sentiment. It might also be true (though I have my doubts) that the origins of the welfare state lie in the ties of national identification European states built and appealed to in the nineteenth century. These are contingent empirical claims about historical and contemporary motivational supports for welfare policies. They do not show that national identification is a *necessary* condition of welfare state policies, and they certainly cannot provide a *moral* argument for nationalism.

Arguments that people have obligations of justice to others cannot depend on their having feelings of identification with those others. At best, feelings of identification can sometimes explain why some people sometimes recognize the obligations they have (or believe they have obligations they do not have). In fact, we most often need to make arguments that some people have obligations of justice to others when those with the obligations fail to recognize them; and people often deny their obligations because they feel no affinity for those others or positively dislike them. Moral arguments for obligations of justice must rest on more objective and normative grounds than feelings of familiarity or cultural affinity.

Writers such as Charles Beitz and Thomas Pogge give more objective criteria for determining the scope of people across whom obligations of justice extend. Wherever people act with a set of institutions that connect them to one another by commerce, communication, or the consequences of policies, such that systemic interdependencies generate benefits and burdens that would not exist without those institutional relationships, then the people within that set of interdependent institutions stand in relations of justice.[20]

Onora O'Neill states a similar objective test. The scope of persons to whom agents have obligations of justice extends to all those whose action the agent presupposes as a background or condition for her own action. The scope of justice includes all those to whom an agent is connected through socially contextualized causal relationships. An agent stands in relations with others where obligations of justice hold when her actions can affect them, or when their actions can affect her even if indirectly through the mediation of the actions of others. In O'Neill's view, this entails a global scope of justice today.[21] If I jump into my car each morning on the assumption that cheap gasoline will continue to be readily available to me on the street corner a few blocks away, then principles and obligations of justice apply to my relations with all those people, from the oil workers in Venezuela to the buyers and brokers who organize the oil industry, to all the others whose actions contribute to the institutions of production, refinement, trade, and transportation that get the gasoline to my car. We all together act within a constellation of interdependent institutions to which principles of justice ought to apply. To the extent that injustices exist within this institutional web, those who benefit from the injustices have obligations to those who are harmed, and their national membership or mutual identification is irrelevant to assessing such obligations. Later I will return to this argument about the scope of justice to support a moral critique of the system of states' sovereignty and envision an alternative system of global governance.

II. The Distinctness of Peoples

Efforts to defend a specific positive value to the idea of nation and distinguish nations from other types of cultural groups fail, I have argued. Claims that the scope of justice extends only to conationals, moreover, and that nationalism is valuable because it motivates redistributive policies are philosophically and politically suspect. These critiques appear to lead us back to the cosmopolitan individualism to which I said that liberal nationalism is an appropriate reaction. If the scope of distributive and institutional justice extends to all those persons with whom we are in institutional relations, and if the distinction between nation and other sorts of cultural affinity groups is relatively arbitrary, then from a moral point of view we are all simply individuals with human rights and their correlative obligations. While persons should be free to associate with one another as they choose, the facts and feelings of membership have no specific moral implications.

This is not the conclusion I draw, however, from this critique of liberal nationalism. The opposition that liberal nationalism expresses to cosmopolitan individualism contains a core of truth. A great many people think of themselves as belonging to a people or peoples whose distinct history, language, values, and practices have helped shape who they are. These usually involuntary affiliations provide not only a background for action but also many of the cultural, moral, and material resources for interpreting the world. People often cherish these group affinities, and insist on recognition and support for their efforts to pursue their group-based way of life without being dominated, discriminated against, or exploited by others. Claims about the global scope of justice and the importance of individual rights do not speak to these powerful, and I believe often legitimate, group-specific claims for recognition and self-determination.

Is it possible to affirm positive claims of group affinity, distinctiveness, and self-determination without accepting the concepts and sentiments of nationalism? It must be, I suggest, for at least the following reason. The claims of many distinct peoples for recognition and self-determination are often thwarted by international acceptance of a unique claim of supposed nations to self-determination in the form of independent sovereign statehood. The claims of indigenous peoples are central for me, but the claims of many other distinct peoples often go unheard within a ruling paradigm of nation-states. While I reject the concept of nation as a specific kind of cultural group, I shall argue that the idea of distinct peoples is appropriate and legitimate. A political theory of distinct peoples relies on a relational social ontology instead of the substantial logic typical of nationalism. In accordance with such a relational logic, moreover, the concept of self-determination should be rethought along lines of autonomy and participation rather than exclusion.

A. Relational Ontology of Distinct People

Both in political theory and in ordinary discourse, "nation" usually appears as an all-or-nothing concept, in two respects. Most generally, a nation is supposed to be a special kind of group with specific political claims that other groups do not have. On this construction, either a group counts as a nation, in which case it has right to self-government, or it is merely an ethnic or religious group, in which case it does not. Second, nationalist ideologies tend to define their groups in either/or terms. They conceptualize the nation as strictly bounded between insiders and outsiders, and seek to define attributes of national identity or character that all members share. Claiming such an essence to the nation sometimes oppresses individuals within who do not conform to these national norms, and sometimes oppresses outsiders against whom national members set themselves in opposition.

If political theorists wish to respond to the complexities of cultural differentiation and recognize legitimate claims of justice, I suggest that we would do better to use a concept of distinct people, rather than nation, and to see distinctness as a matter of degree than of kind. No longer do we need to make a specious distinction between nation and ethnic group, but we can nevertheless follow the observation that some peoples are distinct from others to a greater degree and in more respects.[22] People experience themselves as sharing affinity with some and as distinct from others in many possible respects: language, historical connection with a territory, self-understanding as having a shared history, religious practice, artistic conventions and meanings, a dialogic consciousness of dwelling together distinctly, being segregated and stereotyped by a dominant group, and so on. Some groups are distinct from one another in only some of these ways, and others are distinct from one another in all these respects. The Scots are distinct from the English in respect to historical religious affiliation, history, and territory. Where language once was a major distinction between the peoples, this distinction has lessened, though it is still present to a degree. When they think of themselves in relation to Russians or Chinese, however, I suspect that most Scots think of themselves as more like the English than not.

Replacing the idea of nation with that of distinct people, then, relies on a relational rather than substantial social ontology. A relational conception of difference does not posit a social group as having an essential nature composed of a set of attributes defining only that group. Rather, a social group exists and is defined as a specific group only in interactive relations with others. Social group identities emerge from the encounter and interaction among people who experience some differences in their ways of life and forms of association, even if they regard themselves as belonging to the same society. A group will not regard itself as having a distinct language, for example, unless its members encounter another group whose speech they do not understand. In a relational conceptualization, what constitutes a social group is less internal to the attributes of its members and more a function of the relations in which it stands to others.

On this view, social difference may be stronger or weaker, and it may be more or less salient, depending on the point of view of comparison. A relational conception of group difference does not need to force all persons associated with the group under the same attributes. Group members may differ in many ways, including how strongly they bear affinity with others of the group. A relational approach, moreover, does not designate clear conceptual and practical borders that distinguish one group decisively from others, and distinguish its members decisively. Conceiving group differentiation as a function of relationship, comparison, and interaction, then, allows for overlap, interspersal, and interdependence among groups and their members.[23]

There are thousands of groups in the world today who consider themselves distinct peoples – whose members share cultural characteristics and histories by which they consider themselves distinguished from others, and who recognize one another as in the same distinct group. Some of those who consider themselves distinct peoples in the world today are generally considered what are called nations; many are not so considered but would like to be; some do not claim such a degree of distinctness but nevertheless make political claims against the state under whose jurisdiction they find themselves or on international bodies. Since the concept of nation, as I have argued, is implicitly linked to statehood, and since the international system resists the recognition of new states, many who legitimately consider themselves distinct peoples do not receive the regional and/or international recognition they deserve. Many are culturally, economically, or politically dominated by other peoples within a nation-state, and for this reason they struggle for self-determination. If we abandon the idea of nation along with its association with independent statehood, then distinct peoples can be more easily recognized in their distinctness, because the political consequences of this recognition remain to be worked out.[24] Distinct peoples have prima facie claims to self-determination. A critique of nationalism and attention to the relational distinctness of people, however, leads to a reconceptualization of the meaning of self-determination. Before proposing such a reconceptualization, it is important to explore arguments against the primary mode of self-determination now recognized in international relations, namely, the centered sovereignty characteristic of the states system.

III. Moral Challenges to Sovereignty

I have argued that the concept of nation presupposes the concept of an independent sovereign state. More often than not, nationalism embodies a claim of a people to have a single and unified state of their own, through which that people can claim a right of self-determination over a territory that entails a right of noninterference by all other actors. Such a concept of unified, centered, and independent state sovereignty, however, is coming under question today, both theoretically and practically.[25] In this section I review many of these criticisms of a concept of unified and independent sovereignty. External challenges to such claims of state sovereignty build on the cosmopolitan arguments I cited earlier to the effect that globalization makes peoples interdependent and thereby brings them together under the scope of justice. Internal challenges attend to the fact that most states in the world today have jurisdiction over a plurality of peoples who claim recognition and special rights.

I distinguish the concept of sovereignty from that of *state* institutions. States are public authorities that regulate the activities of those within their jurisdictions through legal and administrative institutions backed by the power to sanction. While only states can be unified sovereigns with no authority above them, they need not be, and many strong state institutions currently exist at a jurisdictional level smaller than sovereign states. State institutions are capable of being subject to review or override without losing their status as states. They can share jurisdiction with other states, and their jurisdiction need not encompass all the activities in a territory. The critique of sovereignty that follows should not be understood as a critique of state institutions as such. There are good reasons to preserve state institutions, and indeed, I shall argue, to extend the functioning of state institutions to a more global level.

A *sovereign state* wields central and final authority over all the legal and political matters within a determinate and strictly bounded territory.[26] Sovereignty entails a clear distinction between inside and outside. Within a sovereign state there are often partial and lesser governments and jurisdictions, but the sovereign government exercises a higher and final authority over them. The sovereignty of the state is partially constituted by the states outside it, moreover, states that recognize it as a legitimate sovereign state. This recognition entails a principle of nonintervention; for a state to have final authority implies that no other state and no transnational body has the authority to interfere with its actions and policies.[27]

Some writers claim that states today no longer have sovereignty in the sense I define here, and perhaps never did. It is questionable, that is, whether states today really exercise centrally coordinated power that is systematically connected over domains of government, and that they exercise it as a final authority. State power today, some claim, is in fact much more fragmentary and limited than the commitment to sovereignty would have one believe.[28] Whatever the factual situation of state powers, however, the *idea* of sovereignty still carries much weight among political leaders and scholars, both regarding the relation of states to internal organization and jurisdictions, and international relations. Many today continue to believe that states *ought* to be sovereign, and that to the degree that their sovereignty is under challenge or in a process of fragmentation, that steps should be taken to reinforce a system of strong sovereign states. Others disagree, and promote either internal devolution or the external evolution of transnational authorities. I shall argue that a principle of state sovereignty lacks moral legitimacy, both regarding external and internal affairs.

A. External Challenges

Considerations of global justice call into question the legitimacy of claims by states that they alone have the right to attend to affairs within their borders and have no obligations to peoples outside their borders. I discussed earlier the arguments of Charles Beitz, Thomas Pogge, and Onora O'Neill, among others, that there are no privileged grounds for limiting the scope of evaluations of justice to relations between people within nation states. Moral evaluation of social relations in terms of justice and injustice apply wherever social institutions connect people in a causal web. The scope and complexity of economic, communication, and many other institutions in the world today constitute a sufficiently tight web of constraint and interdependence today that we must speak of a global *society*.[29] Principles of justice apply to relations among persons, organizations, and state institutions in diverse reaches of global society. These claims of justice constitute a double challenge to the moral boundaries of states. Agents outside states have some claim to judge and regulate the activities of states over affairs within their jurisdictions, on the one hand; states and their members, on the other hand, have obligations to people outside their borders. Considerations of economic regulation, human rights intervention, environmental protection, and migration are among those that raise profound issues of justice that challenge sovereignty in this double way.

The principle of sovereignty gives to states the right and power to regulate for the benefit of their own members. States ought positively to pursue economic gain for their own citizens at the expense of other people in the world if necessary, so long as they do not forcefully invade and conquer the territories of other sovereign states. They have the right to exclude persons from entry into their territory in order to preserve the privileged access their members have to resources and benefits there. States or their citizens owe no general obligation to others outside, whatever their needs or level of relative deprivation. Any efforts states or their members make to help needy people elsewhere in the world are superogatory.

Several moral arguments can be offered against this view of the right of nonintervention in states' policies and their right to be indifferent to the circumstances of those outside their borders. Charles Beitz questions the moral right of states to keep for themselves all the benefits derived from the natural resources that happen to lie within their borders. Resources such as fertile land, economically valuable minerals, and so on are by no means evenly distributed around the globe. Because the placement of resources is morally arbitrary, no state is entitled to treat them as its private property to be used only for its own benefit. Because certain resources are necessary for the productive capacity of all societies, they must be considered a global common. Their use and the benefits of their use should thus be globally regulated under a cooperative framework of global justice.[30]

The global-resources argument is one example of a challenge to the sovereignty claim that outside agents have no claim to regulate the actions of states over activities that take place within their jurisdiction. The state of production, finance and communications in the world has evolved in such a way that many actions and policies internal to a state nevertheless sometimes have profound effects on others in the world. A moral challenge to a principle of nonintervention has come most obviously from environmental concern. States' internal forestry policies, their kind and level of industrial pollution regulation, and similar policies produce consequences for the air quality and climate of many outside their borders. Economic and communicative interdependence, moreover, generate certain international moral claims over other kinds of internal policies. Financial policies of the German or Japanese states, for example, can seriously affect the stability of many other economies. Such interdependencies as these call for some form of international regulatory scheme that aims for stable and just cooperation.

Many argue, furthermore, that current distributive inequality across the globe raises questions of justice that require a globally enforced redistributive regime. The fact that some peoples live in wasteful affluence while many more in other parts of the world suffer from serious deprivation itself stands as prima facie grounds for global redistribution. But these facts of distributive inequality alone do not make a very strong case for global economic regulation. More important is the history of dependence and exploitation between the now poor and now rich regions of the world, and the continuance of institutional structures that perpetuate and even help enlarge global privilege and deprivation. Some scholars argue that the current wealth of Europe and North America compared to societies of Africa, Latin America, and South Asia is due to a significant degree to the colonial relations among these regions that looted for three centuries. While the poorer regions of the world today are composed of independent states with the same formal sovereignty rights as any other states, some argue that the colonial economic relations between North and South persist.[31] The economies of the South depend on capital investment controlled from the North, and most of the profits return to the North. Their workers are often too poorly paid by multinationals or their local contractors to feed their families, and farmers and miners of the South obtain very unfavorable prices on a global resource market. Such deprivation has forced most governments of the Southern Hemisphere into severe debt to northern banks and to international finance agencies such as the World Bank. This indebtedness severely restricts the effective sovereignty of southern states because mighty financial institutions have the power to control those states' internal economic policies, all for the sake of preserving the existing system of international trade and finance and the benefits it brings primarily to some in the North.

The issue is not simply distributive inequality, that some people in some parts of the world are seriously deprived while others in other parts of the world live very well. Rather, the global institutional context sets different regions in relations of dependence and exploitation with others, and this institutional system reproduces and arguably widens the distributive inequalities. Redress of unjust deprivation and regulation of the global economy for the sake of promoting greater justice thus calls for institutional change, and not merely a one-time or periodic transfer of wealth from richer to poorer people.

B. Internal Challenges

Internally, the idea of sovereignty entails that a state has ultimate authority to regulate all the activities taking place within a specific territorial jurisdiction. This often seems to mean, by implication that the same form of law, regulation, and administration ought to apply to all the peoples and locales within the territory. Both these aspects of internal sovereignty are morally questionable, however, because they do not sufficiently recognize and accommodate the rights and needs of national and cultural minorities. Political recognition for distinct peoples entails that they are able to practice their culture and that they can affirm their own public culture in which to express and affirm their distinctness. To the degree that peoples are distinct, moreover, they have prima facie rights of self-governance. These points entail that peoples who dwell with others within a wider polity nevertheless limit the sovereignty of that wider polity over their activities.[32] The limitation of sovereign authority of a wider polity over groups and locales may vary in kind or degree, from local or group-based autonomy over nearly all affairs to self-governance over only a small range of issues, such as family law or the management and utilization of particular resources. As those examples indicate, moreover, local self-determination may vary according to whether it is legislative or administrative or both. Despite the strong claims of most states to be sovereign over all the activities in their particular territories, the sovereign power of many states today is already limited or restricted in many ways that recognize or accommodate national, cultural, and religious differences within their claimed jurisdictions.[33]

Many of these challenges come from indigenous peoples. Most of the world's indigenous peoples claim rights of self-determination against the states that claim sovereign authority over them. These claims are difficult or impossible for states organized in the existing states system to accommodate because they involve claims about the rights to use land and resources, and the right to develop governance practices continuous with precolonial indigenous practices, which are often at odds with the more formal and bureaucratic governance systems of modern European law. The struggles of most indigenous peoples for culture rights and self-determination reveal asymmetries between the indigenous peoples' societies and the European societies that colonized them. This cultural and institutional clash continues to provoke many states to repress and oppress the indigenous people. Despite unjust conquest and continued oppression, however, few indigenous peoples seek sovereignty for themselves in the sense of the formation of an independent internationally recognized state with ultimate authority over all matters within a determinately bounded territory. Most indigenous peoples seek significantly greater and more secure self-determination within the framework of a wider polity.[34]

Despite the locality of their claims, indigenous people have forged a global social movement that has achieved significant success in the past two decades in gaining recognition for the legitimacy of their claims. In some regions of the world, they have had some successes in motivating some social and political changes to accommodate their needs and interests. Properly recognizing the claims of indigenous peoples today, however, requires challenging the international system of sovereign states. Indigenous peoples worldwide have long been aware of the incompatibility of their claims to justice with the concept of state sovereignty that predominates in international relations. Especially in the past two decades they have organized across different parts of the world and have succeeded to some extent in having the uniqueness of their claims recognized by international bodies such as the World Court or the United Nations. Their social movements have prompted some reforms in the policies of some states that claim to have jurisdiction over them. Despite these successes, many nation-states continue to repress indigenous movements. Their accommodation to indigenous demands for self-determination require a degree of institutional change that most states are unwilling to allow, especially if other states in the international system are not doing so. Thus indigenous peoples' movements are both a source of ideas and action beyond the system of sovereign states, and at the same time show the limits of that system.[35]

I dwell on the situation and claims of indigenous peoples because they fundamentally challenge the world order of sovereign states. Nevertheless, there are many other peoples who claim to be oppressed or lack sufficient recognition by the states that the international system recognizes as having jurisdiction over them. Many of these peoples claim a right of self-determination in the sense of wanting a sovereign state of their own. Such claims often create serious conflict, however, especially when different groups seek sovereignty over the same or overlapping territories. Other groups do not claim sovereignty in this sense, either because they are dispersed geographically or because their claims to autonomy do not encompass all governance issues. Whatever the status of the claims resisting alleged domination, I suggest that most are poorly addressed by a concept of self-determination that equates it with central and final sovereignty.

IV. Rethinking Self-determination

At least since the early twentieth century the right of self-determination for peoples has been interpreted as a right for distinct peoples to have a sovereign state of their own with a single contiguous territory enclosed by unambiguous borders. This right of sovereignty entails a principle of nonintervention; a state that is sovereign over a territory and a people has final authority over that territory and people, and no outside state or agent has legitimate claim to interfere with the decisions and actions of that authority. Because this interpretation of a principle of self-determination is so absolute, exclusive, and territorially based, it tends to imply a coincidence of one distinct people for each state. Because distinct peoples are also territorially interspersed, however, that logical implication of a principle of self-determination for a people has often generated violent conflict. This inside-outside noninterference concept of self-determination for peoples was probably always inadequate, but today it is dangerously so.

This concept of self-determination interprets freedom as noninterference. On this model, self-determination means that a people or government has the authority to exercise complete control over what goes on inside its jurisdiction, and no outside agent has the right to make claims upon or interfere with what the self-determining agent does. Reciprocally, the self-determining people have no claim on what others do with respect to issues within their jurisdictions, and no right to interfere in the business of the others. Just as it denies rights of interference by outsiders in a jurisdiction, this concept entails that each self-determining entity has no inherent obligations with respect to outsiders.

Freedom as noninterference assumes that agents, whether individual or collective, are independent of one another except insofar as they choose to exchange and contract. The arguments that I have made above about the scope of justice and global interdependence of peoples, however, challenges such an assumption of the independence of nations or states. Thus a theory of self-determination for peoples should recognize that peoples are interdependent, and for this reason that noninterference is too simple an interpretation of self-determination.[36]

Much feminist theory has criticized a rigid idea of independence as inappropriate for a moral theory of autonomy, and proposes to substitute a relational understanding of autonomy that recognizes the constitution of agents by interaction with others and their interdependencies.[37]

The idea of relational autonomy takes account of the interdependence of agents and their embeddedness in relationships at the same time that it continues to value individual choices. In this concept, all agents are owed equal respect as autonomous agents, which means that they are able to choose their ends and have capacity and support to pursue those ends. An adequate conception of autonomy should promote the capacity of agents to pursue their own ends in the context of relationships in which others may do the same. While this concept of autonomy entails a presumption of noninterference, it does not imply a social scheme in which atomized agents simply mind their own business and leave one another alone. Instead, it entails recognizing that agents are related in many ways they have not chosen, by virtue of economic interaction, history, proximity, or the unintended consequences of action. In these relationships agents are able either to thwart one another or support one another. Relational autonomy consists partly, then, in the structuring of relationships so that they support the maximal pursuit of agent ends.

In his reinterpretation of ideas of classical republicanism, Philip Pettit offers a similar criticism of the idea of freedom as noninterference.[38] Interference means that one agent blocks or redirects the action of another agent in a way that worsens that agent's choice situation by changing the range of options. On Pettit's account, noninterference, while related to freedom, is not equivalent to it. Instead, freedom should be understood as nondomination. An agent dominates another when he or she has power over that other and is thus able to interfere with the other *arbitrarily*. Interference is arbitrary when it is chosen or rejected without consideration of the interests or opinions of those affected. An agent may dominate another, however, without ever interfering with that person. Domination consists in standing in a set of relations that makes an agent *able* to interfere arbitrarily with the actions of others.

Real freedom means the absence of such relations of domination. Pettit argues that institutions should promote and preserve nondomination for everyone. To do so, they must have regulations that sometimes interfere with actions in order to restrict dominative power and promote cooperation. Interference is not arbitrary if its purpose is to minimize domination, and if it is done in a way that takes the interests and voices of affected parties into account. Like the feminist concept of relational autonomy, then, the concept of freedom as nondomination refers to a set of social relations. "Non-domination is the position that someone enjoys when they live in the presence of other people and when, by virtue of social design, none of those others dominates them."[39]

I propose that a principle of self-determination for peoples should be interpreted along lines of relational autonomy or nondomination rather than simply as independence or noninterference. On such an interpretation, self-determination for peoples means that they have a right to their own governance institutions through which they decide on their goals and interpret their way of life. Other people ought not to constrain, dominate, or interfere with those decisions and interpretations for the sake of their own ends, or according to their judgment of what way of life is best, or in order to subordinate a people to a larger "nation" unit. Peoples, that is, ought to be free from domination. Because a people stands in interdependent relations with others, however, a people cannot ignore the claims and interests of those others when their actions potentially affect them. Insofar as outsiders are affected by the activities of self-determining people, those others have a legitimate claim to have their interests and needs taken into account even though they are outside the government jurisdiction. Conversely, outsiders should recognize that when they themselves affect a people, the latter can legitimately claim that they should have their interests taken into account insofar as they may be adversely affected. Insofar as their activities affect one another, peoples are in relationship and ought to negotiate the terms and effects of the relationship.

Self-determining peoples morally cannot do whatever they want without interference from others. Their territorial, economic, or communicative relationships with others generate conflicts and collective problems that oblige them to acknowledge the legitimate interests of others as well as promote their own. Pettit argues that states can legitimately interfere with the actions of individuals in order to foster institutions that minimize domination. A similar argument applies to actions and relations of collectivities. In a densely interdependent world, peoples require political institutions that lay down procedures for coordinating actions, resolving conflicts, and negotiating relationships.

The self-determination of people, then, has the following elements. First, self-determination means a presumption of noninterference. A people has the prima facie right to set its own governance procedures and make its own decisions about its activities, without interference from others. Second, insofar as the activities of a group may adversely affect others or generate conflict, self-determination entails the right of those others to make claims on the group, negotiate the terms of their relationships, and mutually adjust the terms' effects. Third, a world of self-determining peoples thus requires recognized and settled institutions and procedures through which peoples negotiate, adjudicate conflicts, and enforce agreements. Self-determination does not imply independence but, rather, that peoples dwell together within political institutions that minimize domination among peoples. It would take another essay to address the question of just what form such intergovernmental political institutions should take; some forms of federalism do and should apply. Finally, the self-determining peoples require that the peoples have the right to participate *as peoples* in designing and implementing intergovernmental institutions aimed at minimizing domination.

I have argued for a principle of self-determination understood as relational autonomy in the context of nondomination, instead of a principle of self-determination understood simply as noninterference. This argument applies as much to large nation-states as to small indigenous or "ethnic" groups. Those entities that today are considered self-determining independent states in principle ought to have no more right of noninterference than should smaller groups. Self-determination for those entities now called sovereign states should mean nondomination. While this means a presumption of noninterference, outsiders may have a claim on their activities.

Thus the interpretation of self-determination as nondomination ultimately implies limiting the rights of existing nation-states and setting these into different, more cooperatively regulated relationships. Just as promoting freedom for individuals involves regulating international relations to prevent the domination of peoples.

V. Global Democracy

The argument in this paper has taken apparently divergent turns between cosmopolitanism and the recognition of difference. Many problems that cause conflict and require cooperation to solve, such as war, environmental degradation, and global distributive justice, require global regulatory institutions to solve. At the same time, I have agreed with those political theorists who argue that affiliation with cultural and historically differentiated peoples provides a basis for meaning and value in people's lives, and for this reason the distinctness of people should be publicly and politically recognized. The principles and movements of multiculturalism within and across states today challenge traditional ideas of the unity of nationstates and uniformity of the application of their regulations.

From this dual argument I conclude something similar to several others recently writing about these issues: peace and justice in the world today require a transformation in governance institutions that is both more encompassing than existing nationstates and at the same time devolves and decentralizes authority to units of a smaller and more diverse character than many existing nation-states.[40] In this concluding section I sketch some principles for envisioning such transformed institutions of global democratic regulation.

I imagine a global system of regulatory regimes to which locales and regions relate in a federated system. These regimes lay down rules regarding that small but vital set of issues around which peace and justice call for global cooperation. I envision seven such regulatory regimes, though the number could be larger or smaller, and the jurisdictions defined differently: (1) peace and security; (2) environment; (3) trade and finance; (4) investment and capital utilization; (5) communications and transportation; (6) human rights, including labor standards and welfare rights; and (7) citizenship and migration. I imagine that each regulatory regime has a functional jurisdiction separate from those of the others, each with its own regulatory function. Each provides a thin set of general rules that specify ways that individuals, organizations, and governments are obliged to take account of the interests and circumstances of one another. By distinguishing regimes functionally, such a global governance system deterritorializes some aspects of sovereignty.[41]

Each of these issue areas already has an evolving regime of international law and organization on which to build in order to create a global regime with greater enforcement strength and resources for carrying out its purpose. For the most part, however, only the activities of states are subject to regulation under those treaty regimes. An important aspect of decentering governance through global regulatory regimes would consist in making at least some of the activities of nonstate organizations, such as municipalities, private for-profit and no-profit corporations, and individuals, directly addressed in global regulation, with regional and local governments as tools of implementation.

Within the context of global regulatory regimes, everyday governance ought to be primarily local. What defines a locale may vary in accordance with the way people affiliate, their history, priorities, and relationship with others. Locales consist in first-level autonomous units of governance. Some might be defined as selfdetermining peoples. While rooted in place, these might not be associated with a single contiguous territory. The Ojibwa people could count as a self-determining local unit, for example, even if some of the members are dispersed territorially. Many locales ought to be heterogeneous and multicultural, however. Thus metropolitan regions are a primary candidate for self-determining units.

Such autonomous governance units should be institutionalized as *open*, both in a territorial and jurisdictional sense. Autonomous peoples or communities may overlap in territories, and their governance needs to recognize the situations and problems they share with others, as well as how their actions may affect the conditions of action of other units.

Local units, in this vision, are autonomous in the sense that their members construct their own institutions of governance as they choose, within the limits of global regulation. The global level of governance is "thin," in the sense that it lays down only rather general principles. Local jurisdictions "thicken" them into administrable programs and rules by interpreting and applying them according to their own procedures, priorities, and cultural understandings.[42]

A major purpose of global regulatory regimes, in the model I imagine, is to protect local units and their members from domination. Self-determination understood as nondomination, you will recall, does not mean only a presumption of noninterference for the autonomous unit. Even more important, it means that autonomous units are embedded in institutionalized relationships that protect them from dominative threats. Some local units are more vulnerable than others to such threats. Global regulatory regimes should aim to minimize domination both of individuals and of self-determining locales. To the extent that peoples and locales have often experienced domination by neighboring peoples or nation-states that have claimed jurisdiction over them, one purpose of global regulation is to protect such vulnerable peoples and locales. This is one important respect in which local self-determination and cultural self-determination can be understood not as conflicting with but, rather, as requiring stronger global regulation.

A vision of global governance with local self-determination ought to make the inclusion of democratic values and institutions paramount. Those regimes and institutions existing today that coordinate and regulate global interaction beyond the jurisdiction of states are not very democratic. The growing global power of multinational corporations is explicitly undemocratic, for example. Existing tribunals of international law have few channels of democratic accountability. Especially because of the power and structure of the Security Council, the United Nations is not a democratic institution. Scholars and journalists bemoan the "democratic deficit" they observe in the operations of today's most complex and thoroughly developed transnational governance body, the European Union.[43] There are many complex issues involved in such democratization, of course; I will point to just a few.

First, one of the reasons to advocate localism, the devolution of sovereign authority onto more local units in nondiminutive institutional relationships, is to promote democracy. Participation and citizenship are best enacted at a local level. Democratic federated regimes of global regulation, however, do require institutions of representation and policy deliberation at levels far removed from the local. A global environmental regulatory decision-making body, for example, would not need to be any *more* removed from ordinary citizens than many national regulatory bodies currently are. Once we move beyond a local level, any polity is an "imagined community" whose interests and problems must be discursively constructed as affecting everyone because people do not experience most of the others in the polity. I believe that this problem is no bigger for transnational and global regulation than it is for large nation-states.

Activities of global governance ought to be public. Simple as this sounds, the deliberations of some of the most powerful global actors today, such as the International Monetary Fund or the World Trade Organization, are not public. Already the possibilities of transportation and communication in the world today see the formation of incipient public spheres composed of active citizens in global civil society.[44]

Institutions through which distinct peoples and locales can participate in formulating policies of global regulatory regimes would help render such global regulation compatible with a principle of self-determination. Self-determination does not mean sovereign independence, I have argued. It does entail, however, that to the extent that self-governing entities are obliged to follow more encompassing regulation, they have a real opportunity to participate with the others in formulating those regulations.

I have suggested above, for example, that there ought to be a stronger global regime to formulate global standards of individual human rights, and to monitor and enforce compliance with those standards. Having such a human rights regime does not impinge on local self-determination and local autonomy, I am arguing, as long as two conditions are met. (1) The peoples and communities obliged to observe these standards have had the opportunity to participate as a collective in their formulation. (2) They have significant discretion in how they apply these standards for their local context, and the means they use locally to implement them. As I hear their protests, those peoples in the world today who question the application of human rights covenants to their context do not reject general principles of human rights. They argue that the particular formulations of those rights applied today were developed largely by Western powers, and that in these changed times these formulations should be subject to review in a process that includes them.

This paper has criticized theories of liberal nationalism that continue to assume a conceptual distinction between a kind of group that is properly a nation, and thus deserves self-determination, and ethnic groups, which do not. I have argued that the distinction between nation and ethnic group is spurious, and that both ideas should be replaced by the idea of distinct peoples, relationally conceptualized. I have adopted cosmopolitan criticisms of nationalist arguments that claim that obligations of justice should extend only to conationals, even if there are some thinner human obligations to outsiders. Such an idea of the self-sufficiency of nations ignores the complex interdependency of the world's peoples today; obligations of justice are for this reason global in extent. Against the conclusion that affiliation with and loyalty to local and cultural groups is problematic, however, I have agreed with arguments for political recognition of multicultural difference. Distinct peoples should be recognized as self-determining. Self-determination should not mean sovereign independence, however, but relational autonomy in the context of global regulatory institutions that aim to minimize domination.

The purpose of accounts of global democracy to which I have briefly added is to jog the imagination into thinking about possibilities alternative to prevailing ideas and practices in the relations between societies and peoples. Accounts such as these are not and cannot be institutional designs, that is, specific proposals for practices with lawful legitimacy and practical force. The purpose of ideas such as those I and others have outlined is to inspire and motivate individuals and groups who aim to criticize existing international institutions, practices, and relationships, and who engage in actions intended to promote global democracy and justice. Visions such as these are contributions to a discussion of where we should collectively be going and why. Meaningful democratic change in global governance and its relation to local participation will come about only as a result of movements of public leaders and citizen activists pressuring for that change in concerted and thoughtful ways. The global organization of tens of thousands of people to bring positions and demands before several United Nations-sponsored conferences in the past decade is only one sign that such movements may be developing.

Notes

I am grateful to the following people for helpful comments on an earlier version of this paper: Frank Cunningham, Omar Dahbur, Laurel Weldon, Alexander Wendt, Aaron Hoffman, Davis Bobrow, and Reiner Bauböck.

* Rpt. from *NOMOS LXII: Designing Democratic Institutions*, ed. Ian Shapiro and Stephen Macedo (New York: New York University Press, 2000) 147-83, by permission of New York University Press.

1 Jacques Derrida, *The Other Heading*, trans. Pascale-Anne Brault and Michael B. Nass (Bloomington: Indiana University Press, 1991), 48.

2 Julia Kristeva reflects on this coincidence of French nationalism and cosmopolitanism in *Strangers to Ourselves* (New York: Columbia University Press, 1991), especially chapter 7.

3 Elizabeth Kiss attempts to cut a way between nationalism and cosmopolitanism in her essay "Five Theses on Nationalism," *NOMOS XXXVIII: Political Order*, ed. Ian Shapiro and Russell Hardin (New York: New York University Press, 1996). Her essay shows how complicated a critique of nationalism must be but envisions little in the way of an alternative understanding of political community.

4 See, for example, Bhikhu Parekh, "The Politics of Nationhood," *Cultural Identity and Development in Europe*, ed. Keebet von Banda-Beckman and Maykel Verkuyten (London: University College of London Press, 1994).

5 For recent examples of a cosmopolitan position see Martha Nussbaum, "Patriotism and Cosmopolitanism," *For Love of Country: Debating the Limits of Patriotism*, ed. Joshua Cohen (Boston: Beacon Press, 1996); Veit Bader, "Citizenship and Exclusion: Radical Democracy, Community and Justice, or, What Is Wrong with Communitarianism?" *Political Theory* 23.2 (May 1995): 211-46. In more recent work, however, Bader is less unambiguously cosmopolitan, giving more attention to ethnocultural commitments; see "The Cultural Conditions of Transnational Citizenship," in *Political Theory* 25.6 (December 1997); Jeremy Waldron, "Minority Cultures and the Cosmopolitan Alternative," *The Rights of Minority Cultures*, ed. Will Kymlicka (Oxford: Oxford University Press, 1995).

6 See Will Kymlicka, *Liberalism, Community and Culture* (Oxford: Oxford University Press, 1989), especially chapters 4, 5, and 8; Charles Taylor, "Multiculturalism and the Politics of Recognition," *Multiculturalism: Examining the Politics of Recognition*, ed. Amy Gutmann (Princeton: Princeton University Press, 1994); Yael Tamir, *Liberal Nationalism* (Princeton: Princeton University Press, 1993), chapters 1 and 2.

7 David Miller, *On Nationality* (Oxford: Oxford University Press, 1995), especially chapter 4.

8 Will Kymlicka, *Multicultural Citizenship* (Oxford: Oxford University Press, 1995).

9 Miller, *On Nationality* 18-21.

10 Ibid., 172-5.

11   Ibid., 68-70, 172-3.

12   Kymlicka, *Multicultural Citizenship* 11.

13   See Margaret Canovan, *Nationhood and Political Theory* (Brookfield: Edward Elgar, 1996); Mary Kaldor, "European Institutions, Nation-States and Nationalism," *Cosmopolitan Democracy: An Agenda for a New World Order*, ed. Daniele Archibugi and David Held (Oxford: Polity Press, 1995).

14   Tamir, *Liberal Nationalism* 121.

15   The "engine" metaphor is Margaret Canovan's. See *Nationhood and Political Theory*. In this book Canovan does not justify nationalism morally; indeed, she is worried about its potentially destructive consequences today. She argues, however, that nationalism is necessary to the functioning of states.

16   Cf. Miller, *On Nationality* chapter 3.

17   Miller, for one, explicitly distances his argument from the implication that dominant nationals do not have the same obligations of redistribution to members of ethnic or immigrant minorities. See *On Nationality*. As long as one links obligations of justice to national identification, however, the wedge is set to separate those culturally closer from those more culturally distant, and to prefer the former in redistributive policies.

18   See Michael Walzer, *Spheres of Justice* (New York: Basic Books, 1983).

19   Alan Wolfe and Jytte Klausen argue for greater immigration restrictions in the United States on the grounds that they are necessary to renew popular support for redistributive welfare policies. See "Identity Politics and the Welfare State," *Social Philosophy and Policy* 14.2 (Summer 1997): 231-55.

20   Thomas Pogge, "Cosmopolitanism and Sovereignty," *Ethics* 103 (October 1992): 48-75; Charles Beitz, *Political Theory and International Relations* (Princeton: Princeton University Press, 1979).

21   Onora O'Neill, *Towards Justice and Virtue: A Constructive Account of Practical Reasoning* (Cambridge: Cambridge University Press, 1996) chapter 4; see also O'Neill, "Justice and Boundaries," *Political Restructuring in Europe: Ethical Perspectives*, ed. C. Brown (London: Routledge, 1994).

22   I have proposed to replace the dichotomy Kymlicka makes between nation and ethnic group with a continuum of more or less distinct peoples; see "A Multicultural Continuum: A Critique of Will Kymlicka," *Constellations* 4.1 (April 1997). Yael Tamir's suggestion that we think of the idea of a nation as a "cluster" concept rather than a concept defined by a necessary list of essential attributes moves in this direction.

23   Martha Minow proposes a relational understanding of group difference; see *Making All the Difference* (Ithaca: Cornell University Press, 1990) part II. I have introduced a relational analysis of group difference in *Justice and the Politics of Difference* (Princeton: Princeton University Press, 1990) especially chapter 2, and in "Together in Difference: Transforming the Logic of Group Political Conflict," *The Rights of Minority Groups*, ed. Will Kymlicka (Oxford: Oxford University Press, 1995). For relational understandings of group difference, see also William Connolly, *Identity/Difference* (Ithaca: Cornell University Press, 1993), and Chantal Mouffe, "Democracy, Power and the 'Political,'"

Democracy and Difference, ed. Seyla Benhabib (Princeton: Princeton University Press, 1996), 245-56. James Tully proposes a similar deconstruction of substantive understandings of group differences in his idea of cultural difference as "aspectival." See *Strange Multiplicity* (Cambridge: Cambridge University Press, 1995).

24 Cf. Neil MacCormick, "Liberalism, Nationalism and the Post-Sovereign State," *Political Studies XLIV* (1996): 553-67.

25 See, for example, the articles collected in *Contending Sovereignties: Redefining Political Community*, ed. R.B.J. Walker and Saul H. Mendovitz (Boulder: Lynne Reiner, 1990); see also Richard Falk, "Evasions of Sovereignty," *Explorations at the Edge of Time* (Philadelphia: Temple University Press, 1992).

26 Definitions of sovereignty abound, but they vary only subtly. See, for example, Christopher Morris, "Sovereignty is the highest, final, and supreme political and legal authority (and power) within the territorially defined domain of a system of direct rule," *An Essay on the Modern State* (Cambridge: Cambridge University Press, 1998), ms., 166. Thomas Pogge distinguishes degrees of sovereignty. For him, sovereignty is simple when an agent has unsupervised and irrevocable power. Given this distinction, I am concerned with absolute sovereignty. I find it a bit puzzling that Pogge includes the condition that the decisions and laws of a sovereign power are *irrevocable*. This seems quite unreasonable, since in practice many states revoke or revise decisions previously made and no one considers this a challenge to their sovereignty. The condition should rather be put that a sovereign's decisions cannot be revoked or overridden by *another* authority. See Thomas Pogge, "Cosmopolitanism and Sovereignty," *Ethics* 103 (October 1992): 48-75.

27 See Daniel Philpott, "Sovereignty: An Introduction and Brief History," *Journal of International Affairs* 48.2 (Winter 1995): 353-68.

28 See Morris, *An Essay on the Modern State*.

29 Beitz, *Political Theory and International Relations*; O'Neill, *Towards Justice and Virtue*, chapter 4; see also O'Neill, "Justice and Boundaries," *Political Restructuring in Europe: Ethical Perspectives*, ed. C. Brown (London: Routledge, 1994); Pogge, "Cosmopolitanism and Sovereignty." Pogge distinguishes two approaches to social justice, an institutional and an interactional approach. Whereas the interactional approach focuses only on the actions of particular individuals as they affect identifiable persons, the institutional approach theorizes moral responsibility for the fact of others insofar as agents participate in institutions and practices that may or do harm them. An institutional approach as distinct from an interactional approach, Pogge suggests, makes issues of international justice and moral responsibility with respect to distant strangers more visible. I make a similar distinction between a distributive approach to justice and an approach that focuses on the way institutions produce distributions; see Young, *Justice and the Politics of Difference*. Focusing on how structures and institutional relations produce distributive patterns, I suggest, makes a connected international society more visible and the relations of moral responsibilities of distant peoples within it.

30 Beitz, *Political Theory and International Relations*.

31   The work of Samir Amin is classic here; for a recent statement of this argument, see Fernando Henrique Cardoso, "North-South Relations in the Present Context: A New Dependency?" *The New Global Economy in the Information Age*, ed. Martin Carnoy et al. (University Park: Pennsylvania State University Press, 1993) 149-59.

32   Kymlicka, *Multicultural Citizenship*.

33   For one account of different internal challenges to uniformity or universality of the law of sovereign states, see Jacob Levy, "Classifying Cultural Rights," *NOMOS XXXIX: Ethnicity and Group Rights*, ed. Ian Shapiro and Will Kymlicka (New York: New York University Press, 1997) 22-68.

34   Héctor Díaz Polanco, *Indigenous Peoples in Latin America: The Quest for Self-Determination*, trans. Lucia Rayas (Boulder: Westview Press, 1997) especially part Two.

35   Franke Wilmer, *The Indigenous Voice in World Politics* (Newbury Park: Sage Publications, 1993).

36   In the context of conceptualizing the meaning of indigenous people's claims for self-determination, Craig Scott proposes a more relational understanding of the claim. See "Indigenous Self-determination and Decolonization of the International Imagination: A Plea," *Human Rights Quarterly* 18 (1996): 814-20.

37   Anna Yeatman's critique of the idea of independence underlying a contractual view of citizenship is important here; see "Beyond Natural Right: The Conditions for Universal Citizenship," *Postmodern Revisionings of the Political* (New York: Routledge, 1994) 57-79; "Feminism and Citizenship," *Culture and Citizenship*, ed. Nick Stevenson (London: Sage, 1998), and "Relational Individualism," manuscript; see also Jennifer Nedelsky, "Reconceiving Autonomy: Sources, Thoughts and Possibilities," *Yale Journal of Law and Feminism* 1:1 (1989); "Law, Boundaries, and the Bounded Self," *Law and the Order of Culture*, ed. Robert Post; for an application of this feminist revision of autonomy to international relations theory, see Karen Knop, "Re/Statements: Feminism and State Sovereignty in International Law," *Transnational Law and Contemporary Problems* 3.2 (Fall 1993): 293-344; see also Jean Elshtain, "The Sovereign State," *Notre Dame Law Review* 66 (1991): 1355-84.

38   Philip Pettit, *Republicanism* (Oxford: Oxford University Press, 1997).

39   Ibid., 67.

40   David Held, *Democracy and the Global Order* (Cambridge, MA: Polity Press, 1995) part IV; Held, "Democracy and Globalization," *Re-imagining Political Community: Studies in Cosmopolitan Democracy*, ed. Daniele Archibugi, David Held, and Martin Kohler (Cambridge, MA: Polity Press, 1998); Pogge, "Cosmopolitanism and Sovereignty" (Tamir, *Liberal Nationalism,* chapter 7; Tamir argues for federated relations among culturally distinct nations; I think it is a mistake to try to separate the political the cultural in this way, but Tamir's discussion of federalism is much in the spirit of the vision I am promoting here). For reflections directed more explicitly at global governance, see Tamir "Who's Afraid of a Global State?" manuscript; Alexander Wendt offers an account of global functional regulation from the point of view of how such regulatory regimes can promote collective identities for problem solving. See "Collective Identity Formation and the International State," *American Political*

Science Review 88.2 (June 1994): 384-96; Jordi Borja and Manuel Castells propose institutions of greater local autonomy in the context of more global interaction; see Borja and Castells, *Local and Global: Management of Cities in the Information Age* (London: Earthscan Publications, 1997).

41 See John Gerard Ruggie, "Territoriality and Beyond: Problematizing Modernity in International Relations," *International Organization* 47.1 (Winter 1993): 139-74.

42 A federated relationship between self-determining entities might be interpreted as a way of implementing the relationship between "thin" and "thick" principles that Michael Walzer advocates. See *Thick and Thin: Moral Argument at Home and Abroad* (Notre Dame: Notre Dame University Press, 1994) 63-84.

43 See Thomas Pogge, "Creating Super-National Institutions Democratically: Reflections on the European Union's 'Democratic Deficit,'" *Journal of Political Philosophy* 5.2 (June 1997): 163-82.

44 Richard Falk, "The Global Promise of Social Movements: Explorations at the Edge of Time," E*xplorations at the Edge of Time* (Philadelphia: Temple University Press, 1992) 125-59; Ronnie D. Lipschuts, "Reconstructing World Politics: The Emergence of Global Civil Society," *Millennium* 21.3 (1992): 389-420.

Problems and Limits of Multiculturalism:
A View from Québec

Alain-G. Gagnon
(in collaboration with Raffaele Iacovino)[1]

> Je considère [. . .] que nous avons intérêt à mieux voir ce qui nous rassemble, et que les arrivants ont droit à la ressemblance plus encore qu'à la différence.
> Julien Harvey, S.J.[2]

The idea of integrating immigrants or marginalised ethno-cultural groups into established political communities, or "host societies," in the final analysis concerns questions regarding such members' capacity to exercise full democratic citizenship. As Abu-Laban indicates, "multiculturalism ultimately involves conflict and struggle over questions of identity and equity [. . .]. The ongoing debate [. . .] has to do with power, and thus should command the attention of political scientists."[3] Multiculturalism has become somewhat of a catchword in academic and popular circles, yet much normative thought surrounding the notion as a model for citizenship – as a basis for democratic life – remains mired in ambiguity. In examining the concept of multiculturalism in Canada, Mazurek notes that

> as with "justice," "beauty," and "love," everyone seems to approve of multiculturalism, everyone seems to know what it is, yet everyone seems to define and practice it differently [. . .] we have yet to settle upon agreement of what, exactly, multiculturalism is.[4]

Indeed, for Golfman, texts devoted to assessments of multiculturalism have been "engendered by its arguably ontological status."[5]

The aim of this essay is not to engage in a protracted retrieval of the defining characteristics of multiculturalism. Instead, it will be treated as a key marker in a larger discourse in political thought which seeks to address the impact of polyethnicity on prevailing models of citizenship in liberal democracies. In Juteau's words,

> equality and pluralism are values which command some support in occidental liberal democracies. Beyond this point, however, appear disagreements, opposition,

and conflicts. Which pluralism to retain, which measures for redistribution to develop, which policies of cultural recognition to adopt? [. . .] Almost all societies are multicultural, the question is not to know whether we want a multicultural society, rather, it is to decide in which type of multicultural society we wish to live.[6]

Multiculturalism can thus be delineated as an intellectual movement associated with the character of cultural identity as it pertains to democratic citizenship. More specifically, of interest here is the effect of multiculturalism as policy – its manifestation as a model for self-definition, for belonging, in a larger political community – and whether or not it can serve as a marker for identification, an equalising device for polyethnic communities. Thus any evaluation of multiculturalism rests on the value of cultural identity, on citizen dignity, understood here as "empowerment," or "participation," in circumscribed political communities – the identitive, or self-defining aspect of belonging equally to a particular democratic polity. Regardless of strict definitions, multiculturalism, or the "politics of difference," is a response to the late 20th century phenomenon that has been called "the age of migration," challenging countries to redefine the rules of political life.[7] A present case in which the challenge of polyethnicity can be discerned is in Germany, where the post-Kohl era promises to re-evaluate its existing policy of *droit de sang* as a basis for full citizenship status and to incorporate non-German ethnic identities into the political community.

Multiculturalism: A Challenge to Traditional Liberal Models of Citizenship

On a general level, the polemic between universal and particular bases of allegiance demarcates the contours of the debate. With the increasing polyethnic composition of nation-states, the debate has emerged largely as a challenge to the homogenising tendencies of liberal models of citizenship. The idea of multiculturalism can thus be embedded in a wider area of post-national consciousness – some say post-modern, or "identity politics" – as an attack on the assimilation implied by "Jacobin" tendencies of modern nation-states in the name of attaching a sense of common purpose to citizenship status.[8]

A sense of equal citizenship status has long been regarded by liberal theorists as constituting a foundation for democratic political communities – for fostering the civic spiritedness, mutual trust, and allegiance required for meaningful self-government and stability. In recent years, however, traditional liberal thought on citizenship has been challenged by multiculturalism as a response to the increasing polyethnic composition of democratic nation-states around the globe. Kymlicka notes that the traditional liberal response to polyethnicity has been to develop common (undifferentiated) citizenship in a universal vein. In this view, the integrative function of citizenship is to treat cultural differences with "benign neglect," in order that a shared civic identity be forged regardless of collective, or group-based identitive differences. Kymlicka summarises this view:

> Citizenship is by definition a matter of treating people as individuals with equal rights under the law [. . .]. [If it is group-differentiated], nothing will bind the various groups in society together, and prevent the spread of mutual mistrust or conflict. If citizenship is differentiated, it no longer provides a shared experience or common status. Citizenship would yet be another force for disunity, rather than a way of cultivating unity in the face of increasing social diversity. Citizenship should be a forum where people transcend their differences, and think about the common good of all citizens.[9]

The debate centres around the role of culture in a democratic political community, the extent to which cultural identity is reflected in state policy, both symbolically and formally (i.e. representation), and the idea that collective identity or belonging, whether or not formally characterised by "benign neglect," is infused with cultural meaning. For some, the notion of "benign neglect" is simply a preservation of the status quo in many previously homogeneous nation-states – state inactivity reflects a failure to adapt to dynamic polyethnic realities in society. For advocates of multiculturalism as ideology, minority cultures are rendered unequal participants and second-class citizens if their sources of meaning are neglected in the public realm. In this view, the democratic ideal of equality cannot be achieved if citizens are forced to conform to a "civic" denial of identity, a "renewal of self-definition" for individual citizens. Equality demands that state-policy recognises groups in their collective contexts. Isajiw notes that the force of multiculturalism arises out of a particular sentiment in which personal dignity is tied to the collective dignity of one's ethnic community. Recognition of citizen dignity thus requires recognition of the community. Multiculturalism represents a set of values whereby the recognition of identity needs are linked to the instrumental power of members of ethnic communities.[10] Taylor highlights such sentiments:

> The demand for recognition in [the politics of multiculturalism] is given urgency by the supposed links between recognition and identity [. . .]. The thesis is that our identity is partly shaped by recognition or its absence, often by the misrecognition of others, and so a person or group of people can suffer real damage, real distortion, if the people or society around them mirror back to them a confining or demeaning or contemptible picture of themselves. Nonrecognition or misrecogni-

tion can be a form of oppression, imprisoning someone in a false, distorted and reduced mode of being.[11]

From such philosophical roots can be discerned the idea of multiculturalism as *state policy*,

> multiculturalism is construed as a doctrine that provides a *political framework* for the official promotion of *social equality* and *cultural differences* as an integral component of the social order. It is government having the authority in the realm of the mind and an articulation that its responsibilities there are among the most important it has.[12]

The recognition of polyethnicity by the state is thus a call for increased citizen empowerment, a theme which will permeate the discussion to follow. In the final analysis, how are citizens in a polyethnic state equally empowered to share and participate in democratic life, without sacrificing self-fulfilling "modes of being"? This is the challenge posed by the discourse of multiculturalism. How have states adapted to such challenges? Indeed, Wilson argues thus as a challenge to traditional political thought:

> What is truly revolutionary is this attempt to devise a democratic vision by employing the policy instruments of the nation-state in the reconstruction of the symbolic order and the redistribution of social status among racial and ethnocultural groups in Canadian society.[13]

The theoretical contours outlined above reveal that integration requires two separate but related considerations, or criteria for evaluation: one is associated to the idea that citizenship status requires that all collective identities be allowed to participate in democratic life equally – empowerment implies that citizens be permitted to maintain their differences; while the other concerns considerations of unity, a sense of common purpose in public matters in order that deliberation is not confined to pockets of self-contained, fragmented collectivities in juxtaposition. These two basic poles are at issue in any model of integration and subsequent conceptualisations of citizenship status. In short, a balance must be struck between the *equal empowerment of group identity* as active constituents of the larger political community and the need for a *common ground for dialogue* in the name of unity, a *centre* which also serves as an identitive marker in the larger cultural environment and denotes in itself a pole of allegiance for all citizens. The balance resides in maintaining unity while preserving differences.

Having established the normative standard by which to evaluate actual citizenship requirements (markers of identity and their implications for democratic life), and the methods of integration flowing from such policies, the essay will proceed to demonstrate how the United States,

Canada, and Québec have dealt with the issue of polyethnicity. I will argue that the formal (constitutionally entrenched) commitment to multiculturalism in the Canadian case is flawed in its unifying intent, and in its claim to empower ethnic minorities in their cultural contexts. In a multinational federal context, such a model was merely a political strategy. It was based on notions of pan-Canadian identification, or "nation-building," which meant to subvert the recognition of Québec as constituting a distinct national collectivity within the federation. National identity in Québec, as a pole of allegiance, was relegated to occupy the same formal space in the federation as other ethno-cultural groupings. Moreover, the American case, although seemingly a polar opposite of the Canadian "mosaic" vision, actually shares similar features in the end due to an emphasis on a national centre based on individual rights and a denial of a common cultural space in the public realm.

Polyethnicity in the US: The "Melting-Pot" Metaphor

The case of the United States can be deemed a benchmark in evaluating state policy with regard to polyethnicity. To a large extent, the liberal emphasis on "benign neglect" in cultural matters, as a basis for common citizenship status, has permeated American discourse and has been traditionally embraced as somewhat of a founding principle of American identity. The US response to polyethnicity has followed a doctrine of assimilation. John Miller traces this approach as a founding ideal of what it means to be American:

> [America] is a nation dedicated to the proposition that all men are created equal. This extraordinary notion animates the American people, whose very sense of peoplehood derives not from a common lineage but from their adherence to a set of core principles about equality, liberty and self-government. These ideas, recognised at the founding of the United States, are universal. They apply to all humankind. They know no racial or ethnic limits. They are not bound by time or history. *And they lie at the center of American nationhood.* Because of this, these ideas uphold an identity into which immigrants from all over the world can assimilate, as long as they, too, dedicate themselves to the proposition.[14]

Minority cultures of all stripes were expected to shed their values, cultures and languages and unconditionally adopt those of the larger society. This approach can be characterised as one in which the idea of "benign neglect" in the identitive, or cultural sphere, ensures that all citizens may participate equally in democratic life. It is reductionist in the sense that the markers for identity are laid out in a procedural manner – a legalistic approach to citizenship which emphasises the primacy of individual rights in the public sphere. The question of culture itself is relegated to the private sphere – culture is not a political concern. Katz explains,

> our Bill of Rights, in contrast to every other modern bill of rights, is almost entirely procedural. It has virtually no substantive protections [. . .] [it] consists almost entirely of what could be called civil and political rights [. . .] [and] our procedural rights relate almost exclusively to individuals.[15]

Katz argues that the interpretation of equality in the United States is still very much a product of mid-nineteenth century views as espoused in the Fourteenth and Fifteenth Amendments. The former amendment states that "all persons born or naturalised in the United States, and subject to the jurisdiction thereof, are citizens of the United States and of the States wherein they reside."[16] This provision has been interpreted by the Courts in a manner which denied the Amendments' possible use as a basis for addressing minority group rights. Equality demanded that individuals be protected from state intrusions – not designed to eliminate "private" discrimination. The idea of equal citizenship before the law came to represent the "equal" protection of all citizens from discriminatory measures by *state action* – any other form of discrimination experienced by groups was a question of *private conduct* and hence dismissed as constituting a political issue. Katz summarises, "our tradition [. . .] became at least partly one of constitutional discrimination against groups rather than protection of them, and it was based on the growing prescription of individual equality and equal protection of the laws."[17] Such a tradition has been largely upheld in the United States in its formulation of citizenship status. The one significant caveat has been the rather recent attempt to address the reality of groups which have suffered discrimination, historically, through these interpretations of equality. Under the banner of "affirmative action," an attempt was made to grant special access to minority groups to educational institutions, broadcasting, employment, etc., in order that such institutions may better reflect the proportion of group identification in the general population. This was deemed a necessary measure in order to compensate for "lost ground." However, such provisions were qualified to a large degree. The Courts' test of constitutionality of these measures was such that the groups which were discriminated against had to prove that the nature of the intention of particular cases of discrimination was blatant, and not a consequence of the "latent" effects of private actions. In other words, the burden of proof required in order to benefit from such "group based" provisions of equal status rested on minority groups themselves, not on empirical structural inequalities.

In the final analysis, this tradition with regard to citizenship status in the United States prevails. Indeed, the question of the effects of affirmative action on the melting-pot metaphor as a symbol for national identity has resulted in virulent reaction.[18] If multiculturalism has achieved something of an "ontological status" in Canada, in the United States it is deemed by many to run counter to the very defining principles of American democracy. Again, equality in this view rests on reductionist principles – a matter of non-discrimination and the equal opportunity to participate. It is in this light that American sociologist Nathan Glazer describes the role of culture as it pertains to state policy:

> [Immigrants] had come to this country not to maintain a foreign language and culture but with the intention [. . .] to become Americanised as fast as possible, and this meant English language and American culture. They sought the induction to a new language and culture that the public schools provided – as do many present-day immigrants, too – and while they often found, as time went on, that they regretted what they and their children had lost, this was their choice [. . .]. The United States, whatever the realities of discrimination and segregation, had as a national ideal a unitary and new ethnic identity, that of American.[19]

For Schlesinger, Jr. as well, the key to American stability in the face of increasing polyethnicity has and will remain embedded in the melting-pot:

> The United States had a brilliant solution for the inherent fragility, the inherent combustibility, of a multiethnic society; the creation of a brand new national identity by individuals who, in forsaking old loyalties and joining to make new lives, melted away ethnic differences – a national identity that absorbs and transcends the diverse ethnicities that come to our shore [. . .]. The point of America was not to preserve old cultures, but to produce a new American culture.[20]

The basis of such identification is a "civic culture" – the notion that individuals are bound by equal adherence to a set of principles. Jürgen Habermas has labelled this approach "constitutional patriotism." The state here is interpreted as the "domain of law," while collective identity based on national allegiance is the "affective realm." Thus citizenship implies a civic patriotism, void of national identity. Political legitimacy as such stems from the procedures of democracy itself rather than any attachment to historical or cultural attributes.[21] Schlesinger, Jr. calls this set of principles the "American Creed," which is rooted in the practical obligations of civic participation and a patriotic commitment to a "democratic faith." In this view, democracy is not the product of citizen dignity through the recognition of diverse cultural contexts, but the precursor to unity. Procedural democracy comes to be the much heralded symbol of identification which all Americans share. In sum, the American response to polyethnicity has been to deny differences altogether and focus on the symbolic virtue of a "central" American identity, based on a procedurally (legally) defined conception of equal individual rights. Schlesinger puts it succinctly: "[The great unifying Western ideas of individual freedom, political democracy and human rights] are the ideas that define the American nationality – and that today empower people of all continents, races and creeds."[22] Kymlicka argues that Canada is analogous to the United States in its failure to differentiate between national minorities and polyethnic communities. Indeed, he notes that the fundamental difference between national minorities and ethnic communities is that the former seek self-determination while the latter seek inclusion. As will be demonstrated below, Canada has failed to recognise this distinction – multiculturalism becomes a mechanism by which to quell legitimate national aspirations – and thus fundamentally shares with the US model a certain homogenisation, or universalization of identity, albeit through cultural relativism. Kymlicka argues that the US reluctance to recognize minority nations is a direct result of its assimilationist model – a fear that such recognition will trickle down to polyethnic communities and thus undermine any basis for unity.[23] Canada's response stems from similar fears. However, the Canadian strategy was to elevate the status of cultural communities to the same level as national minorities. Both are universal, both are bound by nation-building projects in the name of unity, and both fail in any significant way to recognise group-differentiated rights as a federal principle.[24]

Canada's Policy of Multiculturalism

Multiculturalism as a political force in Canada came into play largely as a result of a negative response to the recommendations of the Royal Commission on Biculturalism and Bilingualism (B&B; Laurendeau-Dunton) in the 1960's by a "Third Force" – groups which represented immigrant ethnic collectivities. The Commission itself was spearheaded by Prime Minister Pearson as a response to the rise of a re-invigorated Québec nationalism through the Quiet Revolution, and the subsequent questioning of Québec's collective place in a federation dominated largely by Anglo-Canadians in economic, cultural and political affairs.[25] To quote Breton:

> The immediate motive [. . .] was the rise of the independence movement [in Québec] and the government's initial response. The transformation of institutional identity, language and symbols to help members of the French segment of the society recognise themselves generated identification and status concerns [. . .] among those of non-British, non-French origin.[26]

Representatives of the "Third Force" sought recognition of their cultural contribution to Canada, and felt that they would be relegated to second-class citizenship status if the country was to be formally defined as "bicultural and bilingual."

Prime Minister Trudeau's response was to alter the recommendations of the B&B commission – which called for a "two nations" conception of the country whereby French- and English-Canada were to be recognised equally as founding nations, with each enjoying majority status. Trudeau's solution was to adopt a policy of official multiculturalism in a bilingual framework. In doing so, he believed that language could be dissociated from culture – and individuals would be free to decide whether or not to endeavour to preserve their ethnic identity. Implicit in such an approach is the primacy of individual rights – the right of all individuals to freely dissociate themselves from their cultural communities. Also, the language of participation in Canadian society – between French and English – was left to individual choice. The idea that language was to correspond to sociological realities, as the B&B commission implied, was abandoned. The community for integration of immigrants was Canada, defined as a bilingual host society. In Trudeau's view,

> we cannot have a cultural policy for Canadians of French and British origin, another for aboriginals, and still another for all the others. Although we will have two official languages, there will be no official culture, and no ethnic group will have priority [. . .]. *All men will see their liberty hindered if they are continually enclosed in a cultural compartment determined uniquely by birth or language. It is thus essential that all Canadians, regardless of their ethnic origins, be required to learn at least one of the two languages in which the country conducts its public affairs.*[27]

Indeed, as Kallen contends, the final policy outcome represented a middle ground to the "multicultural and multilingual" vision espoused by the "Third Force" and the "Two Nations" demand of Québec nationalists.[28] By separating language and culture as such, "Canadian identity" was to be constructed on universal principles, relegating culture to the private sphere. In short, the federal government's policy objectives ran as follows:[29]
(1) The Government of Canada will support all of Canada's cultures and will seek to assist, resources permitting, the development of those cultural groups which have demonstrated a desire and effort to continue to

develop a capacity to grow and contribute to Canada, as well as a clear need for assistance.

(2) The Government will assist members of all cultural groups to overcome cultural barriers to full participation in Canadian society.

(3) The Government will promote creative encounters and interchange among all Canadian cultural groups in the interest of national unity.

(4) The Government will continue to assist immigrants to acquire at least one of Canada's official languages in order to become full participants in Canadian society.

New concerns over racial and ethnic equity led to a reiteration of the policy in the 1988 Canadian Multiculturalism Act by the Conservative government of Brian Mulroney. As Abu-Laban notes, the Act furthered the impact of Multicultural policy by focusing not only on cultural maintenance, but by emphasising more explicitly concerns regarding discrimination. The Act now contained a provision whereby the Minister of Multiculturalism may "assist ethno-cultural minority communities to conduct activities with a view to overcoming any discriminatory barrier and, in particular, discrimination based on race or national or ethnic origin."[30] Such a response by the state emanated from greater concerns surrounding the changing composition of minority ethnic groups due to recent waves of immigration. The new Act, however, did little to change the general thrust of the original policy, and simply refined and strengthened the terms of recognition with respect to the contribution of cultural groups.[31]

Of more significance was the entrenchment of Multiculturalism in the 1982 Canadian Charter of Rights and Freedoms. The existing policy of multiculturalism within a bilingual framework was reinforced. Under the interpretative clause in Section 27, the policy would henceforth "be interpreted in a manner consistent with the preservation and enhancement of the multicultural heritage of Canadians." Multiculturalism thus became a "visible component of the patriated constitution," leading to the perception among ethnocultural groups that they had achieved the status of "legitimate constitutional actors."[32] In Wilson's words, "Armed with long memories and the constitutional gains of 1982, these recently enfranchised "Charter Canadians" took our political decision-makers by surprise in serving notice that they were now serious players in the constitutional stakes."[33] In sum, the Charter

> struck a balance between Trudeau's concept of dualism and the concerns of third force Canadians [. . .]. On the one hand, dualism was constitutionally entrenched in the establishment of English and French as the official languages of Canada, and in the provision of linguistic educational rights to the English minority in

Québec and the French minority elsewhere. On the other hand, Section 27 says that the Charter "shall be interpreted in a manner consistent with the preservation and enhancement of the multicultural heritage of Canadians." In short, the balance between bilingualism and multiculturalism established at the statutory level early in Trudeau's Prime Ministership was duplicated at the constitutional level in the Charter.[34]

As mentioned above, two general considerations are of salience in assessing the models as they pertain to polyethnicity and democratic citizenship. First, the model must consider unity as a basis for democratic stability – which provides a shared sentiment – a common ground for dialogue. In other words, a pole of allegiance which acts as an identitive centre of convergence is required for active participation in a democratic polity. Second, the recognition of difference and a respect for the sources of meaning of minority cultures is an integral element of the equality of citizenship status – of citizen dignity or empowerment. For traditional liberal thought, such goals are incompatible. The involvement of group-differentiated recognition is said to mitigate the former ideal, in which equality emanates from shared adherence to universal principles and culture is treated with "benign neglect" in the public sphere. Recognising cultural distinctions shatters such unity and renders citizens unequal. The Canadian policy of Multiculturalism is a political strategy related to both goals. First, it seeks to achieve unity through a pan-Canadian nation-building project which emphasises the primacy of individual rights in a constitutional Charter and a choice of official language use (French or English) throughout the country. Superimposed on individual rights is the official recognition of all constituent cultures, equally. Such recognition is largely a symbolic concession, the fabrication of an identitive marker based on the principle of voluntary adherence to particular cultural allegiances. In Weinfeld's words:

> In the absence of any consensus on the substance of Canadian identity or culture, multiculturalism fills a void, defining Canadian culture in terms of the legitimate ancestral cultures which are the legacy of every Canadian: defining the whole through the sum of its parts.[35]

In short, while forging a common identity throughout Canada based on the "sum of its parts," it was hoped that the identitive marker for unity could be universal – the recognition of all cultures equally, with a regime of individual rights and bilingualism. In this way, adherence to particular cultural attachments could be voluntary for all individuals, while at the same time claiming to "empower" citizens of minority cultures through reductionist means – Canada's symbolic order was to be based on the negation of any particular cultural definition.

The model, however, is flawed on both counts. Its nation-building project neglected to recognise federal principles, particularly with regard to Québec's national aspirations.[36] As such, Québec national identity was placed, constitutionally, alongside every other minority culture as a basis for identification.[37] In Giroux's words,

> the partial recognition of ancestral rights reveals, *a contrario*, a refusal to recognise the Québec nation [. . .]. Without attributing a hierarchical set of rights [for Québec] vis-à-vis the rights of cultural communities, the representatives of the federal government attempt [. . .] to confuse the criteria of legitimacy of group demands within a multinational state. As such, demands by national minorities, those of cultural communities, and those of the majority group are regarded, without being defined or explicitly taking into consideration the criteria of legitimacy attributed to a nation which allow for a viable and effective democratic order [. . .]. In effect, without valid criteria for inclusion and exclusion, all demands become acceptable; thus it becomes possible to pit group demands against one another and to transform pluralism into a zero-sum game.[38]

In Taylor's terms, multiculturalism as such fails to appreciate the "deep diversity" in Canada, in which difference can be recognised on tiered levels in view of particular groupings' political aspirations and historical/territorial/linguistic realities. National minorities, as opposed to polyethnic communities, seek to provide a "centre" – a pole of allegiance necessary for unity and common purpose. In other words, national identity in Québec assumes a self-determining project for society. The community of reference for all citizens under the banner of multiculturalism is Canada. Bourque, Duchastel and Armony sum up this point succinctly:

> This ideology [. . .] defines itself in its relation to the territorial state: it circumscribes a community of belonging to the state within a country – Canada. It thus privileges, clearly, national dimensions of the production of the community, even though the discourse struggles to find a coherent representation of the Canadian nation. This Canadian nationalism finds its full significance in its opposition to the "counter-nationalisms" of Québec and the Aboriginals.[39]

A second flaw in the Canadian model is related precisely to its predilection towards cultural relativism. While the US pins its identitive centre on a "procedural democratic patriotism," Canada lacks an identitive pole of allegiance. The fact that polyethnic cultures are recognised, *a priori*, in a vacuum of space and time tends towards ghettoization and fragmentation in terms of allegiance to a larger polity. Bissoondath argues this point forcefully, labelling the phenomenon "cultural apartheid." The contention here is that multiculturalism in effect defines culture provisionally – in a static sense – and prohibits full social interactivity. In other words, the dynamic nature of cultural sources of meaning are neglected, resulting in the stagnant "folklorization" or "commodification" of cultural production, reducing culture to "a thing that can be displayed, performed, admired, bought, sold or forgotten [. . .] [it is] a devaluation of culture, its reduction to bauble and kitsch."[40] As such, neither unity nor citizen dignity accrued from cultural recognition is achieved here. Again, this is the result of recognising cultures in juxtaposition without any expectation that such cultures may contribute to the overall direction of the larger society in an evolutionary interplay of ideas. The substantive elements of minority cultures, their bases of meaning – are virtually pre-determined and unchanging, disregarding the very real effects of displacement into a new context. In short, Paquet highlights the general thrust of this line of criticism:

> Citizenship has become a crucible in which a *new identity* is always in the process of being forged, when it becomes understood that any identity or citizenship is always in transition, and therefore *integration sans assimilation* becomes a concept that is not an oxymoron [. . .]. In that sense, citizenship conditions may be negotiated in a manner that would recognize both the *diversity* of the social fabric and the need for some *unifying* concept to provide a linking force. Up to now, multiculturalism as a national policy has emphasized the pluralist forces at the cost of minimizing the centripetal bond. The notion of citizenship would recognize the patchwork quilt social fabric without losing sight of the need to channel the energy of this varied group into a well-defined direction.[41]

"Interculturalism": Québec's Model of Cultural Pluralism

Québec has adopted as its official position a discourse of interculturalism to deal with its polyethnic composition. This view connotes that the incorporation of immigrants or minority cultures into the larger political community is a reciprocal endeavour – a "moral contract" between the host society and the particular cultural collectivity, in the aim of establishing a forum for the empowerment of all citizens – "a common public culture."[42] The Government of Québec describes the general thrust of this model as such:

> The "moral contract" affirms that, in its options for society, it follows that rights and responsibilities apply as much to immigrants, on the one hand, as to the receiving society itself (including Québécois of cultural communities already integrated or on their way to being integrated) and its institutions, on the other hand. Being a Québécois means being engaged in fact in Québec's choices for society. For the immigrant established in Québec, adopting Québec as an adopted land [. . .] requires an engagement like that of all other citizens, and to respect these very choices of society. It is the simultaneous existence of complementary rights and obligations attributed to all parties – and to engage in solidarity in relationships of

reciprocal obligation – which justifies the vocabulary of "moral contract" to designate the general environment governing such relations with the aim of fully integrating immigrants.[43]

The common public culture in this view does not consist solely of the juridical sphere – it is not a procedural definition as in the American model. Instead, the basic tenets of the "moral contract" are such that the established "modes of being" in economic, political and socio-cultural realms are to be respected as a marker of identification and citizenship status, a point of convergence for groups of specific collective identities in order that all may share equally in democratic life. The "moral contract" is summed up as follows:

> (1) a society in which French is the common language of public life
> (2) a democratic society where participation and the contribution of everyone is expected and favoured
> (3) a pluralist society open to multiple contributions within the limits imposed by the respect for fundamental democratic values, and the necessity of intercommunal exchange.[44]

In establishing a model based on the convergence of collective identity, the French language is to serve as the common language of public life, this is seen as an essential condition for the cohesion of Québec society. In this view, language is not conceptualised as an individual right. Rocher et al. elaborate:

> In Quebec, [. . .] the French language is presented as a "centre of convergence" for diverse groups which can nevertheless maintain and let flourish their specificity. While the Canadian policy privileges an individualist approach to culture, Quebec's policy states clearly the need to recognise French as a collective good which requires protection and encouragement.[45]

The notion of "public life" is shady and nuanced – indeed, what constitutes a "public exchange" is not often clear. As a general rule, the confines of "public space" are not relegated solely to the activities of the state, but encompass "the public space of social interaction" as well. For example, students may, as a matter of individual right, communicate in any language they wish on the playground of a francophone school. However, language use in the classroom is considered public space. More examples of what constitutes "private interaction" are relations with family members, friends, colleagues or anyone involved in the social circle of the individual in question in which the choice of language use is of a consensual nature. Again, in Rocher et al.'s words:

> It must be emphasised that valuing French as the common language does not imply in itself the abandonment of a language of origin, for two reasons. The first

is related to the democratic nature of society which must respect individual choices. The second is a question of utility: the development of languages of origin is considered an economic, social and cultural asset. It must be stressed that there exists a fundamental distinction between the status of French as a common language of public life and that of the other languages.[46]

Thus an emphasis on the proficient use of the French language is taken as a minimal condition of the exercise of common citizenship – as an instrument of democracy. To quote Giroux,

> it is of essence that the French language is taken first and foremost as a condition of the exercise of citizen rights, the modern nation cannot claim to be a forum for discussion and decision-making without the existence of a community of language.[47]

Moreover, the host society expects as a matter of obligation that members of minority groups fully integrate into the larger community, with the expectation that all citizens are to contribute and participate in the social fabric of the common public culture. As a democratic community, this implies that once citizenship is attained, all members are equally encouraged to "participate in defining the general direction of our society [. . .] at all stages and in all sectors where the judgment of citizens can be manifested and heard."[48]

With regard to the eventuality of conflict arising between individuals or groups, the method of resolution must correspond to democratic norms. This point is important because it highlights a perspective that is fundamentally different from the American emphasis on procedural judicial channels. The Québec model stresses that in the initial manifestation of conflict, deliberative measures such as mediation, compromise, direct negotiation are preferred, leaving as much initiative and autonomy as possible to the parties in question. Legalistic measures and the recourse to specified rights are to be an option of last resort. In other words, this model values deliberation, mutual understanding, and generally, dialogue as fundamental characteristics of democratic life, in the realm of civil society, and is instrumental in the aim of fostering a cohesive and participatory conception of citizenship.

It is in the model's treatment of pluralism that the idea of "interculturalism" emerges – an idea whereby the notion of difference does not imply a society built on the juxtaposition of ethnic groupings in a "mosaic." Nor does it reduce citizenship status simply to procedural safeguards from state intrusion through the codification of fundamental individual rights and the assimilation of particular identities to such universal principles.[49] The Québec model of cultural pluralism operates fundamentally in the tradition of parliamentary democracy – with an emphasis on deliberation and representation. Within the framework of basic principles – a commitment to the peaceful resolution of conflict, a Charter of Human Rights and Freedoms in order to provide legal recourse to the protection of individual and group rights, equality between the sexes, a secular state, and equality and universality of citizen access to social provisions (i.e. health)[50] – interculturalism attempts to strike a balance between individual rights and cultural relativism by emphasising a "fusion of horizons," through dialogue and consensual agreement. Through the participation and discourse of all groups in the public sphere, the goal of this approach is to achieve the largest possible consensus regarding the limits and possibilities of the expression of collective identitive differences, weighed against the requirements of social cohesion and individual rights in a common public context. The recognition of cultural differences is taken for granted in such a view – the sources of meaning accrued from cultural identity are acknowledged as an explicit feature of citizen empowerment – yet an obligation is placed on all parties to contribute to the basic tenets of a common public culture. Pagé summarises:

> In conceptualising a common civic space, it is common civic norms which constitute the basis for social cohesion. The norms are situated above particular ethnic cultures and have a scope general enough to govern the actions of a society consisting of individuals belonging to a plurality of ethnic groups. *These norms are established by democratic institutions, which are capable of accounting for pluralism in seeking always, through decisions arrived at by democratic voting, as large as possible a consensual base, which does not limit itself only to the majority ethnic group or an ensemble of minority groups.*[51]

The virtue of Québec's model of interculturalism is that it strikes a balance between the requirements of unity – an identitive centre – and a recognition of minority cultures. Québec's model of integration is not assimilatory as that of the US, nor does it fall into cultural relativism and fragmentation in its commitment to cultural pluralism. The idea of empowerment as it pertains to marginalised ethno-cultural groups is such that integration is a necessary prerequisite to participate fully in the construction of a "common public culture" as an identitive centre. Identification with and participation through a variety of cultures is not ruled out as a basis for citizenship status, yet the possibility of enclosure and ghettoization is discouraged because the recognition of particular cultural identities is *de facto* the *recognition of the right and obligation to participate* in the polity, not the recognition of culture as existing in self-contained communities, in a vacuum of space and time. In other words, recognition is an *outcome* of participation, it is in contributing to the development of a common public culture, to larger consensual bases of allegiance and identification, without a rejection of the established symbolic order offered by Québec society as it has evolved historically, that members of minority cultural groups can make a difference regarding their status as citizens.

In the final analysis, the recognition of minority cultures is built into the model, the "moral contract" is an integrative principle whereby ethno-cultural groups are given the empowerment to contribute, in a common language, and to make their mark on the basic principles of the common public culture. Harvey summarizes the model of interculturalism as follows:

> The conservation of a language of origin, a history other than that of the receiving country, the preservation of distinct familial, religious and social commitments, the establishment of welcoming groups to help in the integration of those arriving from the same country, the continuity of relations with the country of origin, are all accepted, welcome, and enriching for the host society. *All of this is also in the domain of negotiation, of active reciprocal tolerance, involving an evolution with the passing of time* [. . .]. Intercultural pluralism is the domain [. . .] in which a host country can and also must encourage originality in the ways of life of those arriving. Sensibilities, aesthetics, and models of belonging and association can remain identical to those within the cultural structures of the countries of origin. Pride in cultural origins must be permitted [. . .] except in the case of contradiction to the common public culture.[52]

Difference is recognised within the limits of societal cohesion and political community, not as a *fundamental starting point* for common identification and unity. Interculturalism as a model for addressing polyethnicity represents a forum for citizen empowerment, not retrenchment. From the initial premise that a national culture consists of a "daily plebiscite," in Renan's conceptualisation, the Québec model rests on the idea that the common public culture be inclusive of all groups in its changing and evolutionary fabric.

Conclusion: Interculturalism as a Model for Export

The political strategy accompanying Canadian multiculturalism as policy, in the name of unity, is not inclusive of Québec's national identity – rather, it constitutes a *competing* vision for society – the forging of a political community where it did not previously exist. As such, there does not exist an identitive centre for citizens of Canada, there is no allegiance to a community called Canada. It is built merely on the basis of a "counter-nationalism" to Québec's collective identity. Canadian multiculturalism is a denial of Québec's distinct identitive status in Canada – more precisely, of Québec as a self-determining political community – with its own instruments for framing citizenship status as a host society. As such, the vision implicit in the policy of multiculturalism was to relegate Québec to the level of a mere administrative unit, equal to all other provinces, and not an identitive pole of allegiance for its citizens. This view implies that there is no such thing as a "citizen" of Québec, if citizenship is understood through a communitarian interpretation, where a sense of belonging and allegiance to a community empowers members to participate in the affairs of the polity.

In contrast to Canadian multiculturalism, a cultural pluralism model characterized in terms of a "fusion of horizons" does not occur through the mere recognition of all cultures given equal status, in a relative manner. It incorporates an understanding of the dynamic and evolutionary nature of cultural identity and its various manifestations by different groups. Québec's model stresses a common public culture as a *foyer de convergence*. Convergence here does not imply assimilation into a reductionist procedural identity, nor does it reduce culture to folkloristic, self-contained pockets of identity. Québec's is a more assertive model which expects all cultures to contribute in a consensual framework towards the development of principles around which the societal cohesion necessary for democratic life can be constructed. As such, the Québec model of interculturalism merits serious consideration as a response to the increasing polyethnicity of states throughout the world.

Notes

[1] Raffaele Iacovino is a Ph.D. candidate in the Department of Political Science at McGill University, Montréal, Québec, Canada.

[2] "Hommage à Julien Harvey: Le Québec, société plurielle en mutation?" *Globe* 1.1 (1998): 51.

[3] Yasmeen Abu-Laban, "The Politics of Race, Ethnicity and Immigration: The Contested Arena of Multiculturalism into the Twenty-First Century," *Canadian Politics*, ed. James P. Bickerton and Alain-G. Gagnon, 3rd edition (Peterborough: Broadview Press, 1999) 463-83.

[4] Kas Mazurek, quoted in Vince Seymour Wilson, "Canada's Evolving Multicultural Policy," *Canada's Century: Governance in a Maturing Society*, ed. C.E.S. Franks et al. (Montreal: McGill-Queen's University Press, 1995) 165.

5   Noreen Golfman, "Locating Difference: Ways of Reading Multiculturalism," *Mosaic* 29.3 (September 1996): 175.

6   Danielle Juteau, "Citoyenneté, intégration et multiculturalisme canadien," *Dual Images: Multiculturalism on Two Sides of the Atlantic* (Budapest: Institute for Political Science of the Hungarian Academy of Sciences, 1996) 173-4, my translation.

7   Will Kymlicka, *Multicultural Citizenship: A Liberal Theory of Minority Rights* (New York: Oxford University Press, 1995) 193.

8   For a more profound assessment of the epistemological challenge of multiculturalism to liberal models of citizenship, see Andrea Semprini, *Le Multiculturalisme* (Paris: Presses Universitaires de France, 1997).

9   Kymlicka, *Citizenship* 174-5.

10 W. W. Isajiw, "Social Evolution and the Values of Multiculturalism," Paper presented at the Ninth Biennial Conference of the Canadian Ethnic Studies Association, Edmonton, Alberta, October 14-7, 1981, cited in Evelyn Kallen, "Multiculturalism: Ideology, Policy and Reality," *Journal of Canadian Studies* 17.1 (1982): 52.

11 Charles Taylor, "Multiculturalism and the Politics of Recognition," *Multiculturalism: Examining the Politics of Recognition*, ed. Amy Gutmann (Princeton: Princeton University Press, 1994) 25.

12 V. Wilson, "The Tapestry Vision of Canadian Multiculturalism," *Canadian Journal of Political Science* 26.4 (1993): 654.

13 Ibid., 653.

14 John J. Miller, *The Unmaking of Americans: How Multiculturalism has Undermined the Assimilation Ethic* (New York: Free Press, 1998) 24, my emphasis.

15 Stanley N. Katz, "The Legal Framework of American Pluralism: Liberal Constitutionalism and the Protection of Groups," *Beyond Pluralism: The Conception of Groups and Group Identities in America*, ed. Wendy F. Katkin et al. (Chicago: University of Illinois Press, 1998) 12.

16 Ibid., 14.

17 Ibid., 15.

18 See for example Arthur M. Schlesinger, Jr., *The Disuniting of America* (New York: Norton, 1992); Dinesh D'Souza, *The End of Racism: Principles for a Multiracial Society* (New York: Free Press, 1995); Alvin J. Schmidt, *The Menace of Multiculturalism: Trojan Horse in America* (Westport: Praeger Publishers, 1997); and John J. Miller, *The Unmaking of Americans: How Multiculturalism Has Undermined the Assimilation Ethic* (New York: Free Press, 1998).

19 Nathan Glazer (1983 and 1978); quoted in Will Kymlicka, "Ethnicity in the USA," *The Ethnicity Reader: Nationalism, Multiculturalism and Migration*, ed. Montserrat Guibernau and John Rex (Cambridge, MA: Polity Press, 1997) 243.

20 Schlesinger, Jr., *Disuniting* 17.

21 Jürgen Habermas, *Écrits politiques* (Paris: Cerf, 1990).

22 Schlesinger Jr., *Disuniting* 147.

23 Will Kymlicka, "Ethnicity in the USA" 240.

24 For more on the distinction between national minorities and polyethnic communities in the framing of citizenship status, see Gilles Paquet, "Political Philosophy of Multiculturalism," *Ethnicity and Culture in Canada*, ed. J.W. Berry and J.A. Laponce (Toronto: University of Toronto Press, 1994).

25 Abu-Laban, "Politics of Race." 466.

26 Raymond Breton, "Multiculturalism and Canadian Nation-Building," *The Politics of Gender, Ethnicity and Language in Canada*, ed. Alan C. Cairns and Cynthia Williams (Toronto: University of Toronto Press, 1986) 48.

27 Pierre Elliott Trudeau (1971), cited in Linda Cardinal and Claude Couture, "L'immigration et le multiculturalisme au Canada: la genèse d'une problématique," *Les politiques publiques canadiennes*, ed. Manon Tremblay (Sainte-Foy: Les Presses de l'Université Laval, 1998) 249-50, their emphasis, my translation.

28 Kallen, "Multiculturalism" 54.

29 House of Commons Debates, (October 8, 1971), Statement of Prime Minister Trudeau.

30 Abu-Laban, "Politics of Race" 471.

31 Cardinal and Couture, "L'Immigration et le multiculturalisme" 251.

32 Abu-Laban, "Politics of Race" 472.

33 Wilson, "Tapestry Vision" 657.

34 Rainer Knopff and F.L. Morton, *Charter Politics* (Scarborough: Nelson Canada, 1991) 88; quoted in Wilson, "Tapestry Vision" 657.

35 Morton Weinfeld, "Myth and Reality in the Canadian Mosaic: 'Affective Ethnicity,'" *Études ethniques au Canada/Canadian Ethnic Studies* 13 (1981): 94.

36 For more on a multinational interpretation of Canadian federalism, in which unity stems from a recognition of the country's constituent political communities, see Alain-G. Gagnon, "Fédéralisme et identités nationales: Le passage obligé de l'État-nation à l'État plurinational," *L'État-nation au tournant du siècle: les enseignements de l'expérience canadienne et européenne*, ed. Panayotis Soldatos and Jean-Claude Masclet (Université de Montréal: Chaire Jean Monnet, 1997); Charles Taylor, "The Deep Challenge of Dualism," *Québec: State and Society*, ed. Alain-G. Gagnon, 2nd edition (Toronto: Nelson Canada, 1993); and James Tully, *Strange Multiplicity: Constitutionalism in the Age of Diversity* (Cambridge: Cambridge University Press, 1995).

37 For more on the idea that official multiculturalism represents a wholesale redefinition of Canada's constitutional order in terms of collective identitive references, see Fernand Dumont, "La fin d'un malentendu historique," *Raisons Communes* (Montréal: Éditions du Boréal, 1995) 33-48; and Gilles Bourque and Jules Duchastel, "La représentation de la communauté," *L'identité fragmentée* (Montréal: Éditions Fides, 1996) 29-51.

[38] France Giroux, "Le nouveau contrat national est-il possible dans une démocratie pluraliste? Examen comparatif des situations française, canadienne et québécoise," *Politique et Sociétés* 16.3 (1997): 141, my translation.

[39] Gilles Bourque, Jules Duchastel and Victor Armony, "De l'universalisme au particularisme: droits et citoyenneté," *L'Amour des Lois*, ed. Josiane Bon Lad-Ayoub, Bjarne Melkevik and Pierre Robert (Sainte-Foy and Paris: Presses de l'Université Laval and L'Harmattan, 1996) 240, my translation.

[40] Neil Bissoondath, *Selling Illusions: The Cult of Multiculturalism in Canada* (Toronto: Penguin Books, 1994) 83.

[41] Paquet, "Political Philosophy" 74.

[42] For more on the conceptualization of the principles of the "common public culture" as it is understood in Québec see Julien Harvey "Culture publique, intégration et pluralisme," *Relations* (October 1991): 239-41; and Gary Caldwell, "Immigration et la nécessité d'une culture publique commune," *L'Action Nationale* 78.8 (1988): 704-11.

[43] Gouvernement du Québec, Conseil des relations interculturelles, "Culture publique commune et cohésion sociale: le contrat moral d'intégration des immigrants dans un Québec francophone, démocratique et pluraliste," *Gérer la diversité dans un Québec francophone, démocratique et pluraliste: principes de fond pour guider la recherche d'accommodements raisonnables* (Montréal: Gouvernement du Québec, 1994) 11, my translation.

[44] Gouvernement du Québec, Ministère des Communautés culturelles et de l'Immigration du Québec, Direction des communications, *Au Québec pour bâtir ensemble. Énoncé de politique en matière d'immigration et d'intégration* (Montréal: Gouvernement du Québec, 1990) 15, my translation.

[45] François Rocher, Guy Rocher and Micheline Labelle, "Pluriethnicité, citoyenneté et intégration: de la souveraineté pour lever les obstacles et les ambiguïtés," *Cahiers de recherche sociologique* 25 (1995): 221, my translation.

[46] Ibid., 225.

[47] France Giroux, "Le nouveau contrat national est-il possible dans une démocratie pluraliste? Examen comparatif des situations française, canadienne et québécoise" 137, my translation.

[48] Gouvernement du Québec 13, my translation.

[49] Julien Harvey: "Intégration dit contact culturel intermédiaire entre l'assimilation et la juxtaposition, tenant compte des deux cultures en contact et constituant une nouvelle synthèse et une nouvelle dynamique." ("Culture publique, intégration et pluralisme," *Relations* [October 1991]: 239).

[50] Gouvernement du Québec, Ministère des Communautés culturelles et de l'Immigration, *La gestion de la diversité et l'accommodement raisonnable* (Montréal: Gouvernement du Québec, 1993) quoted in Rocher et al., *Pluriethnicité* 225.

[51] Michel Pagé, "Intégration, identité ethnique et cohésion sociale," *Pluriethnicité et société: construire un espace commun*, ed. Fernand Ouellet and Michel Pagé (Québec: Institut

québécois de recherche sur la culture (IQRC), 1991) 146-7, my emphasis, my translation.

52 Harvey, "Culture publique" 241, my emphasis, my translation.

Different Drummers, Same Beat: Resistance as Assimilation

Juan Bruce-Novoa

As a World War II Baby Boomer, mine was a generation born of conformity, but marked by resistance, the habit of resistance made possible through relative affluence, security, and access to mobility. Rejecting the powerful mid-century social models of a victorious US, we opted instead for rock and roll and the rebellion of youth culture: Elvis Presley and James Dean set our patterns; come the 60s, we resisted incorporation into traditional US post-high school life of marriage and work by filling university classrooms in record numbers and then the streets to demand just human relations based on equal opportunity, yes, but also in the name of free(dom to) love without social restrictions or social difference: at their best, our mass meetings were called Love-Ins; the most famous anti-Vietnam war motto was "Make Love, Not War." Songs expressed our goals: *What the World Needs Now Is Love, All You Need Is Love* – resistance in the form of invitations to a perpetual Mardi Gras: 67 the Summer of Love, the world lured to San Francisco by Scott McKenzie's voice pied pipering the mantra of the Love Generation – a lucky few who actually made the trip, their bodies ever-after transformed, left the rest of us with perpetual nostalgia – and for a couple of years it flowed and peaked, Monterey Rock Festival cum Woodstock [. . .] but lest we forget, at their worst they were insane riots as cities flamed in the violent venting of the old frustrations, a mixture of much spontaneous, unpremeditated destruction and some calculated rebellion uniting masses of impatient outsiders fed up with society's resistance to letting them share the banquet: 67 the Summer of Burn Baby Burn, Detroit cum Washington D.C., twisting *Light My Fire* from affirmation to resistance, and our love ultimately did become a funeral pyre on the bloody field of Altamont. Two extremes of resistance, running head on into even greater resistance by the status quo: often forgotten is that for every peace-and-love marcher flaunting difference there were two hard hats linking arms with Hells Angels waiting to shunt the flow of rebellion into the side alleys of ethnic neighborhoods, gendered ghettos and ideological home turfs. Resistance to resistance to resistance, and caught in the squeeze, it became progressively more difficult, mostly impossible, to make love survive. Perhaps a generation's virginity was too cavalierly bestowed on undeserving exploiters of our impulsive youth, but looking back only teaches us that something was irreparably lost in the sincere effort to make love indiscriminately to every-and-anyone, and resistance triumphed – not, however, as an achievement of goals – though undeniably some were realized – rather as the institutionalization of a life style.

What we didn't realize then, and reluctantly have considered since, is that this was yet another trap of tradition, more sinister than the conformity to the national consensus of shared customs and values which at least provided a sense of fixed presence from which even outsiders could take their sextant readings; resistance as a way of a life, of constant unsettled otherness, alienation, and juvenile restlessness aging into bitter anxiety. What had once been, if extended beyond the grace period of adolescence, the purview of the few, a sort of perverse elitism of the rare outsider, became the domain of the masses. And resistance flourished as we came to maturity: in the words of Tina Turner, "what's love got to do with [. . .] it's just a second hand emotion."

The painful burden of my generation is that we failed to achieve our highest goal – a harmonious society based on love – and settled for a fragmented one of resistance, cynicism in the guise of social consciousness. Resistance: The word is everywhere, mostly meaningless in terms of actual social praxis, but rhetorically ubiquitous, especially in the realm of academic discourse. Resistance theory can be found rooted firmly across the variegated fields of the humanities and social sciences. I can speak little for the hard sciences, though one hears calls for scientists to resist traditional objectivity and to conduct themselves as responsible citizens, that is, to submit themselves to the politically correct agenda of the moment – for science to resist itself as science.

If you are thoroughly confused by now, it is not surprising. Resistance theory is a hotbed of confusion. This doesn't surprise Latinos: in Mexico and the Caribbean the ultimate form of resistance is called *relajo*, the provocation of amorphous, anonymous disruption that undermines all serious discussion, yet offers no identifiable source of opposition against which the threatened power source might direct its counter attack; a dissemination tactic that scatters the seeds of distraction so widely that counterattack must be spread too thinly to be effective. But true *relajo*, an intellectual guerilla tactic that produces social chaos in order to suspend action, ultimately is a conservative stratagem favoring stasis and retrenchment over progress, the status quo or retrogression over change.

In its structural conformation, resistance calls for a preexisting condition against or in favor of which to position itself, hence it is dependent on the character of the ground, the lay of the land, for its definition of purpose. Whatever one perceives or conceives as the threat or irritation in a field of action will be resisted; in effect, the resisted object is the de facto subject determining greatly the nature and modes of the resistance. Hence, the proliferation of widely divergent writing about resistance theory, that in actuality often attempt to be exercises in resistance themselves to the established patterns in particular bailiwicks; i.e.: in political science, anthropology, psychology, philosophy, cognitive science, sociology, history, English, cultural studies, ethnic studies, gender studies, etc. And, of course, literature and literary criticism. Everybody resisting everybody else, and resistance discovered everywhere until it becomes self-confirming – and perhaps the only thing left unresisted is resistance. This has the same effect as the old leftist dictum, everything is political: if so, then the political ceases to be a distinct category of discourse, and thus useless for analysis. If every action can be seen as resistance, then resistance is the natural pattern of existence.

Perhaps they are right. Time resists permanence, just as movement resists stasis. Nothing is the same from moment to moment, everything perpetually dying and being reborn, yet the desire to maintain and conserve oneself seems universal, if I can be permitted that old fashion expression. And one can focus on this process as resistance to change versus resistance to stasis, although in my experience I was taught, through readings of eastern philosophy and western physics, that even solid objects at rest are actually in movement, and that nothing can prevent inertia.

Beyond this, the world – the given materiality of existence – resists human comprehension in its otherness. The resistance of the world to human comprehension extends trough a long line of the greatest names: Locke, St. Thomas, Augustine, Aristotle. The great tradition of Occidental thought has persistently concerned itself with the stubbornly indifferent world; the difference between that tradition and contemporary academic rhetoric is that those thinkers had a faith in the power of the arts – verbal, corporeal or plastic – to take indifferent, alien matter as its object/subject and reshape it into imagery, a product of human ingenuity, to project, and simultaneously serve as, a source of significance. With the demythification of all grand projects – sometimes called the loss of consensus, or the disappearance of master narratives, or profanation of postmodern, post-colonial existence – we have become masters at deconstructing – a practice only sometimes synonymous with deconstruction – and skeptics if not outright apostates of all Bauhaus ideals.

And yet, in the everyday confrontation with life, human groups, and quite possibly some animals as well, have worked out patterns of interaction within and through which resistance is mediated, minimized and ritualized into manageable and even unnoticeable experiences. This is one of the functions of culture, to create scenarios for the performance of fluid communications and movement. The designs imposed on amorphous nature differ according to circumstances, but they function to cut resistance to a minimum – unless deemed necessary to some greater social, and hence ordering, purpose – and facilitate the flow of productive action.

From the layout of streets, to the etiquette of the market place, to traffic signals, to fashion, to routine greetings, to expressions of affection and hostility, culture dictates the rituals of interaction. Insiders follow the rules unconsciously; outsiders commit blunders when they follow ingrained patterns from another time/space rendered inappropriate by displacement into a different context. We might call this misplaced performance resistance, but more often it is simply a lack of knowledge that once comprehended can be corrected, and there follows at least an attempt to adjust the behavior to the norms of specific locations. It is quite a different story when the sojourner insists on not following the local patterns – this we could call resistance.

However, we should not rush to judgment on the significance of resistance, neither as intent nor as effect. Resistance itself is attributed value by culture. In the United States it is one thing for a beautiful, well-dressed woman or elegant man to speak with a foreign accent – preferably French or Italian – and quite another for a baglady or wino to have a heavy Slavic or Spanish accent. And these situations change. Once it was seen as a sign of Hispanic recalcitrance, or just plain mental inability, for Mexican maids or gardeners not to speak English after years of living in the United States – now, it is has become a matter of pride to have an "Authentic Mexican" who one must address in Spanish, or some semblance of it, to communicate with them. Resistance moves from negative to positive value over time and changing circumstances. Yet, move the children of that maid or gardener to the local school and their resistance to mastering English may or may not be judged as positive, depending on the percentage of ethnic control of the school, the community, or the School Board. It is now an infamous and perturbing fact that Latino voters in California are resisting the efforts of Latino educators to impose bilingual/bicultural teaching on their children. And they are doing it through an institutionalized California ritual: direct voting for or against legislation through propositions, a custom alien to their national origins; but then, even ethnic separatists favor assimilation when it serves their purpose.

Given the above, the positive or negative value attributed resistance to cultural norms will vary. Outsiders perceive that Germany is a culture that marks resistance to social mores and etiquette with a heavy negativity. When first visiting Germany I was fascinated by a sign in a *Postamt* stating that pushing to the front of the line was asocial. My first reaction emerged from my home culture: in the United States to declare something asocial would either have no resonance or be taken as open invitation to do exactly what is being restricted. But then, upon reflection, I wondered why, in a society known for its regimentation of behavior, would it be necessary to post such a conspicuous reminder about what in the United States is a matter of common courtesy, so taken for granted that violations of it assume major proportions – it is no coincidence that pushing ahead in line has been used by Hollywood, at least since *Bronco Billy and the Greaser* (1911), as a surefire visual code to communicate individual deviance or social crisis. However, if a deviant pattern persists in a culture, despite corrective efforts, something in that culture actually is rewarding the behavioral pattern, or the pattern is so ingrained that a much more stringent behavior modification program is needed. One has only to go skiing in the Alps to realize that the latter seems to be the case on the European slopes. However, once again, one must not jump to universalizing conclusions about Germans and lines: for an American it is a wonder of efficiency to watch how cars on the *Autobahn* respect the defined purpose of lanes, performing this visually delightful choreography of movement that allows the more powerful, faster vehicles to take full advantage of their superior power to stream by at breathtaking speeds. This would be impossible in the United States, where everyone assumes they have equal right to any lane at any time, no matter what speed they wish to travel.

In short, resistance to norms is as much a culturally regulated activity as obedience to them. Sacvan Bercovitch's studies of the Puritan tradition show that dissent – or resistance to harmonious collaboration – was rendered meaningful and thus became an ingrained tradition of US culture.[1] The Puritans, themselves proud dissenters from the European norm, needed to control the proliferation of dissent without stifling the character of their project of colonizing the wilderness. Individual resistance to state dominance had to be nurtured, while simultaneously assuring group consensus. Their response: the *errand*, the pilgrimage into the wilderness where individuals indulged self-expression while at the same time serving the community by expanding its sphere of influence through evangelization. They also utilized typology, centered on Moses – an archetypal dissenter/resister turned leader – to constantly reintegrate new dissenters into the fold through topological applications of appropriate biblical models of resistance and re-appropriation.[2]

However, Bercovitch pays little attention in his analysis to the phenomena of dissent/resistance by two major groups: Native Americans and immigrants. Yet, they are implicitly provided for. If resistance is an acceptable mode of behavior, a sort of ritualized performance of Americanization, then resistance should be able to serve both the previous inhabitants and the newly arrived to integrate themselves into the system. Regarding the Native American, Gerald Vizenor has studied patterns of accommodation that are in effect survival tactics through which Native Americans have managed to resist annihilation.[3] The performance of the role of "the Indian" resembles black minstrelsy in its ability to function at multiple levels of signification, simultaneously conveying different messages to different audiences, or the use of palimpsestic writing by gays and women. The use of the costume, be it the proper dress of the master or the assigned dress of the servant or that of the passive companion, becomes a ritualized form of accommodation. When the parties involved realize the element of subterfuge, then they also become ritualized forms of resistance, clever twists on the old norm that have always been considered worthy of a true American.

For the immigrant, there is some of this as well. In his last chapter of *The Rites of Assent,* where Bercovitch deals with the new critical theories of ideological dissent, he does note that many of the practitioners of the new theories emerged from immigrant groups who had not previously had *entrée* into the academy.[4] Playing the resistant minority has a certain cache in contemporary US culture, but then it has had for some time. Stories of Irish political machines or the Jewish lobby are legendary among ethnic groups, especially Latinos who view them as models. Even the post-Puzo transformation of the mafia into a prototypical American ethnic institution glorifies – and to a certain extent justifies – resistance as a necessary survival tactic. And there is something to be said for the logic of playing resistance to the hilt when your ethnic difference becomes a commodity actively recruited on the job circuit. And when legal prescriptions mandate the inclusion of a certain percentage of readily identifiable *OTHERS*, the last thing institutions like a university want is for their hard sought, and often expensive, minorities to become invisible by blending in. They expect ethnics to perform their advertised role: ethnically. And the ethnics who have bought into the role see any dissenters as dangerous. No one wants to be called on the pretense of the game: Resisting the norm is the norm, so no resisting authorized resistance in the form of non-resisting will be accepted; rather, it will be harshly resisted by a cadre of officially sanctioned resisters.

And yet, when different drummers become an orchestra of drummers, differences must be homogenized, like marching bands playing rock music at football game half times – an academic exercise in gap filling, popular entertainment all the rage, but ultimately so boring that it equals dead time on a telecasters schedule.

Before proceding, allow me a parenthetical caveat: I do not denigrate practices of true political resistance. Palestinian writing in Israel is in no way a voguish pose, but a life and death risk, as was pro-Jewish writing in the Germany of the mid thirties, or pro-Catholic writing in the Mexico of the late 1920s or China of the 1950s or Guatemala of the 1970s. However, one must distinguish between being a communist union organizer in the United States and being a Marxist literary critic at a prestigious university – while the former can still put your livelihood, and even your life in danger, the latter no longer has any noticeable ill effects; quite the contrary in fact, if we are to judge by the examples of well-known and highly placed Marxist literary critics.

As Bercovitch demonstrates in *The Rites of Assent*, academic critical dissent has tended to be authorized by the US as the authentic expression of the national spirit or as cocktail leftism. One of the ways to prove one's American credentials is to criticize the system; this appeals to the ideology of renovation, reformation, fidelity to democratic origins, etc. One way to exploit the liberality of the American system is to allow yourself to be displayed as a figure of opposition by the very institutions being criticized. Different routes through the process of appropriation on your way to assimilation – cooptation we used to call it in the sixties; now: strategies of power positioning within the system.

Already having confessed to my own complicity in the habit of resistance, allow me to cross from speculative discussion of it to praxis. In the spirit of resistance I would offer a counter proposal to Bercovitch's placement of origins of the process of assimilative opposition in the Puritans. I would suggest that before the Puritans even landed on the North Eastern coast of what 16th-century French fisherman referred to as Florida, Spanish explorers had already documented experiences of resistance that can serve as paradigmatic of the American tradition. Do not misunderstand: I do not claim that the anecdotes I will relate to you have formed or even informed the US consciousness of dissent or resistance, as the Puritans have, but only that in these incidents from Spanish colonial texts one can find prototypical American experiences.

Anyone familiar with my work will not be surprised that I draw my first example from Cabeza de Vaca. Cabeza de Vaca's position in American writing is assured by the fact that he is the first European to write the American *WE* in his chronicle published in 1547, neither Native American nor European, but a distinct grouping somewhere between, formed through the interaction of both. Cabeza de Vaca becomes a cultural hybrid during his years of living among the Native Americans, serving them as slave, trader, shaman, chief. And his path is marked, at critical junctures, with the sign of resistance. As a member of the would-be conquistadors, Cabeza de Vaca counseled against reckless aggression and in favor of restraint, thus dissenting from the opinions expressed by the Spanish commander of the expedition. Later, when he finds himself shipwrecked and enslaved on the northwestern shores of the Gulf of Mexico, he is forced to become a healer. He has no choice but to obey his Native American masters, but he resists full capitulation to native practice by infusing the ceremony with the sign of the cross and the name of Christ. In so doing, Cabeza de Vaca creates a hybrid cultural practice, neither Native nor European. It is this act, created by resistance in the name of preserving his Catholicism, that he invents the paradigmatic rite of passage into the American self. As with other subsequent resisters in the tradition, Cabeza de Vaca's self-creative act gains him recognition and social mobility among the host people, elevating him to the status of cult figure with hoards of faithful, Native American followers. Later these followers defend his hard won identity as non-Spanish, even at the moment Cabeza de Vaca is attempting to reassimilate himself into the Spanish order. And in the end Cabeza de Vaca will find himself in the difficult position of compromise – a position still much too familiar to professional academic resisters, myself included, in which we recognize that the only thing we have of real value to the dominant culture from which we desire, more than recognition, placement and rewards, the one thing that can win us *entrée*, is the knowledge and control of the culture of otherness we represent that has eluded the hegemonic power of the new masters. In exchange for reorientation into European time/space, Cabeza de Vaca trades his native followers. And then, in what most likely was a futile attempt to protect them from the fate of slavery, Cabeza de Vaca tried to give them the elements with which he had created the hybrid ritual of salvation: the sign of the cross and the name of Christ. He instructs them that they can use the sign of the cross to resist the Spanish enslaving venture. At the same time, he tries to convince his Native American followers to abandon their nomadic customs – ironically adopted by most of them in order to follow Cabeza de Vaca – and take up residence in Christian dwellings. He instructs them that they can resist being abused by any inquiring Spaniard by claiming that they live in the name of Christ and the sign of the sacred cross. However, as Cabeza de Vaca moves southward towards Mexico City, he mentions that his guides are also taking a group of Indians, from all indications captives.

What conclusions are we to draw from this paradigmatic venture into resistance? First, that resistance can actually facilitate acceptance by the dominant culture in that it produces a desirable innovation readily commodified and marketed. Second, the one who benefits from the resistance is the privileged person with knowledge of and access to both cultures, able to manipulate them into integrated forms at the service of the masters of hegemony, and to alter the degree of add-mixture in the performance of the ritual according to the requirements of the specific situation, emphasizing one set of ingredients or another to please different masters. This second conclusion has a corollary: those who so steadfastly believe in the set significance of the hybrid product of resistance that they will fight to the end to preserve it, probably will be swept aside by the ebb and flow of fashion. Third, that while resistance can be parlayed into advantage for the main protagonist – the transculturating mediator – it may well not translate into comparable success for the followers who attempt to imitate the performance. This could well be a useful reminder to those of us who teach students who will spend their lives in a world of pragmatic labor where resistance as a habitual attitude may well lead them to personal disaster. Giving them the elements and tools of resistance, instead of those of accommodation, may be intellectually stimulating and even rewarding for the privileged professional outsider, but counterproductive for those who will inhabit a world where tenure and absolute freedom of expression are anachronistic and even dangerous ideals. As Joseph Alkana suggests in reference to Bercovitch's work, "it is necessary here to add – or, more properly restore – the term *pedagogy* to the debate over Americanist criticism."[5] Gregory S. Jay takes a similar position: "It appears more important than ever to insist on the inseparability of teaching and scholarship, especially in the light of the often ignorant assertions about how indifferent or uninvolved research scholars are when it comes to teaching."[6] While these and other scholars who have raised the same concern refer mostly to the possible effects of shifting the content within the canon, I would focus on the attitude we foster in students by privileging resistance over harmony. While students may quickly forget the content of their readings, many will continue to utilize the fashionable skepticism of confrontational resistance.[7]

Another Spanish colonial text, Gaspar Pérez de Villagrá's *La Conquista de la Nuevo México* [sic] (1616), contains accounts of two confrontations with Native Americans: one near the present day El Paso/ Juárez in which they accommodate, and a second at the Acoma village in which they resist. While the first group engages in an exchange of information-for-goods until they grateful Spanish reward them with European garb and ceremoniously assimilated them into the grand edifice of the universal church, the second rejects *entrée* into Catholicism and stands aloof atop their natural defense tower from which they resists incorporation with violent force. The first group achieves an ephemeral moment of glory within Villagrá's epic, only to disappear rapidly, forgotten by the narrator. The second is given many more verses, as well as the status of characters with specific names, voices and dialogue. True, the Acoma resisters are eventually decimated, the survivors mutilated, enslaved and scattered over the map of Spanish New Mexico, but in terms of the text, they gain a position of prominence denied the non-resisters: they, like the El Paso Indians, are re-costumed, but now by the author; but this time not as Spaniards – a fact that might explain why the El Pasoans are literally and literarily absorbed by the text – but as noble though exotic Renaissance-style epic warriors, with a grand nobility of spirit matched by their gift for oratory. Another way of reading it would be that Villagrá practices one of the first "Indian costuming" acts of American history. On the one hand he dresses one set of natives as Spaniards, assimilating and forgetting them. On the other, by creating the image of the noble dying Indian who recognizes his fatal destiny and chooses death instead of change, Villagrá anticipates by decades one of the archetypal poses of the masters of Indian photography, that of the stoic Indian, usually on elevated ground, standing bravely against time and destiny, against his unavoidable disappearance.[8] In other words, Villagrá's text – the representation of the new hegemonic power of the territory that will endure for three centuries – assimilates the stubborn resisters as distinct, but dispensable entities.

Resistance, in these cases, proves what? The El Pasoans, who followed the path of least resistance, perhaps were wiser in performing as a minstrel chorus during the Spaniards' *Te Deum*; they were allowed to return to their ways after seeing the Spaniards on their way. Vizenor would say they practiced survivance skills, pretending to be what the Spanish wanted them to be, and by so doing resisted incorporation. The Acomas, who chose to resist in the name of maintaining their own culture, were brutally punished, separated from their tribe and enslaved. Which form of behavior was the wiser? Which was the more American? Perhaps some things just can't be reduced to logical answers within binary opposites. But it is a fact that those who resisted at Acoma have come down to us with an identity and a role within the forging of the Americas – ones still debated and capable of stirring passions – while those who did not resist, though they too played a very important, strategically even more significant role – in terms of the epic venture they save the Spaniards, while the Acomas' participation is ultimately not essential – have slipped namelessly into a barely glossed over footnote, a stimulating deconstructive moment of blindness from which to evoke insight, to be resurrected by marginal academicians like me.

Conclusion

I began on a personal note, and begging your indulgence will end with a reprise. Many more historical incidents could be touched on here: the lessons to be drawn from two cases of resistance, one by French Huguenots and the other by African Slaves, during Meléndez de Avilés' founding of the Florida colony in the 16th Century. Jefferson's marvelous essay on Indian mounds documenting the resistance of the Native American subsoil that not only permeates the continent, but surfaces in spite of Jefferson's predisposition to respect the Puritan tradition of vacating the landscape. Américo Paredes' performance of multiple minstrelsy in his legendary *With a Pistol in His Hand*;[9] a reading of *Yo Soy Joaquín* as a reformulation of the Puritan errand through the appropriation of the typology of Moses;[10] a discussion of Oscar Zeta Acosta and Hunter Thompson's creation of Gonzo literature as the performance of resistance for profit and acceptance within a rapidly mainstreaming counterculture;[11] the ethnification of literary scholars in pursuit of tenured, Affirmative Action positions at prestigious universities; the silencing of legitimate dissent in the name of Political Correctness, and most importantly, a discussion of what I see as the most promising proposal for an alternative to the pattern of resistance performances: Sheila Ortiz Taylor's Third Woman utopia as portrayed in her novel *Faultline*, with its floating sense of avoidance of all sides' attempts to force narrative voice into binary opposition of resistance.[12] (Ortiz Taylor's model of the Frontier Family: of loving, non-binary patterning of Queer relationships, neither male nor female, neither dominant nor resistant, neither this nor other, but somewhere between, a loving in which differences are respected but never allowed to congeal into static positions, a continual earth trembler moving with the buried turtle world of the ancients.)

I return, however, to the personal note because the preparation of this paper led me to question the source of my own history of resistance. I justify it by evoking the contemporary practice of positioning. I have performed resistance to the hilt and beyond. Beyond, because I have made it a point – by choice or just from stubborn perversity is difficult to determine after thirty years – to resist especially the accepted paths of resistance. When Chicanismo was following two defined paths: Cultural nationalism or Neo-Marxism, I practiced neither. When calls went out for the preservation of Spanish through bilingual/bicultural education, I took a stand against it, stating publicly that young people should learn the culture and language of their new country, not the old, and develop a culture of the future without feeling obliged to preserve the past. When political issues were accepted as the most relevant, I proclaimed the personal and intimate as more immediately important. And in the face of justification of hatred and racism, of barely disguised ideologies of separatism and segregation in the name of ethnic survival, I have supported all efforts for integration and the erasure of Balkanizing difference.

My habit of resistance is a product of my true ethnicity: the confluence of the specific time and location of my development and the extraordinary family life it was my fortune to be born into. I have come to believe that ethnic movements based on national or racial identities become panethnic; while politically expedient, they harm both the individual and local groups. Ethnicity is always local and time bound; mine is 1950s and 60s North Denver, Catholic Parochial Schools, working class neighborhood with middle class mores, and a multicultural, multiethnic environment. Within this context, however, I led an exceptionally different life due to the influence of my mother, daughter of an upper class Mexico City family, and my Scottish American Father the descendent of the Quaker founders of Pennsylvania. They were both trilingual in Spanish, English and Italian, and my mother fluent in her own mother's native French. I grew up among adults who discussed culture incessantly: history, art, music, religion, politics, and national customs; not only discussed from many perspectives, but argued and fought quite vociferously. A premium was placed on ingenuity, verbal skill, improvisation, and the pleasure of knowledge, not as a commodity, but as an object of play, *diversión*. I traveled to Mexico often, observing the difference in lifestyles, and while I enjoyed the privileges of the elite in Mexico City, I preferred our middle class ways in Denver. When I was five and six I had a Mexican nannie in Mexico City; in Denver, the equivalent to take care of me the summer of 1950 was Cornelia, my great aunt's Black woman companion. I listened to both of them tell me tales, ate their food and played with the toys they taught me to invent from scraps of almost anything. Cornelia showed me how to cast a line for cat fish; Tomasa, to navigate a marketplace, always knowing where the gypsies are, who, although they had the best music, were never to be approached alone, since they kidnapped *guero* children like me.

At eight I learned to drink Scotch with a German American Oil engineer who had worked the drilling fields on both coasts of Mexico in the twenties and later opened in Maracaibo. He recounted tales of the deadly violence committed by sincere men, and discussed World War II at length, as did the Mexican consul, Santiago Suárez, married to a tall, wonderful Transylvanian, or my leftist uncle Germán, an engineer from Georgia Tech, who among many things taught me that stones could speak to me through the pores of my skin if I only let them, that the Mexican ruling party PRI was just another Porfiriato, and that nothing stirred the reason and passion of the human spirit like the brilliance of German philosophy and music.

Much later, when my generation of scholars was turning to Marxism, I would not, could not, having seen the struggle by Mexican artists and writers to free themselves from the stagnant limits of Socialist style realism in Mexico. Nor, after years of studying the history of World War II, could I accept an ethnic cultural nationalism so reminiscent of Fascism.

But mostly, I could not accept the primacy of ideological pragmatism. Difference was everywhere, disagreement rampant, history a fiction from multiple perspectives, no position right for everyone, and the only way to bring it all together was tolerance, good will, generosity and love. Perhaps that was naive, and I confess that in my life and work it much too often has taken a back seat to short terms necessity, but somehow we must return to those 60s ideals. In teaching literature, I recently have returned to a simple message: read the books. Everything starts there. Read for pleasure; literature has a marvelous power of seduction if one lets it be on its own terms. I know there is presently great resistance to accepting that the value of art lies in its utter lack of utility, its existence as an erotic object waiting to be catalyzed into its own subjectivity. You surely will get much more professional mileage out of resisting literature's erotic nature by submitting it to useful programs, but then you could decide to resist the approved pattern of resistance, and at the risk of remaining a perpetual outsider, not *take* literature at all [. . .] but *give yourself to it*. If I could choose at this late date between assimilating into the academy or assimilating into literature, I would resist the seductive benefits of the former and abandon myself to the latter.

Notes

[1] Sacvan Bercovitch, *The Puritan Origins of the American Self* (New Haven: Yale University Press, 1975).

[2] Sacvan Bercovitch, *The Puritan Origins;* and *The American Jeremiad* (Madison: University of Wisconsin Press, 1978).

[3] Gerald Vizenor, *Fugitive Poses: Native American Indian Scenes of Absence and Presence* (Lincoln: University of Nebraska Press, 1998).

[4] Sacvan Bercovitch, *The Rites of Assent: Transformations in the Symbolic Construction of America* (New York: Routledge, 1993).

[5] Joseph Alkana,"Cohesion, Dissent, and the Aims of Criticism," Introduction to *Cohesion and Dissent in America*, ed. Carol Colatrella and Joseph Alkana (Albany: State University of New York Press, 1994), xvi.

[6] Gregory S. Jay, *American Literature and the Culture Wars* (Ithaca: Cornell University Press, 1997), 11.

[7] For positive treatments of resistance pedagogy see: Lesliee Antonette, *The Rhetoric of Diversity and the Traditions of American Literary Study, Critical Multiculturalism in English* (Wesport: Bergin and Garvey, 1998); Paolo Freire, *Pedagogy of the Oppressed* (New York: Continuum, 1993); Henry Giroux, *Theory and Resistance in Education: A Pedagogy for the Opposition* (New York: Bergin and Garvey, 1983) and "Cultural Studies, Resisting Difference and the Return of Critical Pedagogy," *Border Crossings: Cultural Workers and the Politics of Education* (New York: Routledge, 1992) 161-79.

[8] Vizenor, *Fugitive Poses* 145-65.

[9] Américo Paredes, *With a Pistol in his Hand: A Border Ballad and Its Hero* (Austin: University of Texas Press, 1958).

[10] Rodolfo Gonzales, *I Am Joaquín/Yo soy Joaquín* (New York: Bantam Books, 1972).

[11] Oscar Zeta Acosta, *The Revolt of the Cockroach People* (San Francisco: Straight Arrow Books, 1973); Hunter S. Thompson, *Fear and Loathing in Las Vegas: A Savage Journey to the Heart of the American Dream* (New York: Random House, 1971).

[12] Sheila Ortiz Taylor, *Faultline* (Tallahassee: Naiad Press, 1982).

Beyond Multiculturalism?*

Werner Sollors

"Multiculturalism" in American literature still promises something of great interest to me, but I cannot deny that I often tend to be a little disappointed when I read the criticism that travels under that name. One expects new findings from the history of San Francisco's first Chinese newspapers (that Xiao-huang Yin is now investigating) or new collections from New Mexico's long tradition of Spanish-language publications (that Erlinda González-Berry has edited) or of the untapped legacy of writings in many Indian languages (recently assembled, for example, in Mashpee, by Kathleen Bragdon), books about New Orleans Creoles (like Caryn Cossé Bell's), about Norwegian writing in the United States (as Orm Øverland's *The Western Home*), or about the German-language press of New York City around World War I (as did Peter Conolly-Smith in his 1996 dissertation).[1] Or one hopes for more work in the manner of the pioneering and continuing contributions that were made by Jules Chametzky and Berndt Ostendorf, for provocative essays about bilingual poetry from antiquity to the present (as Tino Villanueva's), about forgotten plantation novels (as Simone Vauthier's analysis of *Old Hepsy*[2]), or, perhaps most importantly, about the interaction of all these trajectories in United States culture, which would thus appear more international and connected to "the rest of the world." For it is true that, after a century of professional literary studies of the United States, we still know very little, and though such areas as Black Studies have benefited from the massive work of textual recovery by such leading scholars as my colleague Henry Louis Gates, Jr., there are some other areas in which we know less now than scholars did at the beginning of the century.

Yet my heart often sinks when I dig into the countless collections of multicultural criticism and find again and again a purely contemporary and hermetically sealed national, Anglophone, US focus, and, worse than that, a predilection to debate what are "admissible" approaches, the "positionality" and shortcomings of other contemporary multicultural (or insufficiently multicultural) critics, turgid blueprints that outline which works are permitted to be compared with which other works (without, however, presenting the actual comparisons), and jargon-ridden accounts of the need to resist any attempts at synthesizing. All of this is as exciting as finding out that there are bibliographies of bibliographies, even if the criticism may surround itself by a halo of righteousness. Not very often do I find collections that are as interesting and exciting and fresh as Winfried Siemerling's and Katrin Schwenk's recent *Cultural Difference and the Literary Text*[3] – that grew out of a Berlin workshop; anyone who knows this collection will also understand that I do not here have to comment on it at greater length.

For the present occasion I have taken seriously the call to go "beyond multiculturalism" by opening with comments on some interesting recent book-length contributions to multiculturalism, continuing with a brief passage on multiculturalism in Germany, and concluding with detailed examinations of literary examples that mark directions into which I believe multicultural interests could fruitfully develop – or be transcended.

I.

I have been attracted for a long time to using titles beginning with "Beyond," or to adding the prefix "post-" in front of many words. In fact, David Hollinger's book *Post-Ethnic America: Beyond Multiculturalism* (1995) credits an old essay of mine for having coined the term "post-ethnic."[4] Hollinger's own work may well constitute the most persuasive and sustained brief to transcend and go beyond – *jenseits, au delà, oltre* – multiculturalism. Unlike the demands to go *Beyond Good and Evil* or *Beyond the Pleasure Principle*, going "beyond multicultulturalism" – and I shall be making some suggestions as to *where* we might be going – may express fatigue from journalistic overstimulation rather than constitute the logical endpoint of a sustained argument (which is, however, precisely what Hollinger does offer). Hollinger's proposal is not for us to "return" to a retro-universalism, to the blindness in some scholarship of the 1940s and 1950s when some social scientists could still believe that small ethnically skewed samples taken in the US were representative of mankind. As Hollinger develops his plea, he argues that the past half century has made scholars sensitive to the issues of diversity, so that new forms of stressing commonalities may be called for that show the signs of having gone through the ethnic stage. Hollinger's new, "postethnic" universalism would thus be informed – but not stymied – by the particularist challenges: "A postethnic perspective recognizes the psychological value and political function of groups of affiliation, but it resists a rigidification of exactly those ascribed distinctions between persons that various universalists and cosmopolitans have so long sought to diminish."[5] Thus new scholarship could avoid repeating the mistakes of the old pseudo-universalists as well as the new exaggerations that have been advanced by the ethnicists and multiculturalists. For what good does it do now to imagine group affiliations only within the pattern of what Hollinger calls the "ethnoracial pentagon," according to which Americans belong to one and only one of the five affirmative action categories of white, black, Asian, Latino, or Native American? Wouldn't it be more productive to promote (and for scholars to investigate) voluntary membership in varied and multiple social groupings? Couldn't such a move broaden the circle of the "we" and enhance the cosmopolitan rather than the myopic side of multiculturalism?

II.

By "multiculturalism" we probably mean here a relatively recent phenomenon: a quarter to a half of a century of debate surrounding government policy in Canada, Australia, and some other former Commonwealth countries, a mere decade of mostly educational discussion in the United States, and just a first beginning of examining the interrelations of immigration, citizenship, and rights in European Union countries.

Even the word "multiculturalism" does not seem to be much older than fifty years.[6] It appears to go back to Edward F. Haskell's *Lance: A Novel About Multicultural Men* (1941) whose hero Major Campbell is, as the *Herald Tribune* reviewer noted, "polyglot, bi-national, tied to no patriotic loyalties but ardently a servant of science and of social science particularly" who feels happy only with people who "are 'multicultural' like himself."[7] The reviewer put the brand new term in quotation marks here and when she assessed the books as a "fervent sermon against nationalism, national prejudice and behavior in favor of a 'multicultural' way of life and a new social outlook more suited to the present era of rapid transport and shifting populations."[8] Haskell was the son of a Swiss-American couple of missionaries and grew up in the United States, Turkey, Greece, Bulgaria, and Switzerland, before going to Oberlin, Columbia, and Harvard and becoming an activist aiding political prisoners and an investigator of political trials; and, as the dust jacket tells the reader, Haskell regarded his novel "not only as the statement of a problem, but also its partial theoretical solution." His mouthpiece, Major Campbell, states at a dramatic point in the novel:

> [M]en in all climes and all times live by the narrow little things they know [. . .]. Their contact has been with one language, one faith, and one nation. They are unicultural [. . .]. But we, being children of the great age of transportation and communication, have contacts with *many* languages, *many* faiths, and *many* nations. We are *multi*cultural.[9]

Haskell's characters whose life stories transcend ("go beyond") the confines of individual nation states, of one language, or of a single religion, may be representative harbingers of what has happened in the world at a much larger scale since World War II. Haskell anticipated the anxieties that multiculturalism could unleash in readers accustomed only to the unicultural model of the nation state, readers who might suspect Haskell's "multicultural men" of disloyalty and lack of patriotism. Thus he also lets Campbell stress the similarities between multiculturalists and uniculturalists: "Multicultural people [. . .] are just like unicultural people. They develop faith and loyalty and patriotism too: faith in science, loyalty to world organization, and patriotism for mankind."[10]

Edward Haskell's 1941 novel introduced the word "multicultural" in order to describe the pioneering quality of a few exceptional men. In the meantime, the term has become so omnipresent that Nathan Glazer's 1997 book *We Are All Multiculturalists Now*[11] constitutes a perfect counterpoint to Haskell's *Lance*. Glazer's relatively new endorsement of multiculturalism comes as the result of his recognition that multiculturalism is simply the price America now has to pay for having failed in the past to integrate blacks. Against the historical backdrop of the failed multiracial integration, multiculturalism may be the next best thing to universalism, Glazer argues – in fact, it may be the only way to go. If it weren't for the continued troublesome presence of racial inequality, he'd side with pure universalism any time, he states. But given the real conditions, Glazer is a pragmatic multiculturalist; and he cites approvingly the most detailed brief for multiculturalism published so far, Lawrence Levine's *The Opening of the American Mind*,[12] a 1996 response to the late Allan Bloom. Glazer also quibbles with Hollinger's invitation to go beyond multiculturalism – though he ignores the fact that Hollinger devotes a whole section to "Haley's Choice," in which Hollinger focuses on the constraints placed upon ethnic options by "race." (The question why Alex Haley's *Roots* only constructed a unilateral and monoracial African ancestry had already concerned Leslie Fiedler in

The Inadvertent Epic [1979] – surely a work of multicultural criticism *avant la lettre*.[13])

On Glazer's opposite side is Walter Benn Michaels, *Our America: Nativism, Modernism, and Pluralism* (1995),[14] a scathing critique of interwar pluralist theory and, at least by implication, of contemporary multiculturalist practice. Michaels believes that a paradigm shift from Progressive liberalism and universalist racism to a new mode of cultural pluralism cum nativist modernism qualitatively transformed the older racism in the course of the 1920s. Whereas the old racist belief in a hierarchy of discreet races had still rested on a belief in universal categories *outside* of the races themselves from which judgment could be passed, pluralism and especially, *relativism*, set up a widespread operation that assumed the equal value of different cultures. (*Q:* What joke does one multiculturalist tell another? *A:* It does not matter; they are all equally worthy of our attention.) In the old mode, race was a *fact* and did not imply cultural practice. The new mode, however, did away with any external categories except the different cultures themselves and demanded cultural work to be done, thus setting free race as a project and a source of affect. The various racial and national slots required not merely membership by blood or descent but became the locus of affective cultural work. If the old paradigm allocated race by descent, the new at first *seems* to be replacing "race" by "culture." Yet in fact, as Michaels stresses most forcefully, many of the "cultural" operations were in reality "racial." "For cultural identity in the '20s required [. . .] the anticipation of culture by race: to be a Navajo you have to do Navajo things, but you don't really count as doing Navajo things unless you already are a Navajo."[15] "The modern concept of culture is not," Benn Michaels writes most memorably, "a critique of racism; it is a form of racism."[16] What he has in common with Glazer is the belief that there seems to be no end to multiculturalism, though Benn Michaels would probably find a title such as *We Are All Racists Now* more appropriate to describe this state of affairs.

In a lecture series of 1997 entitled "Achieving Our Country,"[17] Richard Rorty offered a very cautious endorsement of the various movements that later became known under the slogan multiculturalism (though he stays away from the term) as having done much to reduce the forms of *social sadism* (against women, against members of ethnic minorities, against homosexuals, against handicapped people and so forth) that were still commonplace in American life of the 1950s, including the academic world. This is no small accomplishment.

Rorty's central concern is, however, the eclipse of the American reformist Left in the decades since the Vietnam War. Yes, "macho arrogance" led to this disastrous war, and we must be grateful to the angry New Left of the 1960s for helping to stop it and to prevent a possible Orwellian scenario of its long-term continuation. Still, Rorty has argued, nothing that this nation has done makes constitutional democracy improbable. How can shared meaning in social reform be achieved in a secular age, when after all the price to be paid for temporalization is contingency? Not by an academic pseudo-left that in its mocking detachment is in danger of – again Rorty: "sinking to the level of a Henry Adams" in decadence and hopelessness. The literary utopias Rorty reads are full of self-disgust, and the rhetoric of the academic left is inadequate to the task of revitalizing a sense of social engagement that would bring back the visionary project of Whitman or the pragmatic approach of Dewey.

Rorty also sees the danger that the international world of cultural politics has helped to mask the real issues of a growing social inequality in the United States and around the globe (and this is why he is critical of *cultural* studies and multi*culturalism* for focusing on culture at the expense of the goal of social equality). There may now be many multicultural men and women who are completely disconnected from any proletariat anywhere, and multicultural internationalism may even serve as the marker that separates these intellectuals from people, making multiculturalists instead part of a global ruling class (a worry that resembles John Higham's earlier critique of pluralism's ability to reduce the intellectuals' interest in working people except insofar as they embodied authentic cultural practices of discreet ethnic groups. And Michael Lind has also rigorously stressed that the vast majority of poor people in the United States is white, and hence of little interest to multiculturalists). How can new social movements be built, Rorty therefore asks, that would (as did precursors from the 1930s to the 1960s) attempt to fight the crimes of (social) selfishness with the same vigor that multiculturalists have focused on the crimes of sadism?

III.

Such recent contributions to the multiculturalism discussion may help to illustrate the difference between multiculturalism in the United States and in Germany. What Günter Lenz described some years ago may still be true today: in the US, multiculturalism refers to the experiences and demands of the plurality of ethnic group identities *within* the country; in Germany, multiculturalism marks a contrast to the concept of national identity embodied by the *jus sanguinis* (it always sounds like "blood juice" when you say it in English) and consequently a contrast of we/they, of inside/ outside, of "vertraut" and "gefährlich fremd" (as a *Spiegel* cover put it).

The United States has long been viewed as a polyethnic immigrant country with policies and mythologies ranging from the melting-pot of assimilation to the mosaic of pluralism, and multiculturalism is an aspect of this tradition. This has been less the case in Europe, where various states have prided themselves for *not* being immigrant countries, and where the historical excavation of actually existing polyethnicity may not have gone far enough to explain the issues of diversity that the current demographic data force onto the consciousness of Europeans. In 1993 there were about eleven million foreigners legally present in the fifteen member states of the European Union; and the number goes up to sixteen million if one counts citizens of other EU member states as foreigners. In Germany alone, there were nearly seven million foreigners in 1993 (among them about 1.5 million from EU member nations). These appear to be numbers significant enough to solicit political debate and reactions ranging from at times sentimental multicultural advocacy to the brutal hostilities of waves of xenophobia.

How can one make sense of developments which bring many European countries into a growing *union*, while the divisive tendency is pronounced within countries from the former Soviet Union and the former Czechoslovakia to the Basque separatists and the quest for a Northern Italian republic of Padania? Will the different Irish factions become harmoniously united fellow Europeans, or will they interact in the way in which Turks and Greeks continue to do within the shared framework of NATO? How can the complex and historically charged web of blurry terms such as ethnicity, *demos*, race, culture, identity, language, and nation state be disentangled and put into sharper focus so as to arrive at a better understanding of the current debates on citizenship, on legal inclusion and exclusion of political membership in states? Will governments and legislators make concessions to politically significant xenophobic voters or will they remain faithful to the democratic procedures of the previous decades? And what role, if any, might education play in the various countries in which multiculturalism has become a pressing topic of public discussion? These questions loom large at the present moment, and a historical perspective informed by what one might call "comparative multiculturalism" might be helpful in approaching them seriously.

The German multiculturalism discussion has indeed often focused on the clash between "*jus soli*" and "*jus sanguinis*" in extending citizenship rights. And *jus sanguinis* is the "German" model, but it also obtains in many other countries, including most of the East European states, and it is practiced in an even sharper way in Greece, a member country in the European Union that *never* releases Greeks from their citizenhip, even after emigration (unless they are of Turkish ethnic origin – in which case they are not really "Greek" to begin with, even though they and their ancestors may have been born in what is now Greece and speak perfect Greek). The status of "Greek subject" is also hereditary, so that a Bronx-born US citizen with a Greek surname may find himself detained during a Mediterranean cruise and exposed to Greek officials' questioning why he has not yet done his military service in the Greek army.

Jus soli has its home in France, though it has not only been tied to the cultural factor of language, but under Charles Pasqua the Law was modified in such a way that, effective 1 January 1994, children born in France whose parents are not French do no longer acquire French citizenship at birth, but only at age 16. This had the intended effect that illegal aliens (the "*sans-papiers*") can no longer derive from the children to whom they give birth in France a claim for a permit to stay there. (Similar restrictions affect residence rights acquired by marriage.) Thus the *jus soli* has been modified into the direction of a concept in which the citizenship of the parents plays a much larger role than before, hence, in fact, a modified form of *jus sanguinis*. It is this development of the "French model" (subject to new changes under Jospin) that generated the crisis of August 1996 in Paris.

The history of *jus sanguinis* is not always taken into consideration in discussions of the topic; and I shall therefore offer a brief sketch of it.[18] The German model derives from a relatively late departure from the feudal order. In nineteenth-century Germany, territorial membership meant membership in nearly 2,000 feudal units, and in order to overcome the feudal divisions into the direction of the new nation state, the concept of *jus soli* did not seem attractive. Hence *jus sanguinis* emerged as an alternative that was for the first time articulated in Prussia (in 1842). Yet the "Reichs- und Staatsangehörigkeitsgesetz" of 1913 established the *jus soli* as the new national norm for imperial Germany only forty years *after* unification.

In addition to homogenizing a national form of citizenship the legislation had a dual intention: It wanted to make it easier for Germans to retain their citizenship even after long stays abroad. (In fact, a Volga German trying to "return" to Germany before 1913 might have found that much harder than his grandchild would in our days.) And it also wanted to make more difficult the naturalization of strangers at a time that about 700,000 Poles, that is approximately 20% of the Polish population, had become Prussian subjects and hence citizens of the Reich, and many migrated to the Ruhr area and to Berlin; in addition, there were 1.25 million foreigners in the Reich in 1910, not including hundreds of thousands of seasonal workers.[19] The first part of the 1913 law was enthusiastically endorsed by Left and Right (the Left thinking of German working-class emigrants wishing to return, the Right of colonial administrators and German businessmen who lived abroad). The second intention, however, was the pet project of only the ethno-national conservatives, who opposed even the slightest concession to *jus soli*, wished to prevent the assimilation and naturalization of foreigners, wanted an ethnically homogenous German nation state defined by language and race, and thus believed that the only legitimate criterion for membership had to be ethno-cultural, transmittable by descent. (This was a matter of male descent, as the wife's citizenship was tied to that of her husband; only illegitimate birth resulted in the mother's ability to confer her citizenship to the child, a legal problem of some significance to binational married couples, before the law was changed early on in East Germany, and in West Germany only during the Brandt era.) Supported by Poles, Progressives and the Catholic *Zentrum* party, the Social Democrats proposed reforms toward a liberalization of naturalization some of which have not lost their relevance today. Rogers Brubaker summarized that "one proposal would have given a right to naturalization to persons born in Germany and residing there without long interruptions until majority; another to persons born and raised in Germany and willing to serve in the army."[20] The debates of the present suggest who won the battle. The 1913 German citizenship law articulated *jus sanguinis* with a vengeance, firmly established the German citizenry as a "community of descent" (Brubaker), and viewed citzenship as a unique, single quality, and hence could not easily accommodate dual citizenship (about which more later).

    Yet feudal concepts also continued to coexist with the new model of *jus sanguinis*. Aristocrats have always been able to feel at home in a country even if they did not know the vulgar language, and not being descended from local blood was precisely what may have strengthened their legitimacy. And even after the law of 1913, in World War I, as Eric Hobsbawm reported, a Baltic count who taught at Göttingen was summoned by his feudal lord to lead a regiment, and he took a leave from the university, first paid and later unpaid, and continued to read his students' work on the front. There would be little unusual about his case if the feudal lord of this professor had not been the Czar of Russia so that one has to imagine, at the peak of nationalism and shortly after the firm establishment of *jus sanguinis*, a German professor leading a foreign army against his own students – all of which was tolerated because the nation state reached its ideological limit in recognizing the legitimacy of remnants of the feudal order. To put it differently, the coexistence of feudal loyalty and modern nation-state patriotism could lead to the practice of "dual citizenship" even in cases which might be regarded as treason if viewed through the modern lens alone.

Dual citizenship has become a buzzword. In the United States, Randolph Bourne described it in World War I as a cultural ideal marking the way to true cosmopolitanism (very much in the vein that Haskell's *Lance* was to continue 25 years after Bourne): "Dual citizenship we may have to recognize as the rudimentary form of the international citizenship to which, if our words mean anything, we aspire."[21] It is widely believed (and occasionally even stated by German government officials) that, by contrast, Germany adheres to a strict principle of denying dual citizenship. Yet the exceptions to this rule are remarkable, perhaps also as far as numbers are concerned (though I do not have a reliable statistic listing the number of German citizens who are also citizens of another country).[22] First, all children born from binational marriages have two citizenships from birth; they may, but they do not necessarily *have* to, opt for one of the two later on. Second, refugees who left Germany for political, racial, or religious reasons in the Nazi period – and, following the logic of *jus sanguinis*, their descendants, have a constitutional (and hereditary) right to claim their old citizenship without necessarily giving up the new. The same article 116 of the *Grundgesetz* (Basic Law, or Constitution) also regulates the status of the numerically most relevant group of immigrants of German descent, the *Volksdeutsche* or *Aussiedler* from Eastern Europe – the *jus sanguinis* group par excellence. From 1950 to 1993 more than three million were thus "repatriated," more than half of that number arriving from 1988 to 1993. In 1993 alone, 219,000 *Aussiedler* became German citizens (the vast majority of them Russians, and others Rumanians and Poles), and they are not required to go through the complicated bureaucratic process of relinquishing their old citizenships. In the same year 13,000 Turks (of more than 1.8 million living in Germany, two thirds for ten years or more) were also naturalized as German citizens – but they are usually required to give up their Turkish citizenship (though in Berlin, for example, most were, until recently, permitted to keep it after becoming Germans). It is estimated that at least half and perhaps as many as 90% of the 126,000 Turks who have become German citizens also hold Turkish passports.[23]

Dual citizenship has become so much the noteworthy exception to the supposed rule that a recognition of its widespread existence may well ultimately shape the political debate in Germany about a reform of the "Staatsangehörigkeitsrecht." This is all the more the case since the growing European Union will also have a bearing on citizenship in the various member states. As far as dual citizenship is concerned, the most populous countries France, Britain, and Italy do not require that naturalized immigrants relinquish their old citizenships, and neither do the Netherlands, Portugal, Belgium, or Greece. Austria and Luxemburg are the only West European countries with rules similar to those in Germany. European citizenship, though less the subject of public debate, is at least as important as the Euro.

A decade after the end of the Cold War and in the middle of the process of European unification the time may be ideal to take a "secular," unemotional, and pragmatic survey of the possibilities of citizenship. Feudal notions of people "belonging" as "subjects" to their aristocratic liege or to his descendant, the modern nation state, are today at variance with the concept of democratic citizenship, yet the opinion also seems justified that whatever the original emancipatory potential may have been in *jus sanguinis* has been lost with Fascism and become quite inadequate in the age of mass migrations and ever growing streams of refugees. A change of the mode of defining citizenship (away from *jus sanguinis* if not completely into the direction of *jus soli*, which has many problems of its own) might thus profitably be contemplated in present and future discussions, especially in Germany.[24]

IV.

Going beyond multiculturalism might mean somewhat different things in the Old World and the New. As Glazer views it against the history and the scars of racism, American multiculturalism – with all its drawbacks and philosophical weaknesses – still offers a new approach to integration that amends the incomplete assimilationist paradigms of the past. Or as Rorty casts it, multiculturalism's success in curbing the crimes of social sadism may be one of the reasons why crimes of selfishness should now move to the top of the agenda. Perhaps some active multicultural work aimed to reduce the virulent forms of social sadism could also be helpful here at this time, especially if it could be undertaken without the drawbacks of identity politics. In Germany, multiculturalism is directly linked to debates about citizenship and rights of sizeable residential minorities. Going beyond multiculturalism here would thus seem to mean most of all working toward the ratification of the kind of legislation that is most likely to create a stable realistic framework that is needed to reflect the changing composition of the country, its new European context, and the continued need for economic migration and for accommodating those who desperately search for political asylum. My first recommendation then is for Germany to go "beyond multiculturalism" and toward creating easily recognizable avenues toward citizenship. And perhaps some features of the defeated Social Democratic proposals of 1913 could still be of help today. A clear and just system of accepting immigrants and conferring the rights of citizenship to them within a reasonably short time might go further than decades of teaching "citizens" tolerance toward culturally different "foreigners" – who cannot vote.

V.

This might look like one-sided advice to some, and advice coming moreover from someone highly unqualified to offer any. For the sake of balance, then, let me now proceed to make two recommendations to go "beyond multiculturalism" in the US, and here I speak from my professional vantage point as an Americanist interested in literature and culture. These concern first, the unpredicted proliferation of biracial, multiracial, and racially mixed identifications in the American populace (about 10 million at this moment use such a self-designation)[25] and second, the unsung history and continued presence of multilingualism in the United States. In these two aspects the European and American situation may again be seen to diverge.

When the *Nation* reviewed the new *Norton Anthology of African American Literature*, edited by Henry Louis Gates, Jr. and by Nellie McKay, it singled out the surprising short story "The Mulatto" of 1837 for praise. The first published short story by an author of African ancestry born in the United States, it is a remarkable tale, indeed, suggestive of the strength of the whole œuvre produced by the New Orleans-born and -raised writer whose full name was Jean François Louis Victor Séjour Marcou Ferrand (1817-1874). Victor Séjour's father was a free man of color from Saint Domingue; his mother Eloise Phillippe Ferrand was a Mulatto born in

New Orleans; Victor's baptismal record at the Cathedral Saint-Louis identifies him as "quarteron libre" (free Quadroon).[26] The father had a shop on Chartres Street, and Victor studied with the famous tutor Michel Séligny, attended Sainte-Barbe Academy, and in 1836 continued his education in Paris. Yet once there, he must have decided to stay, as he returned to the United States only once more in his lifetime, most of which he spent as a well-known playwright and poet in France. He knew Alexandre Dumas (père), who supported him. His ode "Le Retour de Napoléon" (1841) was included in the famous Creole anthology *Les Cenelles* (1845); and among his many interesting dramas are "The Outlaw of the Adriatic" (1855), "The Brown Overcoat" (1858), and such problem plays as "Diégarias" (1844), and "The Fortune Teller" (1859). He also had connections with Victor Hugo; and the preparation of Séjour's dramatization of the life of John Brown was announced in 1861. He married a New Orleans woman when he returned for a visit, and he also brought his parents back to live with him in Paris. He died of tuberculosis and was buried at Père-Lachaise.

The frame of the tale is provided by a first-person-singular narrator who approaches Saint-Marc, a small town in Santo Domingo, "these days the Republic of Haïti," as the narrator adds so as to suggest immediately the Haïtian Revolution as the significant historical background to the story. The narrator meets Antoine, an old black man who greets him as "master" and who, when reminded of an earlier promise, agrees to tell the story of his friend Georges. The old man's narrative, told from a close to omniscient point of view, and full of vivid dialogues and descriptions, forms the remainder and the bulk of the tale, which does not return to the frame narration at the end.

In the days before the end of slave sales, the estate Saint-M*** that Antoine points out to the narrator, was used as a market where husband was separated from wife, and brother from sister. There the twenty-two year-old Alfred, one of the richest planters of the island was bidding for a young Senegalese beauty and ended up purchasing her for a very high price. She is an orphan whose name is Laïsa, and when Alfred's driver Jacques Chambo speaks with her as he is taking her to the plantation they recognize each other as siblings and embrace each other in tears. Alfred is furious when he sees them in each other's arms and whips Jacques bloody.

A tough and heartless master, Alfred takes violent possession of Laïsa, but finding her proud and cold, loses interest in her before she gives birth to his child, a boy she names Georges and whom Alfred never acknowledges. Mother and child are relegated to the meanest cabin on the plantation. When Georges grows up without ever hearing the name of his father mentioned he becomes curious about the mystery of his origin, but his mother guards the secret, promising him only that he will learn his father's name at age twenty-five. However, Laïsa dies, and leaves Georges as his heirloom only a sack containing a portrait of his father; the son has to promise to his dying mother not to open it before coming of age.

As Georges grows older he keeps this promise despite his curiosity. By coincidence he learns one night that a group of robbers who have been killing planters are planning Alfred's assassination, and Georges immediately warns his master. Alfred, mistrustful like all tyrants, suspects the loyal Georges, but four assassins arrive, and in the ensuing fight Georges saves his master's life, is seriously wounded, and carried to his cabin. Antoine interrupts the flow of his narration because he forgot to mention that Georges had a wife, the young and beautiful Mulatto woman Zélie; and when Georges' life was still in danger, Alfred often came to visit him in his cabin and became enamored of Zélie who rejected the master's advances with humble dignity. Alfred is piqued by the thought that the Sultan of the Antilles would be turned down by a mere slave woman, and he orders her to his chamber where he assaults her, despite all her pleas, and she, as a last resort, pushes him away – but she does it so forcefully that he loses his balance and injures his head falling down. The unfortunate Zélie immediately understands that this means that she will have to die. Alfred obviously calls upon an often-cited paragraph of the *Code noir*. Knowledge of the *Code noir* is so much taken for granted by Séjour's characters and narrator that it does not have to be explicitly named or fully cited in the text.

In tears Zélie tells her incredulous husband what has happened though he, in his weakened state, cannot do anything to help. Ten days later Zélie's execution is being prepared in front of a crowd of heartless spectators. Georges pleads in vain for Alfred's pardon, reminding him of the promises he made when his life had been saved. When Alfred remains unmoveable, Georges accuses him of wanting Zélie hanged only because she had refused him. Georges threatens to kill Alfred, rushes into the forest where he finds and joins the slave rebels, and Zélie is executed.

The ending of the story, set three years later, brings home the violence of the family tragedy to the master's mansion. Georges has heard that Alfred has married and that his wife has given birth to a son; he secretly approaches and manages to enter the master bedroom, having first put poison into the mistress's broth. He makes himself known to the frightened Alfred and congratulates him sarcastically on the birth of his son. Georges also asks him whether it isn't horrible to die when one is happy. When Alfred asks for mercy "in the name of your father," Georges relents for a moment and asks Alfred whether he knows who his father is. But now the wife cries for water, and Georges keeps Alfred from helping his wife whose screams of agony soon fill the room. He shows Alfred the water that could serve as antidote to the poison, but smashes the bottle against the wall because he wants his master to watch his wife dying. Finally Georges takes a hatchet in order to decapitate Alfred whose last pleading words are, "since you have poisoned her, you may as well kill your fa-" – at which moment the head is separated from the body; but rolling away, the father's head audibly mumbles the last syllable, "-ther."[27] Georges cannot believe his ears, opens the bag and exclaims that he is doomed. The next morning his body is found next to that of Alfred. Séjour ends the story abruptly on this high point: what could a return to the frame narrator and Antoine have added at such a moment?

Séjour's tale is a strong concentration of the horrors of slavery told from a point of view of antislavery urgency, and it was published at a time when New England's abolitionist fiction had not yet contributed anything resembling the force of this tale. Especially effective is Séjour's mythic method of locating the deep tragic themes of the son's search for the name of the father and of the father-son conflict culminating in a lurid, unknowingly committed patricide in an interracial family structure in which a modern Oedipus or Job endures the loss of his mother and his wife, and has to make the agonizing discovery that the tyrant and villain he has decapitated in revenge is his own father. As Simone Vauthier has observed in her reading of another text, "oedipal fantasies of parricide and the dream of social redress" may get "fused" in such mythic tales, resulting in images which have, "at the same time, psychoanalytic significance and revolutionary relevance."[28] Georges becomes a political rebel to the extent that he opposes his own father, a fact which heightens the revolutionary spirit of the tale as does the seemingly limitless array of injustices that Alfred is able to commit before – brought about by the master's incestuously toned desire for his own son's wife and his revenge on her through the ruthless application of the *Code noir* – the Faustian Georges finally opposes him with equal violence. The *Code noir* is also the father's law, and Alfred's application of it forces his son to become an outlaw.

While the clash between father and son is central to Séjour and marks the gory climax of the tale, the stark presentation of the fates of the two women at the hand of the master is also remarkable. In Séjour's world the sexual aggression that the tyranny of slavery implies leaves few choices to the enslaved women, single or married: Laïsa's "coldness" prompts

Alfred to banish her, and Zélie's resistance makes him invoke the deadly extremes of the *Code noir*.[29] And the property owner's jealousy toward "his" slave woman's brother (Laïsa's Jacques) or husband (Zélie's Georges) demonstrates the rawness and violence of the possessive urge that is unleashed by slavery. The reference to Alfred as the "Sultan of the Antilles" connects the attack of tyranny with the orientalist critique of the slave owner's desire for a harem. Séjour's "Mulatto" is a brief tale for so much and for such spectacular action; and the characters are defined by their actions and by their constellation to each other more than by psychological depth, but the story is undoubtedly effective in energizing antislavery sentiment toward a revolutionary overthrow of the status quo.

By locating the dramatic development within an interracial family structure of white father, black mother, Mulatto son, Séjour also called attention to the tragic and explosive potential of unrecognized family relations across racial lines. The denial of legitimacy to biracial individuals thus becomes an important building block in the construction of "race." Mediating categories which were commonly used in Latin America, the Caribbean, and in New Orleans, too, were largely absent in the United States where racial dualism obtained and where one could (and still can in Hollinger's ethnoracial pentagon) only be black or white, but not both. (The obvious and explosive exception is constituted by Latinos who, for the census, may be of any race.) Multiracialism (with all its problems for identification and census counting) thus implies a transcendence of multiculturalism: where the additive approach is characteristic of much multiculturalism (with its widespread use of the rhetorical figure of the catalogue, the listing of Native Americans, African Americans, Asian Americans, Latinos, and whites), the multiracial approach is, from the start, more likely to focus on the qualitative consequences of *interactions*.

VI.

Such interactions have, however, run against significant legal and cultural obstacles. In the United States, for example, the little-known Supreme Court decision of *Pace v. Alabama* (1882) set in motion new and powerful patterns of racial segregation longe before *Plessy v. Ferguson* followed suit. In *Pace*, the judges found unanimously that punishing interracial adultery more harshly than illicit intraracial sex constituted no racial discrimination since both the black and the white partner were published more harshly. And such familiar questions as "would you like your daughter to marry one" have functioned as central, and not always ineffective, attacks on racial equality and integration. Widely familiar from American literature, this question was also asked in the Berlin *Reichstag*, not long before *jus sanguinis* was established there, by a Sanskrit scholar, "Wirklicher Geheimer Rat," Dr. Dr. Heinrich Solf who had previously served as Governor of the German colony of Samoa, who in 1911 became the head of the German colonial office (*Staatssekretär des Reichs-Kolonial-Amts*), and soon began to work on his pet project, a *Mischehen-Verbot für Samoa*. In the parliamentary debate on May 8, 1912, Solf used the example of the United States as a threat – "was ist denn die *negro question* – die Negerfrage – in den Vereinigten Staaten anderes als eine Mischlingsfrage?" and appealed to the *Abgeordneten* of all parties to follow their instincts and not social or dogmatic considerations:

> Ich bitte Sie, einfach die nackten Tatsachen auf sich wirken zu lassen. Sie senden Ihre Söhne in die Kolonien: wünschen Sie, daß sie Ihnen schwarze Schwiegertöchter ins Haus bringen? wünschen Sie, daß sie Ihnen wollhaarige Enkel in die Wiege legen?[30]

(It may very well be that the mobilization of such fears is one of the core sources of social sadism.) Yet the *Reichstag* was not swayed. Though the deputies said some of the strangest things about race that day, Solf's government proposal to ban intermarriage in the colonies was defeated (with 202 : 133 votes) and it was resolved in a motion sponsored by Zentrum and supported by Social Democrats, that the *Bundesrat* enact legislation securing the validity of marriages between whites and natives in all German colonies and regulating the rights of illegitimate children.

In some aspects the multiculturalism discussion has replicated the fictions of separable races. While large numbers of Americans still oppose interracial marriage (though the intermarriage rate has been going up very dramatically in the past twenty years – perhaps at a higher rate than the growth of any single ethnic category), multiculturalists sometimes act as if racial mingling – or even the focus on it in literary studies – were a form of caving in to what is sometimes believed to be "the dominant assimilationist ideology." Is it not it more accurate to say that, after centuries of legal bans, cultural ostracism, and historical denial, the time may have come to go "beyond multiculturalism" – toward interracialism, not only on the (most significant) black-white fault line, but on all lines dividing so-called races? Instead of looking at interracial relations as those interactions that are often prohibited between people from " different races" we might also regard intermarriage bans – and the denial of legitimacy to biracial individuals – as important building blocks in the construction of "race." The hackneyed notion of "pure blood" always rests on the possibility and the reality of "mixed blood" – though violent "cleansing" may be deemed necessary to constitute "purity." Investigating interracialism may thus also lead to new understandings of "race." It may help particularly in confronting the emotional core of much racism; but it may also suggest the long tradition of interracial stories that have preceded and are likely to outlast racism – from foundational stories of origin (such as the one Jane Ray's *The Story of Creation* recently retold as part of the impressive contributions multiculturalism has made to children's literature[31]) and multiracial representations of *fraternité* to stories of utopian possibilities in the future.

VII.

Séjour's story is interesting to me also from another point of view. It was written in French, entitled "Le Mulâtre," Alfred actually said "pè-re," and I have here quoted from a translation prepared for the Longfellow Institute by Andrea Lee. It is an interesting sign that the *Norton Anthology* includes at least one non-English text – just like the *Heath Anthology* opened its pages to a very few American texts that needed to be translated into English. This gets me to the issue of multiculturalism and language.

Originally, an "Americanist" was a person who studied American Indian languages. In my student days in Berlin, there was still the likelihood that an "Amerikanist" would be mistaken for an "Altamerikanist." This legacy has been all but forgotten within the largely monolingual and Anglophone American Studies Association of today. According to a 1996 communication from the Executive Director of the American Studies Association, the majority of academic Americanists in the United States is now monolingual in English only, with the exception of "native speakers who happen to be US residents/scholars, or with folks in (mainly comparative) literature or ethnic studies where language is required."[32]

Though perhaps the most significant and fascinating form of "diversity," and certainly the single most important medium for literary expression, the multitude of languages in which literature of the United States has been written has rarely if ever been made the center of readers' attention so that the history and continued existence of multilingualism in the United States remain largely unexplored. This is partly a result of the scaling down of language requirements in the US – ironically just in the period in which the word "multiculturalism" also achieved popularity.

The learning of languages other than one's mother tongue is considered part of an educational agenda that political conservatives as well as radicals in many countries of the world would unhesitatingly endorse. The European Community, for example, which has more official languages than the United Nations, actively supports language acquisition in educational institutions from grade schools to universities. British schools offer an expanded officially approved list of "modern foreign languages" that may be taught privately by immigrant groups, and in Sweden all school children have the right to receive at least two weekly hours of mother tongue (*hemspråk*) instruction with the result that 80 (of an accepted list of 124) languages were taught in Swedish schools in 1993, the less well-known ones by traveling or part-time teachers.[33] There are forms of official bilingualism in European Union countries that might surprise US bilingualists: for example, in Italian South Tyrol/Alto Adige all state and private employees in the public sector must now be able to answer all their customers' questions both in German and Italian. Yet it is also obvious that only *some* European languages are official languages, so that, for example, Catalan and Basque, Welsh and Ladino are not among the elect – only because they are not official languages in a European Union member state. In the discussion of multiculturalism in Germany the hidden significance of language manifests itself in the frequently made casual mention that the nationalized *Volksdeutschen* do not speak German whereas the second-generation Turkish-Germans do. But does that imply that *only*, or that *all*, people who speak German *are*, or should be permitted to become, German citizens? After all, such linguistic minorities as Danes, Frisians, and Sorbs enjoy the protected status of "national minority" in Germany whose non-German language rights are constitutionally guaranteed and do not call into question their German citizenship, their "Germanness."[34] In this case different coexisting models of membership in a nation become apparent.

In the United States, however, an "English only" movement has captured the conservative imagination at the very same time that NAFTA would make the intensified teaching of at least Spanish and French more plausible. Schools and colleges have steadily been reducing their language offerings and requirements, with the support of conservatives who otherwise would make demands for more rigorous edcuational programs. A recent survey by the Modern Language Association shows that foreign-language instruction in such languages as German or French has continued to decline in the 1990s (after increasing a little in 1989, the German-language registration in United States colleges and universities, for example, went down by 27.8% from 133,348 in 1990 to 96,263 in 1996).[35] While liberals and radicals may have paid lip service to a support of bilingual education for Hispanic-Americans, they have remained uninterested in the larger issues of linguistic diversity; and the history of language bans in the United States has hardly seeped into even the most ardent multiculturalists' consciousness. As Gerald Early put it, in commenting on the provincialism of what he calls the multiculturalism craze, "multiculturalists generally do not see learning foreign languages as a major part of their educational reform." Early's point is well taken, yet his use of the term "foreign" also suggests how natural the notion of an Anglophone United States has become even to its critics.[36] Recently voices have been raised that propose, in Mary Louise Pratt's words, "expunging the term *foreign* to refer to languages other than English" for it applies neither to Spanish nor to "French, Cantonese, Italian, or Japanese – to say nothing of Lakota, Navajo, or Cree." Yet the programmatic definitions from 1975 and 1993 of the field of Comparative Literature in the United States make clear that, if anything, it has become *more* acceptable in the last two decades to work only with English translations of non-English originals, in effect making all languages except English more "foreign" than ever.[37]

In the various fields of literary and historical study and in literary histories of the United States, the multitudes of texts written in languages other than English have tended to disappear from view. After World War I, with all its efforts at Americanization in an English mold, there was still a sense left in the world of scholarship that "language and literature of the United States" was a field not limited to English. Thus, the old *Cambridge History of American Literature* of 1919 ff. stressed that the "language of the people of the United States has been English even more prevailingly than their institutions and their culture" – yet it included more than sixty pages exclusively dedicated to "Non-English Writings." Written by Albert B. Faust, Edward J. Fortier, Nathaniel Buchwald, and Mary Austin, these specialized sections focused on German, French, Yiddish, and "Aboriginal" texts, but other parts of the *History* also paid attention to non-English authors so that the old reference work touched upon writers from Lorenzo Da Ponte to Victor Séjour and on texts from Pastorius's *Beehive* to the *Walam Olum* that will now need to be reintroduced to the general reader and the specialist by a new direction in scholarly work. It is also noteworthy that the authors of the *Cambridge History* generally still assumed that their readers were fluent in French, German, and Latin.[38] And it was also in the same period that H. L. Mencken paid notable attention, in *The American Language* (1919), to the non-English elements of its topic. As late as 1946, Robert Spiller's *Literary History of the United States* included a chapter by Mencken on "The American Language," a section by Stith Thompson on "The Indian Heritage," and an entry by Henry A. Pochmann and others dedicated to descibe "The Mingling of Tongues" that followed and abridged the old *Cambridge History* in delineating German, French, and Yiddish writing, while adding new and shorter sections on Spanish, Italian, and Scandinavian texts. In contemporary literary histories, however, readers may be invited to pause for a moment and reflect on the many voices that were silenced, yet will find little space dedicated to descriptions of non-English writings of the past. Literary histories, anthologies, and even bibliographies nowadays inevitably imply a monolingual Anglophone reader. A representative example for the "natural" way in which this exclusion takes place can be found in the volume *Asian-American Literature: An Annotated Bibliography*, a comprehensive publication of nearly 300 pages, which includes the following, telling declaration of limits: "we exclude works written in Asian languages, unless they have been translated into English."[39] As many other examples could illustrate, non-English languages of the United States have been marginalized in the field of American Studies, even when it has intersected with Ethnic Studies or been undertaken with a multicultural focus. This is all the more surprising since multilingualism would seem to be so easily linked with the multiculturalism debate. For example, Hollinger's approach could be strengthened, and Benn Michaels's generalization could appear more questionable if the issue of language were included into their reflections, for language provides a model for an understanding of culture that need not be based on race, and language acquisition may be one way of making voluntary affiliations, widening the circle of the "we," and at least in part "becoming what one is not." Language certainly is a part of "culture" that is not automatically synonymous with "race," and "doing Navajo things" could mean for a non-Navajo to learn the Navajo language.

There are many, many culturally fascinating, historically important, or aesthetically outstanding texts that were written in languages other than English, ranging, for example, from works in indigenous Amerindian languages and from Spanish, French, Dutch, German, and Russian colonial writings to immigrant literature in all European languages and to Arabic texts by African Americans. (At Harvard's Widener Library, for example, a data-base search revealed that there are more than 120,000 imprints published in the United States in languages other than English.) These little-studied texts raise important issues of language policies, national identity, and education, and they are especially suited to international scholarly collaboration.

VIII.

One such example is Victor Séjour's story "Le Mulâtre," that I just spoke about. Another example of the kind of text that a multilingual orientation of multiculturalism might discover is a comedy entitled *Die Emigranten. Deutsch-Amerikanisches Lebensbild in fünf Akten.*[40] The play was published anonymously, it came to be part of the Harvard College Library through a bequest from Evert Jansen Wendell, but its author is not identified in the text or the card catalogue (the item has not yet been entered into our electronic listing.) Thus I do not know who the author was, but some of my readers who have worked in this field may know more about this play or its author.

In *Die Emigranten*, Marie, the young niece of the German-American Schneider who has changed his name to Taylor, has recently arrived from Germany and is urged by her uncle to marry his son, her cousin (though nobody comments on *that*), the worthless gambler James (yes, James Taylor!). Yet she refuses the uncle's authority: she is about to come of age, and his command is palpably wrong and made, though Marie does not know it, only in order to keep the Taylor family afloat, whose wealth secretly rests on Marie's estate "in the West" and on her fortune that Schneider/Taylor has been squandering through his ill-advised speculations. Marie finds an ally in James's sister Ella, manages to escape the disastrous match narrowly, and is betrothed to the good German immigrant Dr. Heinrich Gruner instead. Ella, impoverished by her goodheartedness (though Marie vows to support the Taylors) ends up approaching a marriage with Karl Meyer (who had hesitated earlier only because he saw Ella's money as an obstacle and whose happiness is boundless that the beloved who appeared to be a rich American fortunately turned out to be really a poor German). Yet this double match that provides closure to the comedy plot seems not to be where the playwright's heart is. It seems to be a mere excuse for a sustained game of mixing German and American elements in ever-changing doses and to enjoy what happens. For the true spirit of *Die Emigranten* is not in the success of its plot in saving two couples for "Germanness" and from shallow Americanization, but in its thorough exploration of the language that has been called "Germerican" – a mixed language of the types that are also present in many other American texts. For much of multilingual America has used the "hybrid tongues," or, as one could also say the "melting glots" of Franglais, Portinglês, Yinglish, Italglish, Spanglish, and so forth.[41]

Die Emigranten is remarkable, though it may not be exceptional, in approaching the new language out of old ingredients. At the opening of the play the leading characters (among them our two men destined to be bridegrooms at the end) develop a sense of "heimat" because of the shared journey on the ship, not of their common origin in Germany: allegorically speaking, what ties the characters to each other is not their original locations, but the fact that they have emigrated and recognize that there will be no return to Germany. And Doktor Gruner, who promotes solidarity among the immigrants (or, from the German-language vantage point, among *Emigranten*), exacts the promise from the others that if they ever come to St. Louis they must look him up in order to relive in memory "that important epoch of human life known as ocean journey" (5). And Gruner also presents a counterbalance to a character merely called "S.," a rural critic of America who likes the land but not the people and complains about the speed of pedestrians, not permitting him to light and smoke a pipe in peace. Gruner reminds him (and the spectators) that there is no compulsory military service, no hierarchical bureaucracy in America, creating more egalitarian conditions than in the Old World. Nonetheless, it is S. who introduces the first bilingual pun when he complains about the street here called "Brod-weg" (5) thus Germanizing *Broadway* and inviting such readings as "bread-way" (Brotweg) or "bread-gone" (Brot weg). Two pages later, one of our two heroes sings a song devoted to denouncing titles and ranks, even in the New World in which he ominously rhymes the English "care" and the German "mehr!" The first scene thus sets up a theoretical openness toward German-America against the ideal of the temporary migrant (who wants to make money and then go back and marry his Rosa) and that of the anti-urban villager. It also sings the praises of sophistication and adaptability against the syndrome of what the play will later call "Grünhorner": incredible naïveté, here represented by the Swabian immigrant girl Louischen.

Gruner:	Why don't you rather tell me how all of you like America. After all, – we have been here now for more than a week, and each of you must have had some adventure. How about you, Louischen?
Louischen:	Well! I like the country, and I like this city – but the people – they are so strange, and their language is so strange.
Karl:	It's true that they don't speak Suabian.
Louischen:	And yesterday I met a coalblack woman, and she starts speaking German to me, and then I ask her how long she's been gone from

	Germany, and she says with a laugh: Only five years, but that the sun had burned her so. Well, in five years, I'd be only twenty-one years old.
Karl:	Oh, so you are afraid for your pretty white complexion and believe that you'll turn black, too, and will then not find a husband, or only a black one?
Louischen:	Oh, how terrible.
Karl:	Well, don't worry – this must have been only the joke of a Negro woman who has learned German somewhere. (4)[42]

Turning "black" within five years may well be an interesting way of imagining Americanization, resonating with what Carl Gustav Jung later observed about white American adoptions of Indian and black American ways.[43] (It also brings to mind the more explicit forms of interracialism in Ludwig von Reizenstein's *Die Geheimnisse von New Orleans*, the novel Steven Rowan rediscovered, translated, and is now publishing in the Longfellow Institute[44] series, or the anonymous and fragmentary *Geheimnisse von Philadelphia* that is being edited and translated by Elliott Shore.) But it is not the way advocated by this play which associates an enjoyment of minstrelsy and the use of the slur "nigger" only with the negative foil, Mr. Taylor (12).

When Taylor makes his entry, code-switching also takes command, and we are led to believe at first that the mixed language is only a ridiculous quality that will be rejected by the good German immigrants. Taylor senior: "*You must know*, Sie müssen mich *excusen*, wenn ich Englisch spreche, *but you see*, ich bin schon lange in Amerika, ich bin, was man nennt so ein alter Settler der ist *smart*, der sieht es einem gleich an und dann *move* ich auch blos in *american* und englisch *society*, das heißt Gesellschaft und da vergißt man das Deutsch. – Wenn einer so lange im *country* ist wie ich, na, der spricht nur englisch" (9). One could say, Taylor's motto is as inadequate as redundant: "Ihr müßt Alle Eure deutschen *manners* los werden, *you must get americanised*, das heißt: Ihr müßt Euch amerikanisiren" (11). Yet Taylor's language is only an extreme manifestation of "Germerican," and even though Karl Meyer sings a purifying song about "Muttersprache" und "Vaterland" after meeting Taylor, the interaction of German and American continues and even intensifies. For one thing, Taylor himself has a lot of Schneiderness left in him; for another, the names of the good German characters also alternate from "Carl" to "Karl" and "Marie" to "Mary," and Marie/Mary has to learn the lessons of America in the meaning of such concepts as "Müßiggang" (leisure) and such "American" words as "beau" (rhyming with German "so" and "froh").

What S.'s "Brod-weg" suggested now becomes a full-fledged possibility in the play's focus on the interaction of languages, and the clash of meanings of words that have the same sound. We have become accustomed to read much about Bakhtin's dialogic model for the novel – but *Die Emigranten* offers us a *duet* as the formal expression of the language situation. The following excerpt contains one of the most beautiful passages from the play. One should note the power of the single word "Schoppen"/"*shoppen*" to build up a sustained cultural opposition. Also noteworthy, however, is the presence of a "third language" (not uncommon when two languages interact).[45] Here it is French, which is both "American" (in the case of "beau") and "German" in the case of all those words like "coquettiren," "räsoniren," or "amüsiren," which – unlike "shop" or "stores" do not sound "foreign" in the nineteenth-century German-language text.

Marie:	Why, Ella? Wouldn't you rather go *shopping*? – You said so yourself.
Karl:	Schoppen? What is this? In Germany, too, one goes to drink Schoppen – but only men do it, of course.
Marie:	Oh, Karl, – you mean drinking a Schoppen, Ella means going *shopping*. Why don't you ask her to explain it to you, too? Perhaps in a poetic way?
Karl:	Oh yes, Miss Ella. Please, why don't you start with the song of your Schoppen, and then I'll sing my Schoppen-song for you, or accompany you with it.

Ella:	Oh, yes, there is so much we can learn from each other. I'll start with my song and you'll accompany me:
	    Oh, how lovely 'tis once more –
	    To go *shoppen* in the stores.
	    All the wares are there for trying,
	    And the clerks are there for flirting,
	    For the others there is gossiping,
	    For ourselves there's promenading,
	    All without embarrassment,
	    Such delicious amusement,
	    To fool the lads who love to drop in
	    As we enjoy the lovely art of *shoppen*.

Marie:	Very good, Ella. But now let's hear your German Schoppen-song, Karl.

Karl:	It's quite similar, only completely different. (*Sings:*)
	    Oh, how great it's once again –
	    To have Schoppen at the inn.
	    All the wine is there for trying,
	    With political cavorting,
	    With the others there is disputing,
	    So that wines and beers are soothing,
	    At one's table is much argument,
	    Such delicious amusement,
	    To take much more than one cool drop in

	As we enjoy the greatest art – of Schoppen.
Marie:	(*applauding*) Bravo, isn't this the true German-American Schoppen-song hat glorifies both Schoppen and *shopping*. But don't you have a stanza you can both sing together?
Karl:	Well, if it suits Miss Ella, why don't we sing a duet?
Ella:	Agreed – let's try it. (*Both sing along to the same melody, but with different words.*)

Oh, how lovely 'tis once more –
To go shoppen in the stores.
There young men with friendly eyeing
To receive first, and then nodding,
And their hands so softly pressing,
And their hearts to be caressing,
To entangle them in weaving, tying
Happy knots they find a blessing.
And fool all, yes, all who love to drop in
As we enjoy the lovely art of shoppen.

Karl (*Sings:*)

Oh, how great it's once again –
To have Schoppen at the inn.
All the wine with careful eyeing,
To examine, and then nodding,
And the glass 'gainst lips pressing,
And one's head bent back ingesting,
Then small gulps of this great blessing
Will rejoice heart and intestine.
To take much more than one cool drop in
As we enjoy the greatest art – of Schoppen.

Marie:	Bravo, bravo, that sounds wonderful! But if the husband goes to his German Schoppen, and the wife goes *shopping* American style, then it may not be as harmonious as it sounds in this song. (24-5)

The encounter with Karl reminds Ella of her late mother and her German lullaby – really an exhortation never to give up "die Sprache die die Mutter spricht" (26).[46] Karl, however, in his anger at the moneyed rich, soon sings a mixed song of his own: "Es gibt der Menschen eine sondre Art,/Die dünken sich als *super extra smart*" (34). And though Gruner (always called "Doktor" – a nice contradiction to the play's polemic against the use of titles in America) invokes Darwin in a song that claims that quickly assimilated immigrants are probably the best proof for the theory that the human species is related to the "corps of monkeys" (*Affencorps* – a Franco-German term in its own right), he describes this ideal type in German enriched by an English word:

Bald kann sogar kein Deutsch man mehr
Und Englisch radebricht.

> Dann schilt er auch noch auf die *dutch*,
> Der miserable Wicht. (35)

The word *dutch* in these lines repeats the very phenomenon of speaking in a mixed tongue ("radebrechen") that is being indicted. In another song, Karl similarly mocks quick assimilation and associates it with general infidelity when he sings about Aennchen, an immigrant girl whom Karl sees shortly after she has complained that she could never learn English, but who is now accompanied by a young American man. She answers Karl's polite German question how she is doing with a quick English response: "*I english Lady, dutch not spik*" (45).

The play thus paradoxically – in the polemical speeches and songs of its positively cast protagonists – presents the pitch for language loyalty in (and implicitly, *to*) an "impure" language. The assimilated German-American as the villain may still hold some potential for being reformed (as Taylor senior is), and the pampered, deracinated, and generally unbearable second-generation James who may be the living fear of what the future might hold for immigrants, is the one whom nobody marries, but whose new language, untranslatable into any other language – may somehow prevail. *Die Emigranten* makes the worst offenders only the most extreme representatives of a fairly general practice. The very title page illustrates this, as we find a German title and subtitle followed by "St. Louis, Mo." and (no longer in Gothic *Frakturschrift*) "Aug. Wiebusch & Son Printing Company." Like *Die Emigranten*, many works insist that we should not ignore such "impure" language elements as code-switching and the bilingual pun, or the ethnic negotiations of "German-American" in relationship to other ways of being American.

German-American literature does not exist in isolation but implies in its very hyphenate adjective that it is part of an *interaction*; and that fact may give many works a prophetic quality as they foreshadow aspects of our own transnational period that has all but replaced the nationalist era in which "German America" may have had something unnatural, oxymoronic, or merely comic about it that could only be resolved either by an exilic self-consciousness as *Auslandsdeutschtum* or by a complete immersion into Anglo-America. After two World Wars and the end of the Cold War, the time may have come to go beyond multiculturalism (or more deeply into multiculturalism) – toward multilingualism.

It is now eighty-four years ago that the revelation of the disastrous Zimmermann cable (in which the German government promised Mexico great parts of the US Southwest if Mexico were to join World War I on the German side) led to military confrontation between the United States and

Germany, with its well-known tragic consequences for German-Americans. Five and a half million Germans had emigrated in the century prior to that moment of crisis, most of them to the United States; before the year 1913, in which Germany introduced the new principle of *jus sanguinis* as the basis of citizenship, emigrants automatically lost their German citizenship after a few years abroad. The hopes of many for a compatibility of their past German identification and present American citizenship (which clearly animates *Die Emigranten*) were dashed when they were asked to choose one side or the other; or, rather, when they were really forced to choose one side. Did what Joshua Fishman termed "language loyalty" persist more in the Old World than in the New?[47] Was World War I really the watershed, or was, as Peter Conolly-Smith has argued in his wonderful study of the German-language press of New York City, the dissolution of German-America already in full swing when the War started?[48] *Die Emigranten* and other literary works might well contain the clue to answer such questions, and I am happy to be in the company of scholars who may become, or who are already, engaged in reading and studying such works.

"Beyond multiculturalism?" was my question. I have suggested that for Germany one fruitful direction might be to link up with the German citizenship discussion of the pre-World War I era and with US multiculturalism's focus on curbing social sadism. For the US, promising fields are multiracialism (already growing under such terms as "hybridity" and "Creolization") and multilingualism (which is still at its very beginning and could also profit from examining the World War I scene); it will also be important to find ways in which a new focus on fighting social selfishness might revive the reform tradition. Going "beyond multiculturalism" might finally also mean engaging students and scholars on both sides of the Atlantic to examine critically the history of German-American cultural production and interaction, a project for which the present moment seems ideal.

Notes

* This essay was written in 1997, and it would have been difficult to reflect all the changes that have taken place since then – short of writing a new piece. The reader should at least be alerted to the dramatic changes that have transformed the German citizenship legislation. Some sections from the essay were taken or adapted from "Multiculturalism in an Age of Xenophobia: An Introduction," *Multiculturalism in an Age of Xenophobia: Canadian, American, and German Perspectives*, ed. Abraham J. Peck and Reinhard Maiworm, CD-ROM (Cincinnati: American Jewish Archives and Goethe-Institut – VISTA InterMedia Corporation, 1997); Werner Sollors, *Neither Black Nor*

White Yet Both: Thematic Explorations of Interracial Literature (New York: Oxford University Press, 1997); "For a Multilingual Turn in American Studies," *American Studies Association Newsletter* (June 1997): 13-5; my preface to *Multilingual America: Transnationalism, Ethnicity, and the Languages of American Literature* (New York: New York University Press, 1998); and my reviews of Hollinger's and Michaels's books.

1. For examples of these works and for new criticism see *The Multilingual Anthology of American Literature*, ed. Marc Shell and Werner Sollors (New York: New York University Press, 2000) and *Multilingual America*.

2. Simone Vauthier, "Textualité et stéréotypes: Of African Queens and Afro-American Princes and Princesses: Miscegenation in *Old Hepsy*," *Regards sur la littérature noire américaine*, ed. Michel Fabre (Paris: Publications du Conseil Scientifique de la Sorbonne Nouvelle – Paris III, 1980) 65-107.

3. Winfried Siemerling and Katrin Schwenk, *Cultural Difference and the Literary Text: Pluralism and the Limits of Authenticity in North American Literature* (Iowa City: University of Iowa Press, 1996).

4. David A. Hollinger, *Postethnic America: Beyond Multiculturalism* (New York: Basic Books, 1995).

5. David A. Hollinger, "How Wide the Circle of the 'We'? American Intellectuals and the Problem of the Ethnos since World War II," *American Historical Review* (April 1993): 317-37; here 335-6.

6. The decade from 1940 to 1950 thus seems to have been particularly fertile in producing the terms of our contemporary ethnic debate. In *Beyond Ethnicity*, I have traced the first uses of the word "ethnicity." The term "identity," omnipresent today in connection with such words as "ethnic" or "national," may go back only to Erik Erikson's attempt of 1950 at translating Freud. In a 1926 B'nai Brith address, Freud had opposed religious faith or national pride but described his sense of Jewishness as the result of unconscious elements and of what Freud called "the secret familiarity of identical psychological construction" ("Heimlichkeit der gleichen inneren Konstruktion") – and in *Childhood and Society* Erikson offered the term "identity" as a shortened English formula for Freud's notion. It was a formula that took. See Philip Gleason, "Identifying Identity," *Theories of Ethnicity: A Classical Reader*, ed. Werner Sollors (Basingstoke: Macmillan and New York: New York University Press, 1996) 460-87.

7. I am quoting from Edward F. Haskell, *Lance: A Novel About Multicultural Men* (New York: John Day Company, 1941) and from Iris Barry, "Melodrama, Tract, Good Story," *New York Herald Tribune Books* 12 July 1941: 3.

8. Barry, "Melodrama" 3.

9. Haskell, *Lance* 320-1.

10. Ibid., 321.

11. Nathan Glazer, *We Are All Multiculturalists Now* (Cambridge, MA: Harvard University Press, 1997).

12. Lawrence Levine, *The Opening of the American Mind* (Boston: Beacon Press, 1996).

13   Leslie A. Fiedler, *The Inadvertent Epic: From* Uncle Tom's Cabin *to* Roots (New York: Simon & Schuster, 1979).

14   Walter Benn Michaels, *Our America: Nativism, Modernism, and Pluralism* (Durham: Duke University Press, 1995).

15   Ibid., 125.

16   Ibid., 129.

17   William E. Massey Sr. Lectures in the History of American Civilization at Harvard University; Richard Rorty, *Achieving Our Country: Leftist Thought in Twentieth Century America* (Cambridge, MA: Harvard University Press, 1997).

18   In the next sentences I am following the article by Manfred Hettling, "Schritt nach vorn zurück: Das erste Gesetz zur deutschen Staatsangehörigkeit," *Frankfurter Allgemeine Zeitung* 7 August 1996: N6. See also Rogers Brubaker, *Citizenship and Nationhood in France and Germany* (Cambridge, MA: Harvard University Press, 1992) and Dieter Gosewinkel, "Die Staatsangehörigkeit als Institution des Nationalstaats. Zur Entstehung des Reichs- und Staatsangehörigkeitsgesetzes von 1913," *Offene Staatlichkeit: Festschrift für Ernst-Wolfgang Böckenförde zum 65. Geburtstag*, ed. Rolf Grawert (Berlin: Duncker & Humblot, 1995). Significant excerpts of the 1913 law and of other legal work affecting foreigners from the Constitution to various ordinances are conveniently reprinted in Helmut Rittstieg, ed., *Deutsches Ausländerrecht*, 10th ed. (München: dtv 1996).

19   See Valentina Maria Stefanski, "Die polnische Minderheit," in the most helpful new reference work *Ethnische Minderheiten in der Bundesrepublik Deutschland: Ein Lexikon*, ed. Cornelia Schmalz-Jacobsen and Georg Hansen (München: C.H. Beck, 1995) 386-91; and Rogers Brubaker, *Citizenship* 125, 128-37. See also Max Weber's observations in *Wirtschaft und Gesellschaft*, rpt. as "Ethnic Groups" in *Theories of Ethnicity*, 64.

20   Brubaker, *Citizenship* 120, drawing on *Verhandlungen des Reichstags* of 23 April 1913.

21   "Trans-National America" (1916) in *Theories of Ethnicity* 104.

22   The remarks on this and the next page follow closely the argument made by Günter Bannas, "Ausnahmen bestätigen noch die Regel der Einbürgerung," *Frankfurter Allgemeine Zeitung* 7 April 1993: 5 and "Die Regel ist die Ausnahme: In Europa und auch in Deutschland wird Mehrfach-Staatsangehörigkeit hingenommen," *Frankfurter Allgemeine Zeitung* 16 August 1996: 10.

23   According to Hans-Christian Rößler, "Man kann seine Identität nicht von heute auf morgen aufgeben: Viele eingebürgerte Türken behalten ihre alten Pässe," *Frankfurter Allgemeine Zeitung* 29 July 1997: 3. Rößler also reports that in 1996, 53,000 Turks filed for German citizenship in Berlin and Frankfurt alone.

24   See Michael Schlikker, "Ausländerrecht," in *Ethnische Minderheiten*, 72-5, and Friedrich Heckmann, *Ethnische Minderheiten, Volk und Nation: Soziologie inter-ethnischer Beziehungen* (Stuttgart: Enke, 1992) 236-41.

25   Those who may be disappointed that I am not writing about this topic exclusively, are referred to my book *Neither Black Nor White Yet Both* where I deal with some of these issues in depth. Werner Sollors, *Neither Black Nor White Yet Both: Thematic Explorations*

of Interracial Literature (New York: Oxford University Press, 1997).

26 The discussion of Séjour is adapted from my *Neither Black Nor White Yet Both*. See also Michel Fabre, *From Harlem to Paris: Black American Writers in France, 1840-1980* (Urbana and Chicago: University of Illinois Press, 1991) 14-6; Era Brisbane Young, "An Examination of Selected Dramas for the Theater of Victor Séjour Including Works of Social Protest," diss., School of Education, Health, Nursing, and Arts Professions, New York University, 1979; and David O'Connell, "Victor Séjour: Ecrivain Américain de langue française," *Revue de Louisiane* 1.2 (Winter 1972): 60-1.

27 Sollors, *Neither Black Nor White* 302.

28 Vauthier, "Of African Queens" 90-1.

29 This point was made by Young, "Examination" 95. In the Anglophone part of the African American tradition, it was only Charles Chesnutt who, half a century later, attempted a similarly mythic, but less violently resolved family construction in his short story "The Sheriff's Children" (1899).

30 Quoted from Theodor Grentrup, "Die Reichstagsdebatte 1912 über die Mischehen in den deutschen Kolonien," *Die Rassenmischehen in den deutschen Kolonien* (Paderborn: Ferdinand Schöningh, 1914) 42. For information about Solf, see Robert Volz, ed., *Reichshandbuch der deutschen Gesellschaft* (Berlin: Deutscher Wirtschaftsverlag, 1931), with an introduction by Ferdinand Toennies. See also Solf's *Reichstag* speech of March 6, 1913, in Wilhelm Pflägling, *Zum kolonialrechtlichen Problem der Mischbeziehungen zwischen deutschen Reichsangehörigen und Eingeborenen* (Berlin: Universitäts-Buchdruckerei Gustav Schade, 1913) 59-63.

31 Jane Ray, *The Story of Creation: Words from Genesis* (New York: Dutton Children's Books, 1993).

32 Personal communication from Johns Stephens, December 3, 1996.

33 Ingrid Gogolin, "Sprache und Migration," in *Ethnische Minderheiten* 488-90.

34 See the respective articles in *Ethnische Minderheiten*, with statistical appendices on which I am drawing throughout.

35 "Results of the MLA's Fall 1995 Survey of Foreign Language Enrollments," *MLA Newsletter* 28.4 (Winter 1996): 1-2. For the full report, see Richard Brod and Bettina J. Huber, "Foreign Language Enrollments in United States Institutions of Higher Education, Fall 1995," *ADFL Bulletin* 28.2 (Winter 1997): 55-60.

36 Gerald Early, "American Education and the Postmodernist Impulse," *American Quarterly* 45.2 (June 1993): 220.

37 Mary Louise Pratt, "Comparative Literature and Global Citizenship," *Comparative Literature in the Age of Multiculturalism*, ed. Charles Bernheimer (Baltimore and London: Johns Hopkins Press, 1995) 64. On the issue of translations, see the Greene report and the Bernheimer report in the same volume, 35, 44.

38 William Peterfield Trent, et al., *The Cambridge History of American Literature*, vol. 3 (New York: Macmillan, and Cambridge: Cambridge University Press, 1943) 572-634.

39 King-Kok Cheung and Stan Yogi, eds. *Asian-American Literature: An Annotated Bibliography* (New York: Modern Language Association, 1988) vi. The reason given is that this will help "keep the bibliography to a manageable size" – which implies that the Asian-language publications by Asian Americans must be sizeable. Other excluded items are individual poems, archival and private materials, and student publications.

40 St. Louis, Mo.: Aug. Wiebusch & Son Printing Company, 1882. Page numbers in parentheses refer to this edition.

41 For discussions of "Germerican" – as well as other mixed languages – see *Multilingual America*. The present section stems from an address delivered at the banquet of the Society for German-American Studies, at the Racquet Club, St. Louis, Mo., 18 April 1997.

42 In preparing translations from passages of the play I benefited from a free English adaptation, "The Emigrants," by Gabriele Weber-Jaric.

43 Carl Gustav Jung, "Your Negroid and Indian Behavior," (1930); rpt. in *Theories of Ethnicity* 191-201.

44 For information on the Longfellow Institute, see Daniel Zalewski, "Tongues Untied: Translating American Literature into English," *Lingua Franca* (December/January 1996/97): 61-5, and the world wide web page located at http://www.fas.harvard.edu/~lowinus/.

45 See Alide Cagidemetrio, "Introduction" to Luigi Donato Ventura's *Peppino* (1885), *Multilingual Anthology of American Literature* 214-8.

46 See Steven G. Kellman's comments on the importance of the "mother's lullaby" in literary discussions of mother tongues, "Translingualism and the Literary Imagination," *Criticism* 33.4 (Fall 1991): 527-41.

47 For a quick orientation, see Joshua Fishman: "Language Maintenance." *The Harvard Encyclopedia of American Ethnic Groups*, ed. Stephan Thernstrom (Cambridge, MA: Harvard University Press, 1980) 629-38.

48 See Peter Conolly-Smith, "The Translated Community: New York City's German-Language Press as an Agent of Cultural Resistance and Integration, 1910-1918," diss., Yale University, 1996.

From "Roots" to "Routes": Ethnic Fiction between Comfort Zones and Danger Zones

Rüdiger Kunow

I.

The following argument is an attempt to locate, in a very literal sense of the word, contemporary ethnic fiction within the larger social and cultural manifold of an increasingly post-national United States. This search for location is intended to take us into two different but related problem areas: the first might be designated as "the cultural politics of space," i.e., the attempts by disenfranchised and emancipatory social formations to inscribe themselves into a national cultural geography in which they had previously been little more than blank spots on the map. After all, as Adrienne Rich has observed, "a place on the map is also a place in history."[1] My second area of concern is the poetics of space, more especially the question of how the "identity politics of place"[2] empowers the construction of distinctive discursive spaces whose contours and contents can then be thought about as constituting something like a post-national spatial imaginary. What holds our two perspectives on the making and writing of spaces together is the insight (formulated among others by Henri Lefebvre) that the praxis of a given society and its imaginary geography, that the spaces of representation and the representation of space are dialectically related aspects of the continuing sociocultural construction of space.[3]

The term "post-national" is a useful starting point for such a project. First, it is a conceptual shorthand for the complex geopolitical realities in which questions of representation – political as well as cultural – can no longer be regulated, "contained," as it were, within the boundaries of the nation-state. All those global economic and social forces which are progressively eroding the role of the national state as a primary agent in political, economic, and also in sociocultural matters are at the same time also giving birth to new spatial configurations, to translocal, inter-national formations, "internal external entities,"[4] such as migrancy, diasporic conditions, border crossings, etc. Paul Gilroy's image of "ships in motion across the spaces between Europe, America, Africa, and the Caribbean" is particularly appropriate in this context.[5] While originally referring to the deterritorialization of African American culture, the image is also appropriate in a wider context, designating a post-national subject position, one that is not only constantly in motion, creating changes of values and orientations, but that is itself constituted by motion, "rootless," in transit.[6]

Secondly, "post-national" can be said to refer to an increasing rejection of "the Western nation as an obscure and ubiquitous form of living the *locality* of culture."[7] The idea that culture is "national" has been with us since the formation of nation-states in the sixteenth and seventeenth centuries in Europe. The (then novel) concept of a national culture proceeded from the assumption that the historical experience of the people which made up a unitary, homogenous nation somehow resulted in an equally unitary and national culture. The purpose of this culture, in turn, was "to make the history of the nation part of the personal experience of each of its citizens."[8] Culture, then, was "national" being, the characteristic as well as the possession of, that very nation. As a consequence, such culture needed to be both, constructed and contained, within the confines of that nation.[9] Cultural borders and national borders thus became more or less congruous, requiring constant vigilance and policing. It is in this sense of an equation between political and cultural geography that we still speak today of English, French, or Russian cultures.

Over the last decades, the concept of a "national culture" in the image of the political nation has become complicated, contested, even tenuous. New social and cultural formations have emerged which have successfully challenged the exclusive ownership of culture by the political nation from a decidedly post-national perspective:

> The term postnational indicates [among other things that] [. . .] the socially disenfranchised figures within emancipatory political movements understand that the universality of the national identity depends on their externality for its integrity. In the wake of this recognition, these movement figures offered themselves up not for integration within the national narrative but, by way of what I am calling post-national narratives, actively contested its social arrangements.[10]

Post-national in this sense is not simply that which comes after the national, but rather designates a "minor" position inside the national. From this position it becomes possible to expose and question the "nexus of belongingness"[11] that is always involved in the construction of a national cultural space and that depends on inclusion as much as on exclusion for its creation and subsequent stability.[12] Within this duality of inclusion/

exclusion, the post-national thus can be broadly described as signifying all that which refuses to "be contained within the *Heim* of the national culture and its unisonant discourse [. . .]."[13]

Thirdly, now applied to the United States, "post-national" heralds the end of a peculiar self-representation of culture as both national and natural. In the US, the grounding of culture in the political geography of the nation has not only been traditionally strong, it was, moreover, often quite direct or literal. Given a still "shaky state apparatus, which as yet had no cultural referent whose expression it could authentically say it was"[14] and a comparatively scanty historical record, the physical geography of the country frequently served as a primary referent for the cultural essence of the new nation. This equivalence of the natural and the national continued well into the nineteenth century, when the "wide open spaces" of the American wilderness were not only the physical domain within which the drama of an American Manifest Destiny unfolded itself, but were at the same time also an (as yet) empty cultural space in the process of being filled by an evolving national culture, "a physical means of establishing a moral power," as one contemporary observer put it.[15] Against that background, the closing of the frontier, as Frederick Jackson Turner suggests in his famous 1893 address, became something like the spatial equivalent for the eventual completion of the forming of an American national character.

From the vantage point of our own social and cultural moment, such a convergence, even conflation, of physical, political and cultural spaces appears not only as nostalgic but is also increasingly perceived as part of what has been called the "American ideological consensus."[16] Since the "culture wars" of the 1970s and 80s this consensus has been progressively dismantled by the revisionary energies of new social formations. Their contestation of national culture or their modifying presence within it have changed the cultural geography of the United States in such a way that it can no longer arrange itself around a representative national space. Instead, it has become a geography of dissent and dispersal, of "DissemiNation" (Homi Bhabha),[17] characterized by a multiplicity of social and cultural locations. These locations constitute post-national spaces of representation which reflect new cultural affiliations partly outside, partly in opposition to, the political nation. And while these locations do in this sense ratify the fragmentation of the quondam homogenous national cultural space, they do not simply function as cultural sites on a smaller, post-national or "minority" scale. Rather, they reflect the particular circumstances in which difference is lived and experienced: "[. . .] 'the politics of location' necessarily calls those of us who would participate in the formation of counter-hegemonic practice to identify the spaces where we begin the process of re-vision."[18] In this way difference is no longer an abstract category but is seen as always socially and culturally situated.[19]

Such a politics of space can be shown to have its parallels in, and is in cultural praxis often directly related to, a similar poetics of space. This poetics lies at the heart of a variety of contemporary counter-hegemonic fictions whose post-national orientation is evidenced by their replacement of the grand national narrative of homogeneity and consent with so many small narratives of difference and dissent. These narratives have been understood by some critics as constituting a new and distinct literary genre, variously called "Resistance Literature" (Barbara Harlow),[20] "Diaspora Literacy" (Abena Busia)[21] or "Ethnic American Literature" (Amritjit Singh et al.).[22]

Whatever the specific characteristics of this genre, the writings produced from this specific subaltern subject position can indeed be shown to have in common a definite agenda of representation. In their attempt at "re-sourcing"[23] individuals in a "minority" subject position, they rely less on the temporal dynamics of assimilation or dissimilation (as late 19th-century/early 20th-century immigration narratives often did) but instead on a spatial matrix in which place, territory, the lateral dynamics of proximity and distance, play an important role. In this way they empower narratives of location, so much so, in fact, that the representation of post-national spaces has itself become representative of the project of a post-national literature.[24] In these spaces the subaltern subject finds his/her place in the otherwise amorphous, fragmented social and cultural geography of the contemporary United States. The representation of a given counter-hegemonic identity becomes in this way inseparable (if not indistinguishable) from the representation of a place in which this identity finds – in a very literal sense – its ground. Physical places in the social manifold and discursive spaces are, once again, directly related, this time, however, under a post-national, not a national perspective. The imagined spaces of contemporary counter-hegemonic fiction would then appear as so many such "locations of cultural difference."[25] These imagined locations can then counter the dislocating energies of our time by creating the ground for a "defence against the amorphous freedom and mobility he [the post-national writer] experiences as a national citizen [. . .] he writes because he fears the disappearance of things around him; he records because his world is fading away."[26]

Post-national fiction thus understood becomes "an act of cultural recovery,"[27] and this in more than one sense. First, it literally re-covers lost ground, constituting a subaltern subject position by representing it, by lining out in the mode of fiction "a room of one's own." Secondly, it constitutes an act of recovery by putting it in place: such a *mise-en-scène* of recovery will then provide an imaginary solution to a real sociocultural pathology: the experiences of dislocation and disorientation are sublated into imaginary scenarios of relocation in which a fictive individual is allowed to overcome his/her uprootedness through a return to some kind of safe space or "home."

If we now look at these narratives of recovery from a more narrowly literary-critical point of view, we can see how their representational agenda, the discursive production of a safe minor space, involves a number of recurrent features and strategies. Before I turn to these strategies in more detail, it is necessary to limit my focus somewhat. Since the 1960s there has been a wide variety of reemergent subject positions articulated in fiction so that the following argument will have to restrict itself to a representative literary sample, one particular fictional praxis. My sample will be ethnic fiction. Not only has ethnic writing over the last years been one of the most visible and volatile segments of subaltern literary praxis in the United States, it has moreover relied most directly and consistently on spatial strategies.[28]

II.

My argument will therefore now turn to ethnic writing and more specifically to the question of what is involved in the operations of spacing ethnicity in fiction. I will first briefly focus on an authorial perspective and then offer a reading of a representative text. Toni Morrison has discussed at some length how the spaces of representation accorded to the African American community (or the lack of such spaces) impinge on the representation of spaces in African American writing. In her essay "The Site of Memory,"[29] she describes how the disjunctive spaces of racialized America compel her to a "kind of literary archeology": "you journey to a site to see what remains were left behind and to reconstruct the world that these remains imply."[30] These places are critical locations where the hitherto hidden and repressed cultural heritage of African America can be located and then be brought to surface. What she calls "the archeological site"[31] thus opens up an interplay between de- and re-location, it is a location which empowers recollection and marks the beginning of "[her] route to a reconstruction of a world, to an exploration of an interior life that was not written."[32]

If we turn to the fictional representation of such sites now, the example almost immediately coming to mind (outside Morrison's own oeuvre) is, of course, Alex Haley's *Roots*. However, in order to avoid any suggestion that the search for an "archeological site" is specific to the African American community, I will focus instead on a Native American text written at about the same time as *Roots*, Leslie Silko's novel *Ceremony*.[33] Such a choice justifies itself not least by the fact that Silko has shown a continued commitment to the project tracing the contours of the subaltern space, especially in the American Southwest.[34]

Silko, a Laguna Pueblo writer, tells the story of a World War II veteran, Tayo, a Laguna Indian of mixed Native and white descent who returns from combat with severe psychic disorders. He cannot adjust to American life again. In a veterans' hospital he is diagnosed as suffering from a battle trauma and given tranquilizers. But this treatment does not cure Tayo. He remains psychologically as well as socially disoriented until he returns to the reservation where he had lived as a boy. And here, two medicine men, two shamans, take care of him. By telling him stories about the life of his ancestors they create in a long process an awareness in him not only of who he is but also of where he is. In this novel, not only the place (Laguna Pueblo) but also the psyche of the protagonist become "archeological sites" in Morrison's sense, leading to and empowering excavations of the hidden heritage of Native American culture and identity. These excavations are healing in that they enable Tayo to find a proper place for himself as a Native American in post World War II America. The ceremony mentioned in the novel's title signifies the completion of this healing process and ratifies Tayo's re-turn to his ethnic culture. Silko, moreover, makes clear that location and locution are intimately linked, because after that ceremony Tayo is suddenly able to speak out: He "cried the relief he felt at finally seeing the pattern, the way all stories fit together – the old stories, the war stories, their stories – to become the story that was still being told."[35]

This act of fusion, of becoming one with the tribal nation and its social and cultural space, constitutes a re-location that counters the effects of dislocation, positioning a previously marginalized and disoriented character safely inside the ethnic lifeworld. In the process, the "nexus of belongingness"[36] of which I spoke earlier is allowed by Silko to manifest itself in full force, moving the central character to a centrist position, away from all the borderline conditions (psychic and social) that had previously determined his existence: "He was not crazy; he had never been crazy. He had only seen and heard the world as it always was: no boundaries, only transitions through all distances and time."[37] What the novel textualizes in this way is quite literally a *rite de passage*, transporting its central character from a nomadic and exilic position to the safety of a home place.[38]

Spatial trajectories of this kind can be found in a wide variety of ethnic writing, irrespective of their national or cultural affiliation or narrative content. To pick an almost random example: the autobiographical *Zami: A New Spelling of My Name*[39] by Caribbean-African American feminist Audre Lorde presents an agenda of emancipatory self-fashioning which is mediated by a contrapunctal spatial geography in which places of dislocation are complemented and ultimately superseded by, places of relocation. In the words of the autobiographical "I":

> Once home was a far way off, a place I had never been to but knew well through my mother's mouth. This now, here [Harlem], was a space, some temporary abode, never to be considered forever nor totally binding nor defining [. . .]. For if we lived correctly [. . .] then someday we would arrive back in the sweet place, back home."[40]

And, indeed, the movement of the narrative is towards such an arrival "at home." After growing up in Harlem with feelings of alienation and disorientation, the protagonist goes to visit the Caribbean island of Carriacou (near Grenada), home of her mother's family. In the framework of the narrative, Carriacou functions like an archeological site in that the central character learns about ancestral ways of life, especially about how the women of Grenada fashioned for themselves an autonomous culture, independent of men and filled with love among women. In the end, back in New York, the autobiographical "I," in a very routine moment, suddenly feels how her African-Caribbean ancestry enters her life and places her in the long-desired home space. Listening to an old spiritual she begins to feel "rich with hope and a promise of life [. . .]. The physical realities of the dingy bus [which she is riding] slid away from me. I suddenly stood upon a hill in the center of an unknown country, hearing the sky fill with a new spelling of my name."[41] In this way, the text moves towards a site that is both, location and locution of otherness.[42]

Writings whose direction – geographical as well as narrative – is towards such acts of unambiguous homecoming might be described as "return-to-roots narrative[s]." For Thomas Couser narratives of this kind follow a definable pattern, the main components of which are:

> [T]ake an alienated member of a minority or ethnic group; subject him or her to an unnerving experience that recalls past traumas; introduce a tribal elder, who will

lead the alienated character back into contact and communion with the minority community through traditional ceremony; and so on.[43]

What might be added to Couser's list is a characteristic spatial trajectory which takes the fictional character from de-location to re-location.

Lorde's and Silko's texts do indeed exhibit most of the components of the "return-to-roots"-formula. There is the alienated member of an ethnic group; there is the trauma which is cured by a tribal elder, and this cure leads the alienated characters back into their ethnic communities. And there is also the traditional ceremony. In this way, a new identity is made possible by locating the person within a (fictional) space of belonging. This discursive construction in which dislocation is finally overcome by re-location, in which not only past and present, but also we and I, can be linked inside a significant ethnic locale, has here, as elsewhere in contemporary ethnic literature, a double function. On the level of *histoire*, it solves the identity crisis of a fictional character by reinstating him/her within an ethnic home space. On the level of the *discours*, it provides closure for the fictional narrative, completing its movement across a deterritorialized post-national cultural geography by a moment of ultimate arrival, inside a carefully circumscribed ethnic locality. Here the ethnic narrative becomes a story of homecoming and narrative closure constitutes a veritable enclosure. *Routes ultimately lead to roots*.[44]

It is not Couser's intention, and certainly not my own, to disparage such narratives as merely formulaic or derivative. Rather, his perspective has the advantage of taking us away from the single text and its construction of space to the level of intertextual similarities, to what might be called a post-national poetics of space. On this level, a certain complex of cultural problems (i.e., the politics and poetics of counter-hegemonic spaces) can be shown to express itself not just in a certain subject matter but in structural preferences as well, "in a specific variety of forms and form-problems."[45]

To turn thus from the contents to the contours (the "form") of ethnic spaces is the next necessary step in my argument because this move opens the choices which so far have governed the spatial representation of ethnic fictions to comparison and critique. Such a critical project could take its starting point from the observation that many discursive constructions of subaltern spaces possess a curiously janus-faced quality. On the one hand they register the de-locating effects of our post-national moment, the "DissemiNation," while on the other they construct a re-location in an ethnic domain which possesses many of the features of the quondam national cultural space, above all, definability, homogeneity, and wholeness:

Pilate's home in Morrison's *Song of Solomon*[46] a place which "seemed to be rising from rather than settling into the ground"; or the house that in Sandra Cisneros' *House on Mango Street* functions throughout the different stories as future locale for Esperanza's identity and completeness, "a house quiet as snow, a space for myself to go, clean as paper before a poem;"[47] or the foundational act of "giv[ing one]self up to a particular landscape" in Scott Momaday's *The Way to Rainy Mountain*,[48] together with the examples which I have cited from *Zami* and *Ceremony* are, all differences aside, significations of an ethnic site that is bounded and that enacts boundings.

With the "successful evocation of a cultural inside,"[49] the location of difference as constructed in ethnic fiction at times presents itself as also a location of sameness. Such a representation of ethnic counter-sites is enabling, responds to diasporic desires for belonging, return, for a homeland, for creating a "space of becoming."[50] At the same time, it could be said to rely on a territorial sense of culture – "culture as site of belonging"[51] – that has been declared ideological or obsolete outside the context of subaltern discursive practice. An oppositional poetics of space would thus deconstruct the "ambivalent signifying system of the nation-space [. . .]"[52] only to arrive at an unambivalent signifying system of a post-national, "minor" space.[53] Hence, the proclamation of such places (as part of an identity politics of space) and their representation in fiction (as part of a related poetics of space) have become subject to critique and controversy.

The debate (which cannot be rehearsed in all details here) focuses primarily on two different but related problem areas.
(1) On the one hand it is argued that what started out as a counter-hegemonic project has now itself become hegemonic, relying on strategies of exclusion and centralization. In this way, poetics of space derived from the experience of interaction and migrancy in a post-national world is believed to be once again relying on enclosures and borders. Opposing such reemergence in oppositional writing of constrictive constructions of space, Paul Gilroy calls instead for flexible representations: "The concept of [cultural] space itself is transformed when it is seen less through outmoded notions of fixity and place" and instead as "a space of flows" in which identities are constantly negotiated and renegotiated "in terms of an ex-centric communicative circuity [. . .]."[54] The construction of carefully circumscribed ethnic spaces has even come to be regarded as a colonizing gesture of sorts, one in which as "a pure otherness [is presumed] waiting to be filled by the presence of our desires, a blank page awaiting our words, like the 'empty' wilderness [. . .] waiting to be settled and domesticated [. . .]."[55]

(2) The second field of debate concerns the position of such spaces of pure otherness inside the larger post-national geography. Such an argument has been proposed by the feminist critic and filmmaker Trinh Minh-ha. She is concerned that the self-representations of marginalized cultures repeat in a kind of uncanny historical repetition compulsion all the homogenizing and repressive tendencies of mainstream culture. Minh-ha is arguing as a feminist here, and very often, feminists have been uneasy with undifferentiated essentializing of ethnic culture.[56] For Minh-ha, to counteract the "myths of the tribe" is an important element of any feminist critique of the ethnic politics and poetics of space. It registers in her cautionary remark that such discursive spaces should "avoid reproducing, in the writing itself, the same model of the centre-margin power relationship that has prevailed in the existing system of cultural and political representation." For her, the location of culture is not so much Morrison's "archeological site"; it is rather, in her words, "an 'empty site.'"[57] Moreover, it has been argued that a spatial imaginary in which spaces of privation are regularly complemented by places of plenitude, does indeed provide a neat, clear-cut "geographical counterpoint,"[58] but in so doing relies on a dualistic matrix which essentially reinforces the binary logic of racism or colonialism and at times even comes dangerously close to subscribing to its essentializing and exclusionary logic.[59] My argument cannot presume to act as an arbiter in this debate. It is, however, important for the present inquiry because it brings to the forefront the limiting conditions for the representation of ethnic spaces in a post-national geography. At this point it may be useful to turn once again to an authorial perspective. Just as Morrison's "archeological site" introduced us to the play of dislocation and re-location staged in ethnic fiction, so Wole Soyinka's argument about "the essentiality of our black being" can help understanding how the carving out of an ethnic location of difference may become a project that transcends itself. In his Nobel Laureate Address "This Past Must Address This Present," a speech which he dedicated to Nelson Mandela, who was still in prison at that time, Soyinka insists on the enabling potential of a cultural room of one's own:

> The world which is so conveniently traduced by Apartheid thought is of course that which I so wholeheartedly embrace [. . .]. It is a world that nourishes my being, one which is so self-sufficient, so replete in all aspects of its productivity, so confident in itself and in its destiny that it experiences no fear in reaching out to others and in responding to the reach of others [. . .]. It is the heartstone of our creative existence. It constitutes the prism of our world perception [. . .].[60]

Soyinka's choice of words is significant here. Organic images of nurturing and maturity ("nourish," "replete") combine with a rhetoric of essence and essentialism ("self-sufficient," "confident in itself") to suggest that African culture can indeed be conceived as a space of fullness and wholeness, sufficient in itself, a safe haven. In making this point, the whole passage relies on a clear-cut binarism of the inside vs. the outside, the outside being, as Soyinka makes clear a little further on, the realm of "the enemy on our doorstep." In the face of such hegemonic pressures, the insistence on an oppositional, negated space, the "world that is so conveniently traduced by Apartheid thought," is clearly a defensive strategy and also the precondition of resistance against "centuries-old fantasies [. . .] in Euro-Judaic thought." The cultural inside, by contrast, is not only oppositional but also centrist (Soyinka speaks of "heartstone" [sic]), both location and locution of difference. However, Soyinka's construction of a counter-hegemonic space does not stop here. He sketches a domain in which dislocation is in not simply corrected by re-location, territorial heterogeneity transformed into homogeneity; rather, his insistence on cultural essence can be seen as part of an argumentative move that goes in two directions, from the margins (of hegemonic culture) to the center (of Africanist culture) and also from that center to the far end of the ethnic sanctuary. The "heartstone" is, in fact, destination and starting point, the place which negotiations and exchanges with others can proceed: "and this means that our sight need not be and has never been turned inwards."

Now, Soyinka's argument must not be simply grafted directly onto the situation inside the United States today. But clearly, he responds to a marginalization and a regime of sociocultural difference that has often been regarded as offering obvious parallels to systems of (spatial) apartheid operating in the US.[61] Over against such regimes, Soyinka projects an autonomous subaltern domain that is both *necessary and incomplete*: one which is a unified space of sameness and at the same time a strategic location for negotiations with the adjoining other, "the enemy" at the doorstep.

From such a perspective, ethnic spaces can no longer be regarded as territories in isolation but as part of the overall post-national geography in which relations of sameness and otherness are spatially organized and exist *always in relation*.[62] For such an understanding of spatiality, Foucault's concept of the heterotopic is helpful because it offers a conceptualization of spaces which highlights their generic otherness while insisting at the same time on their inherent relationality. Thus, the heterotopic, for Foucault, is unambiguously "a space that is other, another real space [. . .]."[63] Such sites come into being because every hegemonic construction of space is necessarily incomplete. Hence, in areas which are not controled by the hegemonic regime or incompatible with its functions or interests, "other spaces" can develop and retain a certain stability and functional autonomy. What is important in our context is that these "other" spaces or, as Foucault also calls them, these "counter-sites," are not locations of pure spatial otherness but are sites which are both functional and relational, the terrain of a complex dialectic interplay between power or hegemony and their opposites. More precisely, heterotopias are "counter-sites [. . .] in which the real sites [. . .] are simultaneously represented, contested, and inverted."[64] The forms in which this representation, contestation and inversion occur may vary over time and according to changes in social praxis. All the while, heterotopic spaces remain inescapably linked to, are even part of, the spatial regime whose "other" they are. They have, as Foucault insisted, "a *function in relation* to all the space that remains."[65]

Foucault's notion of the heterotopic as construction of an a-symmetric, dualistic but at the same time dialogic spatial order is pertinent to our inquiry into a post-national poetics of space. For, while representation, contestation and inversion are qualities inherent to all "counter-sites," the topography of return-to-roots narratives has often emphasized only the first two aspects of the heterotopic. This has sometimes promoted an understanding of these spaces as heterotopic in and by themselves. Such a perspective would leave unacknowledged what Foucault called the "function in relation" of locations of difference. Only if this relationality is acknowledged can the heterotopic space become more than a "minor" enclave within an alienating cultural geography.

Such an understanding of the ethnic domain as both different and relational is perhaps best approximated in Arjun Appadurai's concept of the "ethnoscape." For him, ethnic locations are inescapably part of a post-national geography, in which "the link between space, stability and cultural reproduction" has generally become tenuous.[66] Appadurai proposes the term "ethnoscape" as part of a conceptual framework in which the new transnational realities of the current global economy can be understood. This economy privileges "global cultural flows." One of five "dimensions" in which these flows occur is the "ethnoscape"; others are "mediascapes," "technoscapes," "finanscapes," and "ideoscapes." These "dimensions" are not causally related and do not always work in the same direction, nor are they self-sufficient domains. "The suffix *-scape* allows us to point to the irregular, fluid shapes of these landscapes, [. . .] inflected by the historical, linguistic, and political situatedness of different sorts of actors."[67] This situatedness is such in Appadurai's perception that in the ethnoscape "the landscapes of group identity [. . .] are no longer tightly territorialized, spatially bounded, historically unselfconscious, or culturally homogeneous."[68] Hence, "the ethnoscapes of today's world are profoundly interactive."[69] In an argument about the "Contexts of Locality" Appadurai uses the example of ethnic neighborhoods to specify the ways in which the construction of space by social and cultural actors does not only provide a home space but at the same time makes the actors "sometimes recognize that their own logic is a general logic by which Others also construct recognizable, social, human, situated life-worlds."[70] Whenever such an awareness of Other lifeworlds develops, the ethnoscape will be an ethnic location that is necessary and incomplete in the sense we have spoken about. In Appadurai's words: "As ethnoscapes, neighborhoods inevitably imply a *relational consciousness* of other neighborhoods, but they act at the same time as autonomous neighborhoods of interpretation, value, and material practice."[71]

Appadurai himself has insisted that "ethnoscapes" are more than a configuration of space, they are always a representation, "building blocks of what I [. . .] would like to call *imagined worlds*."[72] In the remaining part of this essay I will now return to such imagined worlds. For a discussion of the poetics of space in contemporary ethnic fiction, the concept of the ethnoscape, with its insistence on interaction and relationality, marks the polar opposite to the closed ethnic enclaves to be found in many return-to-roots narratives. By way of a conceptual shorthand we will call the alternative representational modes "comfort zone" and "danger zone."

The former location is the space of what Ben Xu has – somewhat provocatively – called "the cozy view" of the ethnic self.[73] This "cozy" feeling is the result of "an experiential shift" in which "the domain of unknown is shifted toward a domain or field presumably already mastered."[74] "Comfort zones" can be defined as representations of ethnic spaces in which an oppositional social or cultural formation is shown to have found its unproblematic ground. Such a comfort zone functions as an enabling space, making possible the return of the historically and culturally repressed, a return, however, which still bears the mark of cultural marginality in that the space recovered is not only for the marginal but by and of, the marginal.[75] In this way, the comfort zone is always part of what has been called a "cloisonné world."[76]

On the other hand, the ethnic domain can also be a danger zone. "Danger zone" is Toni Morrison's term, in her understanding the location where the "ability to imagine others" (culturally significant others) becomes crucial. A danger zone is thus intrinsically relational, demands that a person project him/herself consciously "into the danger zones such others may represent for me."[77] Morrison's description is reminiscent of Soyinka's argument about the necessity of "reaching out to others and responding to the reach of others" from the "heartstone" of ethnic space. However, the term "danger zone" makes clear that this necessitates a shift in position: danger zones are by their very nature never located in the centers or heartstones of ethnic spaces, they call for, even demand, a movement to the peripheries, the margins, the borderlines of ethnic cultures.[78] In this way, danger zones are not the *mise-en-scène* anymore of ethnic recoveries, rather sites of interaction and relationality, of "encounters that are irreducible to a single point of view [. . .] rather than firmly located in any one culture, place, or position."[79] Understood in this way, the pair "danger zone" and "comfort zone" will in the next section guide our readings of three ethnic fictions which all concern themselves in various ways with the processes of de-territorialization of ethnic cultures and in so doing position themselves at sites of encounters.

III.

This part of my paper will be offering readings of three fictions from different ethnic backgrounds. They all distinguish themselves from the "return-to-roots narratives" in that they no longer carve out and then fill a space for their respective ethnic cultures but instead seek to question the very existence of such spaces. This interrogation involves changes in the overall position of the ethnoscape, it becomes a danger zone, "the site of the intersection of multiple determinations,"[80] one in which identity and meaning have to be constituted always in relation with the Other. The query into the possibility of an ethnic domain furthermore involves changes in representation, which reflect the understanding of the ethnoscape as de-essentialized and de-territorialized.

My first example of a fiction that is in this sense situated in a danger zone is Morrison's *Jazz*, a novel about African American migrants in New York City. The city has always been especially significant for Morrison because here the interrelatedness between race and space became particularly obvious. Her approach to the urban realities of the US is therefore decidedly from a heterotopic perspective, an exploration of "how do the disenfranchised view the cities they inhabit but do not have a claim to?"[81] The tension of which she speaks between inhabiting and belonging is at the heart also of *Jazz*.

The historical donnée of the novel (the 1920s) holds out the possibility of new, self-determined African American identities, even of a place of racial autonomy. That place seems to be Harlem. In the beginning, the narrative voice articulates this optimism: "History is over, you all, and everything's ahead at last. The A&P hires a colored clerk. Nobody wants to be an emergency at Harlem Hospital but if the Negro surgeon is visiting, pride cuts down the pain."[82] The protagonists Violet and Joe Trace are part of this reemergent ethnic community. Like so many other African Americans between 1880 and 1910, they have left the South for the industrial cities of the North to escape racism and begin a new life. As it turns out, however, this migration is not simply the high road "from slavery to freedom," especially since the city turns out to be an unexpectedly dangerous terrain.

In the South, the contours of African American existence were clearly drawn. The attempts by African Americans to clear a space for themselves were brought to nought in acts of racial violence: "Red fire doing fast what white sheets [that is the Ku Klux Klan] took too long to finish: cancelling every deed, vacating each and every field; emptying us out of our places so fast we went running from one part of the county to another – or nowhere"(151). After thus literally losing their ground in the South the newcomers come to the North, to New York City. At first they are excited by the options which the City as "a space of concupiscent possibility"[83] seems to be holding out: "The minute they arrive they know they are born for it. There, in the city, they are not so much new as themselves: their stronger and riskier selves" (46). For a while it appears that New York is a place which the ethnic self can affiliate itself with. Here, they "feel more like themselves, more like the people they always believed they were" (48). But this turns out to be an illusion, New York is not an exemption from, but rather an extension of the racialized geography of the country at large.

Morrison makes this point by highlighting the interrelation between possible representations of space in the city and the spaces of representation which it accords to African Americans. Roland Barthes' observation that the city is a sign system[84] speaking to its inhabitants is particularly pertinent here. At first Violet and Joe are excited "[that] the city is speaking to them" (44). But Morrison soon makes clear that this language is not innocent. In a gesture reminiscent of Döblin in *Berlin Alexanderplatz*, she presents the discourse of the city, its abundance of signs and messages:

"The City is smart at this: [. . .] sending secret messages disguised as public signs: this way, open here, danger to let colored only single men on sale woman wanted private room stop dog on premises [. . .]" (82). And, to be sure, among these messages, the motley array of private and public signs, is a racial signifier: "colored only." The discourse of the city is not racially neutral but always already infused with racist signifiers which define and delimit access to the various urban spaces. The cityscape is thus saturated with practices of racism, as is the case on 5th Avenue, "where whitemen leaned out of their cars with folded dollar bills peeping from their palms" (70), to buy themselves cheap, i.e., black sex. Thus the northern city is not simply the place of liberation, a comfort zone for the displaced victims of racism; rather it is a veritable danger zone: "the streets will confuse you, teach you or break your head" (92 f.). There is throughout the novel no ethnic sanctuary, even the ethnic neighborhoods are, as the East St. Louis riots show, no safe place. Their existence and their survival depends on an acute "relational consciousness,"[85] the ability of African Americans to anticipate the logic by which the Others construct their lifeworlds.

Jazz marks a departure from Morrison's previous novels in that the "archeological site" of ancestral presence is repeatedly invoked but never really attained as a position from which the remains of personal or collective life can be successfully reassembled. The routes of the displaced characters do not take them (or, for that matter, the novel) back to ethnic roots; life in the modern metropolis effectually makes African Americans rootless people. So one of the characters remarks in a resigned note: "Before I came North, I made sense and so made the world" (241). The two protagonists, Violet and Joe Trace, thus keep on looking for a trace of their ethnic identity, a place as African Americans in the danger zone of the modern city, but in vain. What they experience instead, is a constant play of dualities, between South and North, old discrimination and new, traditional and new habitat. As a result, their identity never finds its place, but remains constantly in the making: "if you was colored you had to be new and stay the same every day the sun rose and every night it dropped" (162). In the absence of any ethnic enclave, the novel ends in a vision of private, very private, space: "when grown people whisper to each other under the covers. They reach, grown people, for something beyond, way beyond" (263). But this "beyond" is never attained, as a matter of fact it remains curiously inexpressible, both inside the fictional world and in the text.

My second example is taken from Chinese-American literature, Maxine Hong Kingston's *Tripmaster Monkey: His Fake Book*.[86] Kingston situates her protagonist precisely in the danger zone where the hegemonic and the subaltern must constantly be mediated by the ability to imagine the Other: Wittman Ah Sing comes from an assimilated Chinese-American family, his father, Zeppelin Wadsworth Ah Sing, was a strong advocate of assimilation and the melting pot. His son, Wittman, lives in the 60s, in Berkeley, CA, at the time of the students' movement. At first he takes something like the "cozy view" (Xu) of his ethnic existence, regarding himself as "fellow ethnick" (sic, 73; 245). His de-centered location is already highlighted in his name, Wittman Ah Sing. It recalls Walt Whitman, the 19th century singer of democratic and pluralistic America. Whitman's programmatic "I sing," i.e., "I sing America," found its proper poetic *sujet* in the ethnic diversity of America, in his words from *Song of Myself*, "[. . .] the Nation of many nations, the smallest the same and largest the same."[87] And, indeed, a little bit of the original Whitman's synthesizing vision resurfaces in his latter-day counterpart. Wittman Ah Sing dreams of becoming an artist, "the first bad-jazz Chinaman Bluesman of America" (27), synthesizing the best of both cultural traditions.

Kingston portrays Wittman as something like an empty ethnic site waiting to be filled. He constantly urges himself "to let it come in [. . .]. He would let it all come in" (4). But this ideal of cultural amalgamation is constantly subverted by the realities of America as a racialized society which forces on Wittman a growing awareness that he is not only Wittman-Whitman but also Ah Sing. However, the Chinese cultural tradition, as Wittman discovers, does not offer him an ethnic sanctuary since the "brief and dying culture" (6) of Chinese America has left behind little more than a vacuum. Addressing the Chinese American community he accuses them of having withdrawn into the no-man's-land of assimilation: "Who are we? It's our fault they call us gook or chinky chinaman. We've been here all this time, before Columbus, and haven't named ourselves" (326). At the same time, he criticizes white America for placing Chinese-Americans in the realm of the merely exotic: "What's so exotic? We're about as exotic as shit. They [the Whites] think they know us – the wide range of sweet to sour – because they eat in Chinese restaurants" (308).

The only alternative left to him is to take a position that is by definition open and incomplete, and for such a position Chinese culture does indeed offer a model. Thus Wittman declares himself to be "the present day U.S.A. incarnation of the King of the Monkeys" (33; thus the title *Tripmaster Monkey*). In Chinese mythology the monkey is a figure which constantly changes identities and positions and in this fashion undermines existing orders. Some of these "monkey powers" are also to be found in

Wittman Ah Sing, especially "outrage and jokes" (241). These subversive powers make it possible for Wittman, as the novel progresses, to position himself playfully in various cultures and to develop a relational consciousness that unmasks and plays with identity constructs from both sides of the ethnic dividing line. At the same time this means that there is, as in Morrison's novel, no way back from here to cultural comfort zones. Belonging really nowhere, Wittman asks himself: "O home-returning powers, where might home be? How to find it and dwell there?" (284).[88]

There is one instance in the novel when Wittman does seem to find an ethnic homeland of sorts. In the rooms of his grandmother he discovers a "memory village" (191), a miniature model of a Chinese village, with houses, fields, trees, and animals. This memory village is itself the product of a massive historical displacement, Chinese immigration into the US The prospective immigrants would study this model so that they could tell US immigration officials credible stories about their home places. The memory village combines all the features of a Chinese village, but it is not a representation of any specific village. As Wittman explains to his (Caucasian) wife, Taña: "It is not a model *of* anything, do you understand? It's a memory village" (192). In other words, it is a simulation, the memory/model "of a real without origin or reality."[89] Such a simulacrum of the ethnic home space can evoke and support memories but is not a place to live in.

Throughout the novel, Wittman consistently rejects essentialist definitions of ethnicity ("I am not going to the prom with the only Chinese girl in the class" [59]) and, at times, even positions himself inside the national cultural space. On one occasion he even declares: "We are allthe-same Americans" (282). This "Americanness" is present as a frame of reference throughout the novel, but it never becomes a position which Wittman can unambiguously make his own. Twice removed from both the national cultural space and the terrain of his own culture, Wittman remains positioned on shifting grounds, in the danger zone between cultures, a position that is presented in this novel not so much as limiting than enabling. It provides Wittman with a perspective that is "irreducible to a single point of view" (Chambers), and this perspective finds its final realization in the realm of art: "Got no home. Got story" (110). That "story" is transformed into a play written by Wittman and put on the stage as a collaborative effort of people from various ethnic backgrounds. This play is a veritable danger zone of unprepared for and unguarded intercultural encounters and cross-references. It is based on ancient Chinese myths and tales combined with the myths and tales of American popular culture, including John Wayne, Bugs Bunny, Groucho Marx, and the slapstick act of the "banana-peel run, slip-sliding around the room" (258). This cultural hybrid of myth and media creates in the world of the theater what will in the world outside remain a utopia. Wittman exclaims enthusiastically: "We make theater, we make community" (261). Such a provisional community has no proper location, no territory of its own. Its site is not archeological so much as its processual, constantly in-the-making: "He was defining a community, which will meet every night for a season. Community is not built once-and-for-all; people have to imagine, practice, and re-create it" (306).

My third example is a novel written for the quincentennial of Columbus' (re)discovery of America. Gerald Vizenor, fiction writer and professor at UC Berkeley wrote *The Heirs of Columbus* to celebrate the resourcefulness of Native American culture while questioning the fundamentalist implications of ethnic comfort zones.[90] The polarities of Old vs. New World, discoverer and discoveree, majority and minority, which one would expect in such a novel – and which are, in fact, present in other Native and Euro-American fictions written for that occasion (and are subverted in some[91]) – are here turned upside down. To begin with, Columbus is portrayed as a creation of the Maya, hence his "discovery" of the "New" World is actually a return to an old one; his "heirs" (cf. the novel's title) are thus not white but Native Americans. These Native Americans are crossbloods, true to Vizenor's conviction that all Native Americans living today have hybrid heritages, both racially and culturally.[92] Crossbloods are in his view located forever in the danger zone of critical transcultural interactions, they are "a postmodern bloodline, an encounter with racialism, colonial duplicities, sentimental monogenism, and generic culture."[93]

The novel focuses on various searches for origin and location, staged by a group of such crossbloods who live at the margins of both, tribal and white civilizations. Contrary to the return-to-roots formula, they do not at all feel alienated, but rather enjoy their marginal status, especially since they are also tricksters. A trickster, in Native American mythology, is a person living both in the spiritual and the empirical worlds, a magician who can switch identities, conjure up things, etc. For Vizenor, tricksters are not persons so much as "a semiotic sign in a comic narrative that denies presence."[94] This denial of presence is articulated by the tricksters in the novel in various ways, their preferred field is the postmodern world of multi-media simulation. Their annual tribal festivals are not reconstructions of an ethnic past but feature "laser light show[s]" of a truly intercultural kind, featuring, for example, "Jesus Christ, Joan of Arc, Crazy Horse and the Statue of Liberty."[95]

How far this novel is going in its self-reflexive play with ethnic cultural heritage, can be shown by comparison with Silko's *Ceremony*. In that novel, Native American shamans play a central role: as healers they save a traumatized Indian by re-locating him inside his ethnic home. *The Heirs of Columbus* also features shamans but they have a totally different mission. One of them, Luster Browne, is paid by the California Transportation Department, but not to heal people. His magical powers, more exactly his voice, are employed for more mundane purposes, namely "to shout over the weeds on the highway medians, and sure enough the wild flowers bloomed the next morning [. . .]" (23). In addition, his shouts are broadcast over the state parks and recreation areas where they help conserve water. Another shaman, Stone Columbus, is the star of a successful midnight talk show on the radio. One day, in his show, he announces the formation of a new Native American state on the west coast between the United States and Canada. Symbol of this new nation is a statue standing at the entrance to its territory, the "trickster of liberty." Of course, as object of ethnic pride, the statue is "taller than the Statue of Liberty." Unlike its more prominent namesake, however, this statue does not signal a safe haven for the displaced migrants from all over the globe. Rather than calling, in Emma Lazarus' famous words, the "tired [and] poor, yearning to breathe free," tribal Miss Liberty answers to another call: What awaits the visitor is a kind of tribal Disney World featuring, for example, replicas of the three ships of Columbus' fleet. The flagship, the Santa Maria, now functions as "Santa Maria Casino," equipped with all the modern Las Vegas gambling gadgets (7). It is, in other words, a "bingo flagship," the Niña a restaurant and the Pinta a floating duty free shop (6). This new Native American state is thus more of a tribal theme park than a subaltern ethnic homeland of the kind inscribed by Silko.

But the novel does not simply play with topical references to gambling on the reservations, Native American independence movements, etc. More importantly, Vizenor's novel is concerned with something that Stone Columbus defines at one point. He declares: "The essence of [Native American] sovereignty is imaginative" (7, 16). Accordingly, "[t]he Heirs of Christopher Columbus created one more New World in their stories" (5) and the creation of such a narrative space is indispensable, because this is the only terrain available to Native Americans. Such an imaginative terrain is indeed "lightly territorialized" in Appadurai's sense. The crossbloods generate virtual spaces, "tribal simulations" (84), not with the help of ancient magic but through the modern computer. These simulations, while often entertaining and funny, are generated not just for fun, but rather, as part of an attempt by Native Americans to win back "[their] realities stolen by cold reason and manifest manners" (84). For this purpose the tricksters throughout the novel use the most advanced means of hegemonic, "white" civilization, even genetic engineering. This "high-tech Indian" is the very opposite of the archaic, mythical prototype conjured up by both ethnic fundamentalists and white "tourist civilization" alike.[96] By placing his Native American tricksters outside both, the tribal as well as the hegemonic worlds, Vizenor's novel not only deconstructs the option of a subaltern space but at the same time even subverts the contrapuntal geography on which much subaltern writing depends. Tricksters are central for this project, as they are for Vizenor's story-telling, because by denying presence, they deny the presence also of closure, both of physical spaces and of discursive spaces. Hence the narrative of *Heirs of Columbus* never reaches a proper closure, neither in spatial nor in diegetic terms. Like the tricksters, it "imagine[s] the starts but never the ends"(173) – indefinitely so, as the novel suggests.

Denied presence is also at the heart of the novel's self-conscious play with cultural stereotypes of "Indianness."[97] American history, in Vizenor's view, has subjected Native American culture forever to inauthenticity, made it an empty site that can be filled only by what he calls "absolute fakes,"[98] the simulacra of Native American identity produced by tribal nostalgia and hegemonic misconceptions. In the presence of these "fakes," the only available counter-strategy – the strategy on which *Heirs of Columbus* relies – is not the return to the *cloisonné* world of tribalism (that would be a fake in itself), but instead a position in the danger zone, by means of what Vizenor has called willed "cultural schizophrenia."[99] Schizophrenia of this kind is capable of negotiating the multiple and contradictory cultural identities which define Native American reality today without reducing them to a single point of view. As Vizenor once explained (outside the novel): "[t]he trick," is, he says, "to elude historicism, racial representations, and [yet] remain historical."[100]

IV.

This essay has been an attempt to discuss the cultural empowerment of emergent social formations inside the United States by looking at the spaces they imagine and create for themselves in fictional discourse. The three texts discussed in the previous section are particularly relevant for such an inquiry, since they are – all other differences aside – centrally concerned with a "counter-hegemonic cartography,"[101] the politics and poetics of space in a post-national context. This concern registers in their representations of subaltern spaces in such a way that the project of locating ethnic identity in(side) such spaces becomes a self-reflexive, contradictory and ultimately inconclusive process: *Jazz, Tripmaster Monkey* and *Heirs of Columbus* never inscribe their ethnic protagonists (nor, for that matter, themselves) firmly within the sanctuaries of their respective ethnic culture; instead they focus on critical encounters generated by overlapping or conflicting localizations, by "the simultaneous presence of multiple spatialities."[102] For this purpose the novels prefer spaces which are not "tightly territorialized" (Appadurai) but inflected by ethnic presence, the metropolis, the theater, the world of media simulations. The inconclusiveness of ethnic placements in such fluid spaces is also reflected in the trajectory of movements represented in the texts: these movements are never really "homeward bound" but instead lead to positions *in transit*, positions where the multiple determinations of a post-national topography make themselves felt. Borrowing Shelley Fisher Fishkin's terms, one could say that these texts "interrogate" whiteness but at the same time "complicate" their own ethnic terrains.[103]

These observations should not be construed as definition of a new trend in ethnic writing but, rather, as a cautionary proposition against too limited a view of its options. As my readings have indicated, we would unduly restrict the representational dynamics which subtends most ethnic fictions in the United States today if we only saw these texts as so many instances of writing ethnic enclosures, "always less than one nation and double."[104] My sample texts, on the contrary, refuse to be contained by the absoluteness of such a neat spatial counterpoint. Instead, they present subaltern spaces as locations-in-relation, in which different and often contradictory cultural affiliations and determinations co-exist and contend. I have sought to capture this uneasy co-existence with the term "danger zone."

What is ultimately at stake in these fictions is "culture's equation with location or place."[105] This equation has been fundamentally disrupted by the post-national processes of migrancy and dislocation which I have sketched at the beginning. Instead of offering geopietistic projections of a *cloisonné* ethnic world, the novels discussed above privilege scenarios of transition, marginality or in-betweenness. This representational shift involves a further shift in the relations which persons have with the spaces surrounding them, a change in emphasis from location to negotiation. Ethnic characters are no longer *in* a place but instead they must *make* one, in a way that Trinh Minh-ha alluded to when she suggested that the subaltern location functions as an "empty site" in which "the meaning of marginality remain[s] constantly in progress or in-the-making throughout the text."[106]

This "making" is indeed what the three novels keep focusing on, the relations in them between place and meaning remain thus deferred. Rather than representing a full-fledged ethnic location of difference, my sample texts inscribe a danger zone, exact (from their imagined characters as much as from their readers) efforts of mediation and coordination between self and space under the post-national conditions of deterritorialization and displacement.[107]

The self-reflexive position of these fictions in the danger zone expresses itself not only in terms of content but in the very narrative structure of the texts as well. As we have been arguing before, following Jameson, specific cultural problems find their expression in specific "forms and form problems."[108] In the novels under investigation here, the "formal" equivalent of the deferral of ethnic placement is a rejection or at least suspension, of narrative closure. Instead, we find a situational orientation pervading these texts, a concern with moments of transition, of identity crisis, of reorientation. These moments can be regarded as the narrative correlate of a re-configuration of the ethnic location of difference as inconclusive and open-ended. In this way, Morrison's, Kingston's and Vizenor's novels represent a move beyond the evocation of a cultural inside, by involving the ethnic location in a series of critical encounters and negotiations, turning it from a comfort zone into a danger zone, or from roots to routes.

Such a position in the danger zone is not only an option for fiction, it is also a place from which cultural criticism might speak. As Chicano critic Juan Bruce-Novoa argues, the position at the juncture of signifying systems is empowering:

> [W]e are the space (not the hyphen) between the two [Anglos and Latinos] the intercultural *nothingness* of that space. [. . .] We continually expand the space, pushing the two influences out and apart as we claim more area for our reality, while at the same time creating interlocking tensions that hold the two in relation.[109]

In a similar way, Salman Rushdie has recently positioned himself in the title of his collection *East, West*.[110] He says, "when I started thinking of calling the stories *East, West*, the most important part of the title was the comma. Because it seems to me that I am the comma – or at least that I live in the comma."[111] This in-between position is for Rushdie a necessary prerequisite for what he calls (elsewhere) "stereoscopic vision,"[112] a vision which refuses to be contained by the enclosures on both sides of the cultural divide.[113]

Our inquiry closes with a text that positions itself exactly in the danger zone between two cultures, Anglo and Chicano, and understands this positioning as a problem as well as a chance. In Gloria Anzaldúa's *Borderlands/La Frontera* we read:

> I am a border woman. I grew up between cultures. I have been straddling that Tejas-Mexican border, and others, all my life. It's not a comfortable place to live in, this place of contradictions. However, there have been compensations and certain joys. Living on borders and in margins, keeping intact one's shifting and multiple identity and integrity, is like trying to swim in a new element being a participant in the further evolution of mankind.[114]

Notes

1. Adrienne Rich, *Blood, Bread, and Poetry: Selected Prose 1979-1985* (New York: Norton, 1986) 212.

2. Michael Keith, and Steve Pile, "Introduction Part 1: The Politics of Place," *Place and the Politics of Identity*, ed. Michael Keith and Steve Pile (London: Routledge, 1993) 20.

3. The distinction goes back to Henri Lefebvre and his differentiation between "[r]epresentations of spaces" as "conceptualized space" and "[r]epresentational space" as "the space of 'inhabitants' [. . .], the dominated [space] [. . .]" (*The Production of Space*, trans. Donald Nicholson-Smith [Oxford: Blackwell, 1991] 38-9). Both are variously connected (116-7; 230-1). By reiterating Lefebvre's insistence on the functional interrelatedness of the two spaces, on the "[r]eference from one to the other, and back again" as part of social and cultural praxis (233), the present argument also registers dissent with Keith/Pile's deconstructive reading of the same relationship according to which the "spaces of representation subvert the representation of spaces so that the ground we stand on becomes a mongrel hybrid of spatialities; at once a metaphor and a speaking position, a place of certainty and a burden of humility [. . .]" (*Place and Politics* 23).

4. Paul Virilio, "Critical Space," *The Virilio Reader*, ed. James Der Derian (Oxford: Blackwell, 1998) 59.

5. Paul Gilroy, "Route Work: The Black Atlantic and the Politics of Exile," *The Post-Colonial Question: Common Skies, Divided Horizons*, ed. Iain Chambers and Linda Curti (London: Routledge, 1996) 23.

⁶ The argument concerning globalization and the de-territorialization of culture cannot be presented in all detail here. The brief outline given above is indebted to Paul Virilio's description of "the generalized incontinence of transfers and transmissions" ("Critical Space" 58); and especially to James Clifford, to his "attempts to trace old and new maps and histories of people in transit [. . .] human difference articulated in displacement, tangled cultural experiences, structures and possibilities of an increasingly connected but not homogenous world" (*Routes: Travel and Tanslation in the Late Twentieth Century* [Cambridge, MA: Harvard University Press, 1997] 2). For a non-totalizing view of globalization that registers the interplay of global and local forces cf. the collection *Global Visions: Beyond the New World Order*, ed. Jeremy Brecher et al. (Boston: South End Press, 1993).

⁷ Homi K. Bhabha, *The Location of Culture* (London: Routledge, 1994) 140, emphasis original.

⁸ Frantz Fanon, *The Wretched of the Earth*, trans. Constance Farrington, preface by Jean-Paul Sartre (Harmondsworth: Penguin, 1979) 200.

⁹ The idea of a functional interrelation between the culture and the politics of the emerging nation goes back to Frantz Fanon, especially his chapter on "The Pitfalls of National Consciousness" in *The Wretched of the Earth*. In a more contemporary context, the idea of a possible "collusion" between cultural practices and the creation of nations as "imaginary constructs that depend for their existence on an apparatus of cultural fictions" has been explored by Timothy Brennan in his *Salman Rushdie and the Third World: Myths of the Nation* (New York: St. Martin's Press, 1989) 1-31; 8.

¹⁰ Donald E. Pease, "National Identities, Postmodern Artefacts, and Postnational Narratives," *National Identities and Post-Americanist Narratives* (Durham: Duke University Press, 1994) 3.

¹¹ Ibid., 4.

¹² Pease turns this doubleness into a characteristic of the post-national in general: "Postnational forces understand every social category as the ongoing antagonism between internalized models and external forces. As such, they are productive of an internal divide (the contamination of the excluded/external), whereby the structures underwriting the stability of the national narrative can undergo transformations" ("National Identities" 5). "Minor" is here used in the sense suggested by Deleuze/Guattari, as designating not an essence but "the revolutionary conditions for every literature within the heart of [. . .] great (or established) literature" ("What Is a Minor Literature?" *Kafka: Toward a Minor Literature*, trans. Dana Polan [Minneapolis: University of Minnesota Press, 1986] 16-27; 18).

¹³ Bhabha, *Location* 164, emphasis original.

¹⁴ Lauren Berlant, *The Anatomy of National Fantasy: Hawthorne, Utopia, and Everyday Life* (Chicago: University of Chicago Press, 1991) 21.

¹⁵ Francis Grund, in his *The Americans in Their Moral, Social and Political Relations* (1837); quoted in John P. McWilliams, *Hawthorne, Melville, and the American Character: A Looking-Glass Business* (Cambridge: Cambridge University Press, 1984) 8. McWilliams' "Introduction" offers a useful overview regarding the development of US national

culture in interaction with a homogenous national as well as natural space. Brian Jarvis has shown how the development of early American national culture centered around "the promotion of a sense of national identity rooted in the land [. . .]" (*Postmodern Cartographies: The Geographical Imagination in Contemporary American Culture* [London: Pluto Press, 1998] 3). Donald Pease has argued that the United States were programmatically "Nature's Nation." Thus, "[t]he image repertory of the [19th century] US national community [. . .] [connects] an exceptional national subject (American Adam) with a representative national scene (Virgin Land) and an exceptional national motive (errand into the wilderness)" ("National Identities" 4).

16 Sacvan Bercovitch, "The Rites of Assent: Rhetoric, Ritual, and the Ideology of American Consensus," *The American Self: Myth, Ideology, and Popular Culture,* ed. Sam Girgus (Albuquerque: University of New Mexico Press, 1981) 20.

17 Bhabha, *Location*.

18 bell hooks, *Yearning: Race, Gender, and Cultural Politics* (London: Turnaround, 1991) 6.

19 On "the historical and cultural 'situatedness' of difference" see Peter McLaren, "White Terror and Oppositional Agency: Towards a Critical Multiculturalism," *Multiculturalism: A Critical Reader,* ed. David Theo Goldberg (Oxford: Blackwell, 1994) 52; an extended argument has also been made by Abdul Jan Mohamed and David Lloyd in their "Introduction: Towards a Theory of Minority Discourse: What Is To Be Done?" to their collection *The Nature and Context of Minority Discourse* (New York: Oxford University Press, 1990): "Becoming minor is not a question of essence [. . .] but a question of position: a subject-position that in the final analysis can be defined only in political terms – that is, in terms of the effects of economic exploitation, political disenfranchisement, social manipulation [. . .]" (9). For an elaborate analysis of a spatial politics which recognizes this situatedness cf. the collection *Place and the Politics of Identity,* ed. Keith/Pile, especially the editors' "Introduction Part 1: The Politics of Place" 1-21; also Clifford on the methodological implications of a "situated analysis [which] means to become aware, always belatedly, of limits, sedimented meanings, tendencies to gloss over differences" (*Routes* 11).

20 Barbara Harlow, *Resistance Literature* (New York: Methuen, 1987).

21 Veve Clark quoted in Abena Busia,"What is your Nation?," *Changing Our Own Words: Essays on Criticism, Theory, and Writing by Black Women,* ed. Cheryl A. Wall (New Brunswick: Rutgers University Press, 1989) 197.

22 *Memory, Narrative, and Identity: New Essays in Ethnic American Literatures,* ed. Amritjit Singh et al. (Boston: Northeastern University Press, 1994).

23 William Boelhower, "Ethnographic Politics: The Uses of Memory in Ethnic Fiction," *Memory and Cultural Politics: New Approaches to American Ethnic Literatures,* ed. Amritjit Singh et al. (Boston: Northeastern University Press, 1996) 35.

24 A theoretical argument concerning the "articulation [of space] as both a descriptive and a political practice" can be found in Lawrence Grossberg, "The Space of Culture, The Power of Space," *The Post-Colonial Question: Common Skies, Divided Horizons,* ed. Iain Chambers and Linda Curti (London: Routledge, 1996) 169; esp. 176-80. For a

25 Bhabha, *Location* 148.

26 Paul Christensen quoted in Wolfgang Karrer, "Nostalgia, Amnesia, and Grandmothers: The Uses of Memory in Albert Murray, Sabine Ulibarri, Paula Gunn Allen, and Alice Walker," *Memory, Narrative & Identity*, ed. Amritjit Singh et al. 128-44.

27 Stuart Hall quoted in "Introduction" to *Memory, Narrative & Identity*, ed. Amritjit Singh et al. 19.

28 For an overview of the creation of cultural locations in contemporary ethnic fiction see the "Introduction" to *Memory, Narrative & Identity*, ed. Amritjit Singh et al.; this essay also gives an overview about the structural options involved in such projects of spacing. For a theory of "ethnic semiosis" in contemporary ethnic fiction that relies on "a topological hermeneutics" as its basic operation cf. William Boelhower: Ethnic semiosis, he argues, "takes the territory of the United States and converts it into a memory theater [. . .]. In other words, the nation's corpus – its Chicagos, Detroits, and Los Angeleses – is examined not as history but as metahistory; not as the procedural landscape of political democracy but as the topology of a people's dwelling. It is at the topological level [. . .] that the exclusively temporal horizon of hermeneutics gives way to archeological operations of the local mind" ("Ethnographic Politics" 36, 38). Wolfgang Karrer has shown how the pattern of "flight from the ethnic community to return to it as well as the ambivalent relation to it [. . .] have become a central tradition in contemporary multiethnic writing. To go home again is the spatial equivalent of recall [. . .]" ("Nostalgia, Amnesia and Grandmothers" 135).

29 Toni Morrison, "The Site of Memory," *Inventing the Truth: The Art and Craft of Memoir*, ed. William Zinsser (Boston: Houghton Mifflin, 1998) 185-200.

30 Ibid., 192.

31 Ibid., 195.

32 Ibid. For an assessment of Morrison's oeuvre as "constitut[ing] a counter-hegemonic cartography of colour, one that charts key spaces within the geographical experience of African-Americans" and for a reading of Morrison's key novels in terms of "race and space" see Jarvis, *Postmodern Cartographies* 113-35; 113. Also Gurleen Grewal, "Memory and the Matrix of History: The Poetics of Loss and Recovery in Joy Kogawa's *Obasan* and Toni Morrison's *Beloved*," *Memory and Cultural Politics*, ed. Amritjit Singh et al. 140-74.

33 Leslie Marmon Silko, *Ceremony* (New York: Signet, 1977).

34 See her *Almanac of the Dead* (New York: Simon & Schuster, 1991).

35 Silko, *Ceremony* 258.

36 Pease, "National Identities."

37 Silko, *Ceremony* 258.

38 A reading of *Ceremony* that also traces the spatial contours of the novel is given by Edith Swann, "Laguna Symbolic Geography and Silko's *Ceremony*," *American Indian Quarterly* 12.3 (1988): 229-49; on the shifting relations in *Ceremony* between "exterior

landscapes" and "interior landscapes" cf. also Robert M. Nelson, "Place and Vision: The Function of Landscape in Ceremony," *Journal of the Southwest* 30 (1988): 281-316. My thanks to Marc Priewe who brought this essay to my attention.

39 Audre Lorde, *Zami: A New Spelling of My Name* (Watertown: Persephone Press, 1982).

40 Ibid., 13, emphasis original.

41 Ibid., 239.

42 A more detailed reading of *Zami* in terms of Lorde "creat[ing] a home, as well as a mythic place of origin, for herself" is offered by Jennifer Browdy de Hernandez, "The Plural Self: The Politicization of Memory and Form in Three American Ethnic Autobiographies," *Memory and Cultural Politics*, ed. Amritjit Singh et al. 43.

43 G. Thomas Couser, "Oppression and Repression: Personal and Collective Memory in Paule Marshall's *Praisesong for the Widow* and Leslie Marmon Silko's *Ceremony*," *Memory and Cultural Politics,* ed. Amritjit Singh et al. 117.

44 I owe this wordplay to Clifford's *Routes*; on numerous occasions in this book Clifford explores the relationship between the two, he shows how (in traditional cultures) "roots always precede routes" (3) and (in an argument more directly related to my own project) he analyzes diaspora discourse as a textual practice which "articulates, or bends together, both roots *and* routes to construct what Gilroy (1987) describes as alternate public spheres, forms of community consciousness and solidarity that maintain identifications outside the national time/space in order to live inside, with a difference" (251).

45 Frederic Jameson, *The Geopolitical Aesthetic: Cinema and Space in the World System* (Bloomington: Indiana University Press, 1992) 1.

46 Toni Morrison, *Song of Solomon* (New York: Knopf, 1977).

47 Sandra Cisneros, *The House on Mango Street* (1984; New York: Knopf, 1995) 132.

48 N. Scott Momaday, *The Way to Rainy Mountain* (Albuquerque: University of New Mexico Press, 1969) 83.

49 Boelhower, "Ethnographic Politics" 37.

50 Grossberg, "Space of Culture" 182.

51 Iain Chambers, "Signs of Silence, Lines of Listening," *The Post-Colonial Question,* ed. Chambers/Curti 47-62; 53.

52 Bhabha, *Location* 145-6.

53 This tendency towards carefully circumscribed counter-hegemonic spaces has been commented upon in both literary and cultural criticism; cf. Karrer, "Nostagia, Amnesia, and Grandmothers" 135-41; Keith/Pile, *Politics of Place* 6; the libidinal investment into such projections of a counter-hegemonic empty space waiting to be filled surfaces repeatedly in fiction; cf., e.g., Lorde, *Zami*: "But underneath it all as I was growing up, *home* was still a sweet place somewhere else which they had not managed to capture yet on paper, nor to throttle and bind up between the pages of a schoolbook" (14).

54 Gilroy, "Route Work" 22. A related critique of ethnic spaces as enclosures has been articulated by Guillermo Gómez-Peña: "This tendency to overstate difference, and the unwillingness to change or exchange, is a product of communities in turmoil who, as an antidote to present confusion, have chose to retreat to the fictional womb of their own separate histories" (*The New World Border: Prophecies, Poems and Loqueras for the End of the Century* [San Francisco: City Lights, 1996] 11). These "wombs" are once again characterized by "the localism of many common assumptions about culture" and especially in constructions of homogenous national cultures: "In these assumptions social existence is, or should be, centered in circumscribed places – like the gardens where the word 'culture' derived its European meanings" (Clifford, *Routes* 3).

55 Chambers, "Signs of Silence" 57-8.

56 Thus, e.g., Gloria Anzaldúa, a Chicana, argues: "I abhor some of my culture's ways, how it cripples women, como burras. [. . .] No, I do not buy all the myths of the tribe into which I was born" (*Borderlands/La Frontera: The New Mestiza* [San Fransisco: Spinster/Aunt Lunte, 1987] 78).

57 Trinh Minh-ha "The Undone Interval: Trinh T. Minh-ha in Conversation with Annamaria Morelli," *The Post-Colonial Question,* ed. Chambers/Curti 3-16; 9.

58 Jarvis, *Postmodern Cartographies* 116.

59 Such a construction of subaltern spaces would be "mimic[ing] the worst aspects of European thinking about self and community" (Gilroy, "Route Work" 25). Gilroy throughout is very critical of the processes by which "desparate theories of selfhood, kinship and community drawn from nineteenth-century sources [. . .] have begun to circulate and create a model of identity politics [. . .]," more especially "an imploded ethnicity [. . .] [in which s]ome of the terms of white supremacist thinking are modified, but important elements of its conceptual and tactical logics are retained and confirmed" (25); for a related critique of any "assertion of marginality as mere opposition to a locatable centre" cf. again Minh-ha, "Undone Interval" 10; and Jan Mohamad/Lloyd, *Nature and Context*: "[. . .] the nonidentity experienced by minorities [. . .] is the strongest reason that a rigorously criticial minority discourse [. . .] should not merely fall back on the oppositional affirmation of an essential ethnic or gender identity" (16).

60 Wole Soyinka, "This Past Must Address Its Present," Nobel Lecture, Swedish Academy, Stockholm, 8 Dec. 1986 <http://www.nobel.se/literature/laureates/1986/soyinka-lecture.html>.

61 For arguments made on behalf of the "emergence of an internal Third World" inside especially the metropolitan centers of the US cf. the arguments by Frederic Jameson "Modernism and Imperialism," *Nationalism, Colonialism, and Literature,* ed. Terry Eagleton et al. (Minneapolis: University of Minnesota Press, 1990) 51; as the Indian historian Gyan Prakash argues, "[t]he Third World, far from being confined to its assigned place, has penetrated the inner sanctum of the 'First World' in the process of being 'Third Worlded' – arousing, inciting and affiliating with the subordinated others in the First World [. . .]" (quoted by Bhabha, *Location* 247).

62 These relations (as Soyinka's argument has also made clear) must not be understood as simply conforming to binary subject-object models. With regard to the African American community, Gilroy argues for "mak[ing] the pluralising inner logic of the diaspora idea [the] starting point for theorising black identity, refusing its simple negation in return to the motherland or fatherland" ("Route Work" 21); cf. also the arguments presented by Minh-ha, "Undone Interval" 9; as well as by Vijay Mishra and B. Hodge, "What is Post(-)Colonialism?" (1991), quoted by Martina Michael, "Postcolonial Literatures: Use or Abuse of the Latest Post-Word," *Postkoloniale Literaturen: Peripherien oder neue Zentren? Gulliver* 33 (1993): 6-23; cf. also McLaren, "White Terror" 58; for the primacy of spatially configured social and cultural differences-in-relation cf. David Harvey, *Justice, Nature and the Geography of Difference* (Oxford: Blackwell, 1996) esp. 207-326.

63 Michel Foucault, "Of Other Spaces," *Diacritics* 16.1 (1986): 22-7; 27. As Foucault argues, these counter-sites have a critical potential directed at the given order of things. They "have the curious property of being in relation with all the other sites, but in such a way as to suspect, neutralize, or invert the set of relations that they happen to designate, mirror or reflect" ("Other Spaces" 24). Foucault's concept of the heterotopic has been widely adapted in analyses of the post-national topography; cf. José David Saldívar, *Border Matters: Remapping American Cultural Studies* (Berkeley: University of California Press, 1997) 13f.; also, in the context of the postcolonial metropolis, especially in the work of Edward Soja (most distinctly in his "Heterotopologies: A Remembrance of Other Spaces in the Citadel-LA," *Postmodern Cities and Spaces*, ed. Sophie Watson and Kathrine Gibson (Cambridge: Blackwell, 1995) 13-34; or Benjamin Genocchio, "Discourse, Discontinuity, Difference: The Question of Other Spaces," ibid., 35-46. Lefebvre also uses the term "heterotopia" without reference to Foucault to designate "mutally repellant spaces" (*Production of Space* 366; cf. 163, 294).

64 Foucault, "Other Spaces" 24.

65 Ibid., 27, my emphasis.

66 Arjun Appadurai, "Global Ethnoscapes: Notes and Queries for a Transnational Anthropology," *Recapturing Anthropology: Working in the Present,* ed. Richard G. Fox, (Santa Fe: School of American Research, 1991) 49.

67 Ibid., 33.

68 Ibid., 48; cf. 183.

69 Ibid.

70 Ibid., 183.

71 Ibid., 186 (emphasis added). Ethnoscapes, in Appadurai's understanding reflect and compensate for "the cultural dynamics of what is now called deterritorialization" since "the homeland is partly invented, existing only in the imagination of the deterritorialized groups" (ibid., 49; cf. 178). Thus, what is much more important in Appadurai's argument than the reality status of ethnoscapes is their ability of grounding experience in a representation of space that is by nature dialogic and that disturbs or decon-

structs, the neat pattern of dislocation and relocation that governs the spatial imaginary of return-to-roots narratives.

72 Ibid.

73 Ben Xu, "Memory and the Ethnic Self: Reading Amy Tan's *The Joy Luck Club*," *Memory, Narrative & Identity*, ed. Amritjit Singh et al. 261-77; 275.

74 Ibid., 265.

75 I am borrowing the term from Sandra Jackson and José Solís who define "comfort zones" as an ethnic space that is ideological, falsely suggesting the possibility of occupying a niche in the vast area of national culture. "The task before us," they argue, "is to force the parameters of those comfort zones outward, pushing for broader and more liberating constructs [. . .] not merely a recognition and acknowledgement of difference" (*Beyond Comfort Zones in Multiculturalism: Confronting the Politics of Privilege*, ed. Sandra Jackson and José Solís [Westport: Bergin & Garvey, 1995] 2). My interest in the term has been sparked by Jackson's and Solís' conceptual and analytical impetus to move beyond the comfort zones. However, my use in the present context is much more limited than theirs; for me comfort zone is primarily a conceptual shorthand for the result of a counter-hegemonic construction of space in which the interplay of de- and re-location is suspended in favor of spatial closure.

76 Janet Abu-Lughod, "Going Beyond Global Babble," *Culture, Globalization and the World-System: Contemporary Conditions for the Representation of Identity*, ed. Anthony D. King (Binghampton: SUNY Press, 1991) 131-7.

77 Toni Morrison, *Jazz* (New York: Signet, 1992) 3.

78 That this movement implies a turn towards a more interactional orientation of home spaces has been argued by Geoffrey Bennington: "At the centre, the nation narrates itself as *the* nation: at the borders, it must recognize that there are other nations [. . .]" ("Postal Politics and the Institution of the Nation," *Nation and Narration*, ed. Homi Bhabha [London: Routledge, 1990] 121, emphasis original).

79 Chambers, "Signs of Silence" 51, 53. At this point our argument ties in with a related discussion centered around the notion of a contact zone. The term "contact zone" has been introduced by Mary Louise Pratt to designate "the space of colonial encounters, the space in which peoples geographically and historically separated come into contact with each other and establish ongoing relations, usually involving conditions of coercion, radical inequality, and intractable conflict" (*Imperial Eyes: Travel Writing and Transculturation* [London: Routledge, 1992] 6). By speaking of contact, Pratt argues, she wants "to foreground the interactive, improvisational dimensions of colonial encounters so easily ignored or suppressed by diffusionist accounts of conquest and domination. A contact perspective emphasizes how subjects are constituted in and by their relations to each other. It treats the relations among colonizers and colonized, or travelers and 'travelees,' not in terms of separateness or apartheid, but in terms of copresence, interaction, interlocking understandings and practices, often within radically asymmetrical relations of power" (6-7). While similarly concerned with relations of interaction, the argument presented here – directed less at colonial than postcolonial or post-national encounters – will prefer the pair "danger zone" and "comfort zone." First, these terms allow for differentiation between various forms and intensities of contact; secondly, my argument positions itself, not so much at a neutral

"third space," "the *in-between* space" between cultures (Bhabha, *Location* 38), but instead highlights the problematic nature of the contact. In this way, I attempt to contextualize the spatial model which subtends most of ethnic writing today, viewing it from the outside, as it were, in order to determine less the extent of a contact space than the (often problematic) relations with other existing spatial configurations enacted in this location.

80   Grossberg, "Space of Culture" 177.

81   Toni Morrison, "City Limits, Village Values: Concepts of the Neighborhood in Black Fiction," *Literature and the Urban Experience: Essays on the City and Literature*, ed. Michael C. Jaye and Ann Chalmers Watts (Manchester: Manchester University Press, 1981) 35.

82   Morrison, *Jazz* 16. Further page references to the novel are given in parentheses.

83   Jarvis, *Postmodern Cartographies*, 133. Instead, as Jarvis emphasizes, Morrison "recognises the City as a space of disconnection between black people and their past" (133). Jarvis offers a reading of the novel in terms of race and space that differs from the one presented here; for him, "the urban present of the black community is shown to be haunted by the refrain of their shared rural past of miscegenation, violence and need" (135).

84   Cf. especially Roland Barthes, "Semiology and the Urban," (1970); rpt. in *The City and the Sign: An Introduction to Urban Semiotics*, ed. M. Gottdiener and Alexandros Ph. Lagolopoulos (New York: Columbia University Press, 1986) 87-98. The text above alludes to Barthes' suggestion that the city "speaks to its inhabitants [. . .] simply by living in it, by wandering though it [. . .]" (92); an interpretation of Morrison's novel along semiological lines is offered by Jocelyn Chadwick-Joshua, "The Rhetoric of the City in Toni Morrison's *Jazz*," in *The City in African-American Literature*, ed. Yoshinobu Hakutani and Robert Butler (Madison NJ: Fairleigh Dickinson University Press, 1995) 168-80.

85   Appadurai, "Global Ethnoscapes."

86   Maxine Hong Kingston, *Tripmaster Monkey: His Fake Book* (New York: Knopf, 1989). Page references to the novel are given in parentheses.

87   Walt Whitman, "Song of Myself," *Leaves of Grass*, ed. Sulley Bradley and Harold W. Blodgett (New York: Norton, 1973) 44.

88   At another point, Wittman expresses his conviction that "[t]he ethnos is degenerating" (255); on Kingston's exploration of the location "at significant remove from at least one of the home places" cf. Debra Shostak, "Maxine Hong Kingston's Fake Books," *Memory, Narrative & Identity*, ed. Amritjit Singh et al. 234; also 251.

89   Jean Baudrillard, "The Precession of Simulacra," (1983); rpt. in *Art After Modernism: Rethinking Representation,* ed. with an introduction by Brian Wallis, Foreword by Marcia Tuctio (Boston: Godline, 1984) 253.

90   Gerald Vizenor, *The Heirs of Columbus* (Hanover: Wesleyan University Press, 1991).

91   For instance in Stephen Marlowe's *The Memoirs of Christopher Columbus* (New York: Scribner's, 1987), a novel written from a non-Native American perspective; or especially in Michael Dorris and Louise Erdrich's *The Crown of Columbus* (New York:

Harper Collins, 1991). Cf. Helmbrecht Breinig, "(Hi)storytelling as Deconstruction and Seduction: The Columbus Novels of Stephen Marlowe and Michael Dorris/Louise Erdrich," *Historiographic Metafiction in Modern American and Canadian Literature*, ed. Bernd Engler and Kurt Müller (Paderborn: Schöningh, 1994) 325-46.

[92] On this encounter perspective cf. also Vizenor's description of crossbloods as "transitive contradancer[s] between communal tribal cultures and those material and urban pretensions that counter conservative traditions" (*Interior Landscapes: Autobiographical Myths and Metaphors* [Minneapolis: University of Minnesota Press, 1990] 4). On the crossbloods "act[ing] between two worlds," see the argument in Christoph Irmscher, "Crossblood Columbus: Gerald Vizenor's Narrative 'Discoveries,'" *Amerikastudien/American Studies* 40.1 (1995): 83-98; 88.

[93] Gerald Vizenor, *Crossbloods: Bone Counts, Bingo and Other Reports* (Minneapolis: University of Minnesota Press, 1990) vii.

[94] Ibid., 225.

[95] Vizenor, *Heirs* 45, 61. Further page references to the novel are given in parentheses.

[96] On Vizenor's rejection of "any view of traditional Indian cultures as fundamentally centred and fixed" cf. David Murray, "Crossblood Strategies in the Writings of Gerald Vizenor," *The Yearbook of English Studies* 24 (1994): 213-27; 226.

[97] In both his fictional and his critical writings Vizenor consistently argues against holistic notions of Native American culture or identity. "The American Indian Movement" Vizenor argues, "was a radical urban organization whose members tried from time to time to return to the reservation as warrior heroes" (Murray, "Strategies" 222). These notions are for him little more than simulations: "Tribal peoples have in this sense been invented as 'absolute fakes' in social science models, cinema and popular media" (Vizenor, *Crossbloods* 55); on the novel's withholding the possibility of a return to authenticity cf. Irmscher, "Crossblood Columbus" 96-7.

[98] Murray, "Strategies" 215.

[99] Vizenor, *Crossbloods* 223.

[100] Quoted in Murray, "Strategies" 227.

[101] Jarvis, *Postmodern Cartographies* 113.

[102] Keith/Pile, "Introduction Part 1" 19.

[103] Shelley Fisher Fishkin, "Interrogating 'Whiteness,' Complicating 'Blackness': Remapping American Culture," *American Quarterly* 47.3 (1995): 428-66; 429, 447.

[104] Bhabha, *Location* 168.

[105] Grossberg, "Space of Culture" 169. "On the "crisis of territorial citizenship, of localization" cf. Virilio, "Critical Space" 60; for a critique of the "fetishisation of the local [. . .] the identification of the local and agency [. . .]" in postcolonial discourse cf. Grossberg, "Space of Culture" 176.

[106] Minh-ha, "Undone Interval" 9.

[107] Bhabha has repeatedly emphasized this dislodgement of meaning from its traditional (national) location and has – interestingly enough in the context of literary analysis – identified "the conflictual articulation of meaning and place [. . .]" as characteristic of post-national formations (*Location* 60); in an argument about migrancy as enabling condition of postcolonial writing Bernd-Peter Lange has argued that "[i]n this centrifugal movement geographical mobility was never quite synchronised with cultural affiliations" ("Dislocations: Migrancy in Nabokov and Rushdie," *Anglia* 117.3 (1999): 395-411; 399). Clifford suggests that contemporary interculturality should be reflected methologically in "[c]ontact approaches" which proceed from the assumption that "sociocultural wholes [are not] subsequently brought into relationship, but rather systems already constituted relationally, entering new relations through historical processes of displacement" (*Routes* 7).

[108] Jameson, *Aesthetic* 1.

[109] Juan Bruce-Novoa, *RetroSpace: Collected Essays on Chicano Literature, Theory, and History* (Houston: Arte Público, 1990) 98, emphasis original.

[110] Salman Rushdie quoted in *Salman Rushdie*, D.C.R.A. Goonetilleke (London: Macmillan Press, 1998) 131.

[111] Salman Rushdie, *Imaginary Homelands* (London: Granta, 1992) 131.

[112] Ibid., 19.

[113] This may also be one of the reasons why there has been a renewed interest in cultural hybrids from the past such as Canadian Métis or the Mestizo/a in Latin American cultures. In a wider political context, the location in the danger zone must be understood not only as enabling but also as cautionary and defensive, because the ideal of a pure ethnic culture might carry with it sinister implications. Homi Bhabha has recently reminded us "that the very idea of a pure, 'ethnically cleansed' national identity can only be achieved through death, literal and figurative" (*Location* 5).

[114] Anzaldúa, *Borderlands* 22.

Interimage Simulations:
Fugitive Poses of Native American Indians

Gerald Vizenor

The ethnographic discoveries and translations of native cultures are *interimage* simulations, the unbidden, ascribed names and fugitive poses of dominance; not the tricky stories of natural reason, the ironies of tragic wisdom, or survivance.

Anterior simulations of the other are cited in the generative *interimages* of the "discovered" *indian,* and without a substantive reference; one simulation becomes the specious evidence of another. Simulations are not mimicry, imitations, or reduplications, not even ironies or parodies, but rather, "substituting signs of the real for the real itself," wrote Jean Baudrillard in *Simulations.* "For ethnology to live, its object must die."[1]

Photographic and iconic enactments of the other are seen without a native presence or referent: *interimage* simulations are causal reason and, in many translations, serve as ethnographic evidence. One situation and circumstantial simulation subserves another in the course of *interimage* portraiture.

The dominance of simulations may be overturned by the pleasures of virtual images more readily than the pretensions of substantive, "authentic" evidence. For instance, the technologies of virtual reality create, by choice and interaction, situations that are their own essence. The fugitive poses in ethnographic photographs are the ransom of *interimage* simulations, but not in the interactive world of electronic contrivance and virtual realities. Such motion creates a virtual presence out of the burdens of manifest manners and dominance.

The recent digital manipulations of photographic images, however, are comparable to the pretense of *interimage* simulations. Computer "software can generate completely synthetic photorealistic pictures," wrote William Mitchell in *Scientific American.* "Unlike drawings and paintings, which we regard as inherently trustworthy products of human intention, these fakes can easily trick us into false beliefs."[2]

Forrest Gump, for instance, is *seen* in the cinematic presence of three presidents at the White House. John Kennedy is *heard* in a conversation on screen with the artless hero in the film of the same name. This is interactive entertainment, not *interimage* simulation. Industrial Light and Magic created the scenes by the digital manipulations of archival newsreel footage.[3]

"Virtual reality is older than sin," wrote Hillel Schwartz in *The Culture of the Copy*. "It is the hallucination of heaven, the peyote vision, the dionysiac stupor. It is the play, the novel, the film, the radio mystery, the panorama, the pastoral symphony, the soap opera, any system devised for losing oneselves in another world."[4]

Many natives once endured in the visionary; in a world of tricky creation, totemic associations, imagic moments of survivance, and for some, chancy shamanic journeys. Clearly, natives were better lost in the virtual realities of another world than abated by the ethnographic simulations of the social sciences.

Photographs are *poselocked*, still to be sure, but not "totally passive." Elizabeth Edwards pointed out in the introduction to *Anthropology and Photography* that photographs "suggest meaning through the way in which they are structured, for representational form makes an image accessible and comprehensible to the mind, informing and informed by a whole hidden corpus of knowledge that is called on through the signifiers in the image."[5] The fugitive poses of natives, and latent *interimage* simulations, serve the reductive evidence and the "hidden corpus" of dominance.

"Jean Baudrillard has suggested that simulation is the ultimate telos of the postmodern esthetic," wrote Eric Gans in *Originary Thinking*. Gans touched on the notion that the production of simulations are esthetic representations of scarce realities. "Here 'form' has ideally no concrete expression at all; the perfect simulation is indistinguishable from the original. Presumably we know it to be a simulation only because we have paid to experience it [. . .]. The esthetic of the age of simulation would seek to create a utopia of plenty not merely in material but in interactive terms, as though human beings were finally able to forget the deferred violence of the originary event."[6]

Baudrillard observed that "representation tries to absorb simulation by interpreting it as false representation," and that "simulation envelops the whole edifice of representation as itself a simulacrum." He named three "successive phases of the image." The first is the "reflection of a basic reality," the second "masks and perverts a basic reality," the third "masks the *absence* of a basic reality," and the last "bears no relation to any reality," the image is "its own pure simulacrum." He noted that in the "first case, the image is a *good* appearance: the representation is of the order of sacrament. In the second, it is an *evil* appearance: of the order of malefic." The third "*plays at being* an appearance: it is of the order of sorcery. In the fourth, it is no longer in the order of appearances at all, but of simulation."[7]

Native origin stories are the tricky realities of visionary transmotion, otherwise the elusive motility of "a basic reality." Native ceremonies, and imagic moments, create a sense of presence, and, at the same time, mask an absence: the rites of presence are ecstatic unions of time and place, and the absence, virtual masks of sorcery. Alas, the images of *indians* are simulations.

"Culture is now dominated by simulations, Baudrillard contends, objects and discourses that have no firm origin, no referent, no ground or foundation," observed Mark Poster. "In a commodity the relation of word, image or meaning and referent is broken and restructured so that its force is directed, not to the referent of use, value or utility, but to desire."[8]

Ethnographic *interimages* are the narrative closures of the *seen* over the heard, the simulation of icons over chance, and the desire of the scriptural over the ironies of oral narratives. "Writing puts a distance between man and his verbal acts," wrote Jack Goody in *The Domestication of the Savage Mind*. Writing, "and more especially alphabetic literacy, made it possible to scrutinise discourse in a different way by giving oral communication a semi-permanent form; this scrutiny favoured the increase in scope of critical activity, and hence of rationality, scepticism, and logic to resurrect memories of those questionable dichotomies."[9]

Theodore de Bry, Russell Means, and Joan Halifax, for instance, are three nonce overtures to *interimages* in the common course on native cultures. The artist, the radical actor, and the humane author, have in common at least the narrative closures of circumstantial simulations.

Theodore de Bry never encountered more than a gruesome simulation of the native people he depicted in his engravings. Published in the late sixteenth century his pictures have been used as ethnographic portraiture. He created *interimage* savages for an international audience and heightened previous simulations. "Europeans had always known that cannibals and other monstrous races inhabited the fringes of the known and *ipso facto* civilized world," wrote Anthony Grafton in *New Worlds, Ancient Texts*. "European publishers, illustrators, writers of firsthand accounts, and compilers of compendiums made cannibalistic images virtually emblematic of America."[10]

Theodore de Bry created new engravings for the republication of the *True History of His Captivity* by Hans Staden, which first appeared in Germany in 1557. "The account contains much ethnographic detail, including a complete and horrifying account of the cannibalistic acts he witnessed." Bry's "much more elaborate versions" and "masterly reworking" of the original crude woodblock prints in his 1592 edition of *America* "hightens the horrors of scenes in which Staden himself appears, often in an attitude of prayer."[11]

Bry's other engraved *interimage* simulations of the tribes were based on the watercolors by John White who, in turn, used "images of Virginia Indians as the models for his depiction of the ancient Picts and Britons." De Bry depicted a "female warrior of the ancient Picts" in *America*. Grafton pointed out that in the introduction of this first volume, "de Bry writes that he was directed to append these illustrations based on a 'certain old English history' to those of the Virginians 'to demonstrate that the inhabitants of Britain had been no less forest dwellers than these Virginians.'"[12]

Grafton wrote that the "tendency of Europeans to equate the alleged barbarism of the American populations they encountered with the cultural life of their own ancestors would eventually lead some people to believe that human societies, rather than inevitably deteriorating, progressed through increasingly sophisticated stages of civilization."[13]

At the same time that colonialism dominated much of the world, and native communities were driven onto exclaves, the new technologies of photography captured the other in the structural representations of savagism and civilization. The surveillance of colonialism and desires of objectivism were the manifest manners of anthropology and the new social sciences. "In encountering countries that were being transformed through the impact of social change, the photographer paradoxically chose to focus on unchanging representations of peoples and cultures," wrote Iskander Mydin in *Anthropology and Photography*. "For it was the 'exotic,' the culturally different, which fascinated, in both scientific and popular terms." Christopher Pinney pointed out in the same book that "photography appears as the final culmination of a Western quest for visibility and scrutiny. It stands at the technological, semiotic and perceptual apex of 'vision,' which itself serves as the emulative metaphor for all other ways of knowing."[14]

Russell Means posed in photographs with the new *interimage* warriors of the American Indian Movement during the occupation of Wounded Knee in South Dakota. A decade later, he landed in motion pictures and a laudable postindian *interimage* simulation, a studio production of a silk screen portrait by Andy Warhol. The fugitive poses of the *postindian*, the poses that come after the discoveries and inventions of the *indian* and the portraiture of dominance, are the simulations of survivance that undermine ethnographic evidence and manifest manners.[15]

"How about the *American Indian* series?" asked Patrick Smith in *Warhol: Conversations about the Artist*. "Was that any particular Indian?"

"Yeah. That was Russell Means," said Ronnie Cultrone who was, at the time, a studio production assistant to Andy Warhol. "He was involved with the Wounded Knee Massacre, which I don't really know too much about, to tell you the truth. But I think he's still in court. I don't know. Something like that."[16]

Andy Warhol pictured the narrative closures of the obvious, and the most noticeable simulations of the *indian*. Indeed, his studio production of Russell Means is an artistic, not ethnographic, *interimage* simulation in several obscure dimensions: the absence of the other at a *massacre*, the pasticcio warrior, and the *postindian* poses of the American Indian Movement.

Means has demonstrated notable ambitions as a speechmaker and radical politician. He was a candidate for the presidency of the Oglala Sioux Tribal Council in South Dakota and later he aspired, with Larry Flynt, the hustler publisher of *Hustler*, to become the presidential executives of the United States. Means lost both elections, but his desires to bear uncommon simulations were heartened as Chingachgook in the film *The Last of the Mohicans*.

"When we sever ourselves from society in a rite of change, there is an invisible door that we pass through that has no words on the other side," wrote Joan Halifax in *The Fruitful Darkness*. "I believe it is through stillness and silence that the door opens. Inside the secret room, we weave the threads of understanding into the cloth of culture."[17]

Halifax praises an aesthetic metashamanism, a paradise that would be heard in silence and would be woven into the "cloth of culture." Once more native cultures are burdened with silence and the simulations of a lonesome civilization; the romantic *interimages* in the literature of dominance. "Tribal peoples are natural experts in interspecies communication," she wrote. "Many times I have found myself sitting with an elder who speaks for hours in a language totally unfamiliar to me, and yet the pictures come, and the energy of Presence holds the time together like a well-woven blanket."[18] The burdens of translation from oral stories to the scriptural, the uncertainties of nature, and the cast of the sacred, are not heard in these simulations of the passive presence of the other. Pacific silence is a simulation of dominance.

Thich Nhat Hanh "invited people to put photos of their deceased relatives in a book placed on the altar," wrote Halifax about her Buddhist teacher in Plum Village, France. "Practicing Buddhism is about discovering ourselves to be in a great flowing river of continuities [. . .]. It was in Plum Village that I began to question our relationship to the dead. I wondered if we can see beyond personal histories of loss and grief to an autobiography that includes the loss of forests and rivers."[19] The *interimage* simulations and pictures of the native dead have been on the altar of dominance for several centuries.

The notion that a photograph is worth a thousand words is untrue in any language. Narratives create a sense of presence, but even stories can be simulations and separations when they serve the manners of unbidden dominance. Photographs are specious representations, the treacheries of racialism, neither cultural evidence nor the shadows of lost traditions.

Photographs were the new conceptions and simulations of realities, a common choice by the end of the nineteenth century. Painting and other forms of representation had been the foundations of visual consciousness, but the camera captured motion. The portraiture of natives became a transposed desire of *interimage* dominance. "Photographic information made people more aware of speed and time," wrote Donald Lowe in *History of Bourgeois Perception*. "Such perceptual interpretation would have been incomprehensible to people from other cultures. They would have had to acquire the bourgeois perceptual emphasis on visual information in discontinuous, mechanical time, before they could have translated static traces into motion."[20]

Moreover, "whatever it grants to vision and whatever its manner, a photograph is always invisible: it is not it that we see," wrote Roland Barthes in *Camera Lucida*. The photograph is the "advent of myself as other: a cunning dissociation of consciousness from identity." He noted that "photography transformed subject into object, and even, one might say, into museum object."[21]

Native American Indians bear their memories, sense of presence, and chance of solace in narratives not cameras. Natives posed in silence at the obscure borders of the camera: fugitive poses that were secured as ethnographic evidence and mounted later in museums. The silence could have been resistance at the altar of simulations. Fugitive poses are not without some humor, but when photographic representations became the evidence of a vanishing race, irony was lost to the assurance of dominance.

Could the bourgeois sanctions of *interimage* simulations be based on the cultural nostalgia of representation and dominance? Indeed, the possession of a native pose is a romantic desire to maintain representations. The "wonder and illusion of representation is different from the wonder and illusions of reality. In this respect representation is exactly the opposite of what it has always been supposed to be. Representation is miraculous because it deceives us into thinking it is realist, but it is only miraculous because it is something other than what it represents," wrote David Freedberg in *The Power of Images*.[22]

"The photographic semblance of eternal, universal Truth and innocent, uncomplicated pleasure is what always potentially links the medium to institutional power; it seems to reproduce so easily those grand narratives of our culture," wrote Linda Hutcheon in *The Politics of Postmodernism*.[23]

What can we *see* in the photographic representations of the racial other that is not dominance? Portraiture as evidence, or even *postindian* pasticci, must be more than the eternal silence of a fugitive pose: there, in the stare of the shadows, is an elusive native presence. The true stories of pictures are in the eyes, not in the costumes or simulations of culture; the eyes are the tacit presence, the costumes are the racial enactments of the other. Clothes, masks, and decorations are changeable, and borrowed clothes are prosaic *interimage* simulations, neither cultural codes nor representations of conversion stories. The eyes that meet in the aperture are an obscure assurance of narratives and an ironic native presence.

"What is the content of the photographic message? What does the photograph transmit?" asked Roland Barthes in *Image – Music – Text*. "Certainly the image is not the reality but at least it is its perfect *analogon* and it is exactly this analogical perfection which, to common sense, defines the photograph. Thus can be seen the special status of the photographic image: it is a message *without a code*."[24]

What could the absence of a code that has a message of racialism and dominance mean in portraiture? The destinies of the nation are burdened with racial *interimage* simulations and the captious warrants of civilization; at the same time, there is incontrovertible evidence of the actual removal and termination of real native communities. The camera became a new weapon in the representations of manifest manners. The fugitives of dominance learned how to pose in silence as an act of survivance.

John Tagg pointed out in *The Burden of Representation* that the camera has the power of surveillance and representation. "Like the state, the camera is never neutral. The representations it produces are highly coded, and the power it wields is never its own."[25]

Ethnographic photographs, besides the simultaneous cuts of time and motion, are the manners and counts of surveillance, the causal simulations of dominance. Those captured in the eternal pose of the other, are the fugitives of desire and dominance.

"The systematic study of societies different from one's own has been undertaken only within the Western tradition," wrote Eric Gans. "But this quest for diversity is also, despite itself, a reduction of diversity. The fascination with the ethnological Other only hastens the revelation that the Other is just more of the Same."[26]

Natives are the *interimage* fugitives of the camera; the decorated simulations, captured and compared, are the public evidence of dominance, not the private metaphors of survivance, courage, or the ironic stories of an uncertain native nature.

"When we are afraid, we shoot. But when we are nostalgic, we take pictures," wrote Susan Sontag in *On Photography*. "Still, there is something predatory in the act of taking a picture. To photograph people is to violate them, by seeing them as they never see themselves, by having knowledge of them they can never have; it turns people into objects that can be symbolically possessed."[27]

The pictures of the native other, the wounded fugitives of the camera, are not the same as those nostalgic photographs of homesteaders and their families in a new nation. The manifest camera created *interimage* fragments of fugitive poses that separated native people from their communities and ancestral land; the simulations of the other turned the real into the unreal with no obvious presence in time or nature. For these reasons, and more, the native other in photographs should be seen in the shadows of the eyes, an invitation to underived narratives rather than public representations and closure.

Native American Indians have been eye to eye with occidental predation and the ironies of civilization for more than five centuries. The same nations that celebrated political and religious liberties embraced racialism, objectivism, and master evidence over the humor of creation, natural reason, and the tragic wisdom of native families.

The eyes of the fugitives in photographs are the sources of stories, the traces of native survivance; all the rest is ascribed evidence, the representations of dominance. The eyes have never been procured in colonial poses, never contrived as cultural evidence to serve the tropes to institutional power.

The eyes are the narrative presence of natives, and the poses are the simulations of the other, the unreal representations of the other as causal evidence of *indianness*: the state, conditions, and instance of simulations that take over the real; at the same time, even romantic simulations are overcome by the wicked closure of savagism and civilization.

Closure is another name for the nescient representations of the other, and in this sense, the extreme closure of the *indian* in photographs. "Representation is what determines itself by its own limit. It is the delimitation for a subject, and by this subject, of what 'in itself' would be neither represented nor representable," wrote Jean-Luc Nancy in *The Birth to Presence*. "But the irrepresentable, pure presence and pure absence, is also an effect of representation."[28]

The eyes are the underived narratives not the ruins of native bodies. "Photographs in themselves do not narrate. Photographs preserve instant appearances," wrote John Berger in *About Looking*. "No painting or drawing, however naturalist, *belongs* to its subject in the way that a photograph does."[29] The eyes in a photograph are the secret mirrors of a private presence, not the closure of public representations; indeed, the eyes hold the obscure presence of the photographer on the other side of the aperture. The instances of the eyes in the aperture are continuous narratives that counter the closure of discoveries and cultural evidence in photographs.

Jean-Luc Nancy argued that the "body first was thought *from the inside*, as buried darkness into which light only penetrates in the form of reflections, and reality only in the form of shadows." Literature mimes bodies, and bodies are shadows, and shadows are the wounds of representation in photographs. "The body is but a wound," he wrote in *The Birth to Presence*.[30]

The eyes are the secret stories of wounded bodies, and the poses are the absence of the other, an ironic exposure because the representation of bodies as cultural evidence is the certain death of the other, death by photographic exposure.

"Whatever it grants to vision and whatever its manner, a photograph is always invisible: it is not it that we see," wrote Roland Barthes in *Camera Lucida*. The eyes, in this sense, are the presence we see in photographs. "Every photograph is a certificate of presence. This certificate is the new embarrassment which its invention has introduced into the family of images."[31]

Quanah Parker, for instance, is pictured in both native clothes and in a morning coat with an umbrella, pocket watch chain and derby. In one photograph he is supported by a rustic wall, in the other by a classical stucco simulation. He is posed near the same ornate column in both photographs. These could be fashion pictures of a native fugitive; indeed the obscurities of modes and costumes could be a much better interpretation of native histories than the rush to cultural evidence.

The costumes in photographs are not the same as either real clothes, ceremonial vestments, or the languages of clothes and fashions, because the stories of each appearance are never the same as the simulations of *indianness*. Costumes are the seasons, the fashions and measures of time; the species of costumes in pictures are not the monotheistic closure of creations.

Parker was Comanche, a wise crossblood leader at the turn of the last century who defended the use of peyote as a religious freedom. The narratives of his religious inspiration, his crossblood uncertainties, are not obvious in either of the photographs. His hair is braided in both pictures but the poses seem to be the causal representations of then and now, tradition and transition, or variations on the nostalgic themes of savagism or civilization. His eyes, not the costumes, are the narratives, his presence in the picture; his eyes are the sources of imagination, not the mere notice of an umbrella, a derby, or bound braids. His eyes are the presence of the pictures, the stories of resistance, and traces of native survivance. His eyes dare the very closure of his own fugitive poses.

Quanah Parker was an inspiration to the native people of the plains. "The great warrior established his bravery when he and a group of Comanches refused to accept the dictates of the Treaty of Medicine Lodge and battled to the end at Adobe Wells in Texas in 1874," wrote Rennard Strickland in *The Indians of Oklahoma*. "Parker then led his people down the new road, became a famous native judge, and as a member in the Native American Church was a widely identified peyote figure. While willing to adjust to farming and the new economic ways, Parker continued to practice the old Comanche family way of having a number of wives. Ironically, while Parker remains to the present a controversial figure in his own tribe, the Parker pattern of selective adaptation and resistance became the one Oklahoma's Indians generally followed."[32]

The decorative feathers, beads, leathers, woven costumes, silver, turquoise, bone, and other native representations have turned humans into the mere objects that bear material culture in photographs. Moreover, peace pipes, medals, trade axes, bows and arrows, rifles, and other weapons, are the obscure simulations of *indianness*. The native other is seldom pictured with families, children, or in situations of humor, chance, or at work. Most photographers of natives focused on the fugitive warrior pose and decorative costumes as traditional, the occidental simulations of the *indian*; such closures of presence would be mimicked several generations later by *postindian* leaders as the traditional sources of radical identities. *Postindian* "traditions" are the ironic *interimage* simulations in the ruins of representations. The imitations of the fugitive poses are the double closures of presence, an ironic separation with no wisdom or sense of the real; the fugitive remains are the perpetual victims of dominance.

Edward Curtis, for instance, one of the most dedicated pictorial photographers of *indians*, altered some of his photographs to preserve the fugitive poses of native traditions. Some of these poses have become the evidence of traditions in the new simulations of urban *indianness* and *postindian* identities.[33]

Curtis removed umbrellas, suspenders, the tracks of civilization, and any traces of written languages. This was unfortunate because at the turn of the last century thousands of native scholars had studied at federal and mission schools and were teachers on the same federal exclaves that photographers visited with their costumes and cameras. Curtis was the best of the portrait photographers, to be sure; nevertheless, his portraits enhanced the image of the noble savage as the antithesis of civilization. He visited hundreds of native communities and processed more than forty thousand pictures that simulated *indians* in fugitive poses. Alas, his dedication proved that ethnographic photography is an oxymoron. The last aversions, however, are overturned with the evidence of new *interimage* simulations.

Native American Indians were simulated in portraiture generations before the invention of photography. George Catlin, Karl Bodmer, Charles Bird King, and others, have been praised for their exotic and ethnographic portraits of the tribes. King recorded personal names with most of his portraits, but the ethnic noses, hands, and costumes were homogenous.[34] Other painters created innominate ethnographic simulations. The native persons in most portraits and photographs became mere ethnographic simulations, silenced without names or narratives; the pictures were the coincidence of discoveries in the cause of dominance.

Richard Brilliant pointed out in *Portraiture* that the notions of ethnographic portraits "seems to cause some critical difficulty in assessing their worth as portraits because the subjects are so often ignored as subjects of portraiture or they are strongly subordinated to other agendas of representation." The other is the simulation of ethnographic portraiture. "Of course, portrait artists working in their own culture rarely think like ethnographers, nor is it customary to apply anthropological techniques to the portraits of those with whom one shares a common culture."[35] Ethnographic portraiture is an oxymoron of dominance.

"The photograph both loots and preserves, denounces and consecrates. Photography expresses the American impatience with reality," Sontag argued in *On Photography*. "After the opening of the West in 1869 by the completion of the transcontinental railroad came the colonization through photography. The case of the American Indians is the most brutal." Tourists invaded the privacy of the tribes, "photographing holy objects and the sacred dances and places, if necessary paying the Indians to pose and getting them to revise their ceremonies to provide more photogenic material."[36]

The public at the time seemed to be more interested in the exotic warriors who had fought the soldiers than in the service of native historians, artists, and medical doctors. Many of the first photographers learned their craft during the Civil War and at the end of the war were hired by government surveys, the military, and railroads; their pictures of the plains tribes, the Sioux and Comanche in particular, "helped create the image of an Indian in a long headdress, made so familiar later by Hollywood films," wrote Dorothy and Thomas Hoobler in *Photographing the Frontier*. "Studio photographers went so far as to keep on hand what was regarded as 'typical' Indian dress to supply to Indians who might otherwise come to be photographed in nondescript, more practical attire."[37]

What might have been the watchwords of the entrepreneurs on the other side of the camera? Hundreds of photographers created simulations that would menace the tribes for more than a century, but the men armed with cameras were seldom burdened in native communities. The natives were the observers; the men with cameras and notions of surveillance were the agents of dominance.

How were the native observers in the aperture to know that the pictures of them would be obtained by surveillance, possessed as cultural evidence, sold as postcards, and then established in new museums of desire and dominance as the representations of native traditions? Only mythic ironies and some incredible watchword could touch the obvious contradictions, the occidental obsession to render the natives unreal in their own sense of time and place.

How would these photographers of *indians* explain the distinctions between public and private simulations of the other? Clearly there are more serious troubles to consider, but remember the eyes, and the stories that the loss of privacy is the loss of freedom. Photographers abused the native sense of privacy, and then either sold or distributed the simulations to various agencies. How should we now respond to the photographs that violated the privacy of the subjects? Cover the eyes?

Today, is aestheticism enough to absolve the heirs and curators of cultural dominance? Must the underived native be celebrated in a museum to be real? Digital manipulations of photographs could overturn the fugitive pose, and create an aesthetics of desire and ironic surveillance. Virtual realities are interactive entertainment, new situational observations and narratives, but the noble savages of the past are now the romantic victims of consumer cultures, and once again, without irony. Nonetheless, the eyes of natives are a shadow presence, and, on the other side of the aperture, the virtual eyes of the photographer are caught forever in the same ironic stories of the pictures.

"Privacy is usually considered a moral interest of paramount importance. Its loss provokes talk of violation, harm, and loss of agency," wrote Julie Inness in *Privacy, Intimacy, and Isolation*. "Privacy is defined as a variety of freedom, a freedom that functions by granting the individual control over the division between the public and the private with respect to certain aspects of life."[38] Native privacy and freedom were seldom considered in the simulations of the other; the representations of natives in photographs were the sudden closure of the rights and liberties to privacy. The pictures of nude native women on postcards, for instance, are ironic teases in a nation that associated nature, and the natural body with savagism, a monotheistic separation of sex and culture.

Those who discover the other in pictures, the simulations of the *indian* in the absence of the real, have denied their own presence in the histories of representations; moreover, natives must forever bear these unbidden, treacherous documents of dominance. Otherwise, the curious other would be a presence on either side of the aperture, an aesthetic closure of dominance.

"The only thing left for me to do is to find a refuge in the *other* and to assemble – out of the *other*," wrote Mikhail Bakhtin in *Art and Answerability*, "the scattered pieces of my own givenness, in order to produce from them a parasitically consummated unity in the *other's* soul using the *other's* resources. Thus, the spirit breaks up the soul from within myself."[39]

The most obvious search for the other is in the simulations of the *indian*; the eyes are stories in the same aperture, and the closures of representation are the evidence of the other. The pictures of natives are haunted by the absence of the photographer in the eyes of the other; natives, by their virtual gaze, are ironic representations of the photographer. "The *I* hides in the other and in others, it wants to be only an other for others, to enter completely into the world of others as an other, and to cast from itself the burden of being the only *I* (*I-for-myself*) in the world," wrote Bakhtin in *Speech Genres and Other Late Essays*.[40]

Native American Indians have practiced medicine, composed music and poetic narratives, won national elections, and traveled around the world before the turn of the century, but their experiences were discovered as the other, the antithesis of civilization in photographs and motion pictures. The simulations of the other in the cinema, in fact, continue to be an established bourgeois source of notions about *indians*; in other words, *interimage* simulations, the absence of the real, have become the popular cultural evidence of the *indian*, the ersatz *indian* over the actual presence of natives.

"More than any other medium, photography is able to express the values of the dominant social class and to interpret events from that class's point of view, for photography, although strictly linked with nature, has only illusory objectivity," wrote Gisèle Freund in *Photography and Society*. "First catering to the intellectual elite, photography next reached out to the bourgeois middle class. But when commercial photographers made pictures to please an uneducated public, even the initial supporters of photography became vehement critics."[41]

The fugitive poses and *interimage* simulations of *indians* are the eternal ironies of photography and the literature of dominance; all the more tricky and incisive because the simulations of *indians* have overturned the real presence of natives. The shadows of the eyes are the stories of an elusive presence.

Notes

[1] Jean Baudrillard, *Simulations* (New York: Semiotext(e), 1983) 2, 5, 130. "Simulation is no longer that of a territory, a referential being or a substance. It is the generation by models of a real without origin or reality [. . .]. To dissimulate is to feign not to have what one has. To simulate is to feign to have what one hasn't. One implies a presence, the other an absence [. . .]. Unless you admit that the natives are perfect naturals, incapable of simulation, the problem is the same as here: the impossibility of obtaining for a *directed* question any answer other than *simulated* (other than reproducing the question). It isn't even certain that you can interrogate plants, animals, nor even inert matter in the exact sciences with any chance of 'objective' response." "Ethno-

graphies work against themselves in that establishing the fieldworker's credentials as an empirical scientist requires depicting a passive observer existing nowhere in reality," wrote Paul Roth in "Ethnography without Tears," *Current Anthropology* 30.5 (1989): 556. "They are rendered unbelievable by the impossibility of this authorial pose."Artistic simulations are not the same as ethnographies. Arthur Kroker pointed out in *The Possessed Individual* that "art must always be forgery – a perfect counterfeit. This is the secret of its fatal seduction, and the promise of its aesthetic destiny. Here, art only succeeds to the extent that it compels the disappearing order of the real – real subjects, real sex, real space – to vanish into a virtual world of perspectival simulacra. Art, then, as an enchanted simulation of trompe l'oeil" (New York: St. Martin's Press, 1992) 134.

2. William Mitchell, "When Is Seeing Believing?" *Scientific American* (February 1994): 68-73. "We are approaching the point at which most of the images that we see in our daily lives, and that form our understanding of the world, will have been digitally recorded, transmitted and processed."

3. "Tom Hanks as an Innocent Interloper in History," a film review by Janet Maslin, in *The New York Times*, July 6, 1994. Forrest Gump visits the Kennedy White House and "winds up drinking too much Dr. Pepper. Typical of the film's magic is a brief glimpse of Forrest writhing uncomfortably and telling the President that he has to go to the bathroom." President Kennedy chuckles. "The President's voice sounds authentic, his mouth movements match his movie dialogue, and he and Mr. Hanks appear to be on precisely the same film stock, in the same frame. Special kudos for this go to Ken Ralston, the film's special-effects supervisor, and to Industrial Light and Magic, pushing the technical envelope further than ever."

4. Hillel Schwartz, *The Culture of the Copy* (New York: Zone Books, 1996) 360, 362. "We grant machines humanity by default. Once we have such perfect servants as intelligent machines promise to be, then we may discover who we really are."

5. Elizabeth Edwards, ed. *Anthropology and Photography 1860-1920* (New Haven: Yale University Press, 1992) 8, 11, 12. "Nevertheless, because the photograph is assumed to be unmediated and analogical," she wrote, "there is a danger in photographic analysis that the retrospective construction of intention, rather than substantiable analysis, will be used to legitimate the interpretive appropriation of the image into a specific discourse."

6. Eric Gans, *Originary Thinking* (Stanford: Stanford University Press, 1993) 212, 213. "Postmodernism," he pointed out, "may well be the era of simulation, but it is no accident that it has been so far an era dominated by theory rather than esthetic practice."

7. Jean Baudrillard, "Simulacra and Simulations," *Jean Baudrillard: Selected Writings*, ed. Mark Poster (Stanford: Stanford University Press, 1988) 170, 171.

8. Mark Poster, "Introduction" to *Jean Baudrillard: Selected Writings*, 1, 8. "His work shatters the existing foundations for critical social theory, showing how the privilege they give to labor and their rationalist epistemologies are inadequate for the analysis of the media and other new social activities. In these regards his critique belongs with Derrida's critique of logocentrism and Foucault's critique of the human sciences."

9   Jack Goody, *The Domestication of the Savage Mind* (Cambridge: Cambridge University Press, 1977) 37, 150.

10 Anthony Grafton, *New Worlds, Ancient Texts* (Cambridge, MA: Harvard University Press, 1992) 108.

11 Ibid., 108, 111. Grafton pointed out that "Staden's primary goal is to tell a traditional Christian moralizing tale both to edify and to inspire devotion." How ironic that a monotheistic moral tale becomes the *interimage* simulation of savagism.

12 Ibid., 126, 130. De Bry's illustrations based on the watercolors of John White "cleverly combines ethnographic detail about the native Virginians' way of life with details of New World flora and fauna, and attempts to provide detailed and accurate images of non-European life."

13 Ibid., 129.

14 Iskander Mydin, "Historical Images – Changing Audiences" and "The Parallel Histories of Anthropology and Photography" by Christopher Pinney, *Anthropology and Photography 1860-1920*, ed. Elizabeth Edwards (New Haven: Yale University Press, 1992) 74, 249.

15 Gerald Vizenor, *Manifest Manners: Narratives on Postindian Survivance* (Lincoln: University of Nebraska Press, 1994, 1999) 4, 5, 6, 17. "Manifest manners are the simulations of dominance; the notions and misnomers that are read as the authentic and sustained as representations of Native American Indians. [. . .] Simulations are the absence of the tribal real; the *postindian* conversions are in the new stories of survivance over dominance. The natural reason of the tribes anteceded by thousands of generations the invention of the *indian*. The postindian ousts the inventions with humor, new stories, and the simulations of survivance."

16 Patrick Smith, *Warhol: Conversations about the Artist* (Ann Arbor: UMI Research Press, 1988) 359. Smith asked, "Did Andy do anything in particular for the Bicentennial?" Cultrone responded, "Yeah. Around that time. Yeah, we just skipped that over. It was too much like jumping on a bandwagon."

17 Joan Halifax, *The Fruitful Darkness* (New York: HarperCollins Publishers, 1993) 26, 27. "I, like many others, sought fresh answers in ancient fields, not only in the old Ways of elder cultures, East and West, but in old forests and old river bodies," she wrote in the preface. "I looked for root-truth in language, in food, in social institutions, and in mind itself, what one Lakota elder calls 'the root that has not end.' This self that is coextensive with all of creation holds within it the sense of a continuum as vast as the oceans flowing around Earth." The metaphors are the *interimage* simulations of monotheism and dominance.

18 Ibid., 98, 99.

19 Ibid., 187, 188.

20 Donald Lowe, *History of Bourgeois Perception* (Chicago: University of Chicago Press, 1982) 39, 135.

21 Roland Barthes, *Camera Lucida* (New York: Hill and Wang, 1981) 6, 12, 13.

22 David Freedberg, *The Power of Images* (Chicago: University of Chicago Press, 1989) 438, 439. "For all the return to what critics may want to call representational art, one of the lessons of art and of image making now (and over the last fifty years) is that much of it cannot by many means becalled representational - at least in any useful sense." He pointed out that the word "figurational" might better serve the critic.

23 Linda Hutcheon, *The Politics of Postmodernism* (London and New York: Routledge, 1989) 123.

24 Roland Barthes, *Image – Music – Text* (New York: Hill and Wang, 1977) 17.

25 John Tagg, *The Burden of Representation* (Amherst: University of Massachusetts Press, 1988) 63, 64.

26 Eric Gans, *Originary Thinking* 46. "For the inevitability of intercultural dialogue suggests that the diversity of ethical principles springs from a ground of unity." He noted that this may be a reassurance to ethnographers. "The paradigm for this unity-in-diversity is the originary articulation between morality and ethics that we seek." Indeed, and originary discourse would deconstruct *interimage* simulations.

27 Susan Sontag, *On Photography* (New York: Farrar, Straus and Giroux, 1973) 14, 15, 97. "It is a nostalgic time right now, and photographs actively promote nostalgia," wrote Sontag. "Photography is an elegiac art, a twilight art. Most subjects photographed are, just by virtue of being photographed, touched with pathos [. . .]. Once they began to think photographically, people stopped talking about photographic distortion, as it was called."

28 Jean-Luc Nancy, *The Birth to Presence* (Stanford: Stanford University Press, 1993) 1, 2.

29 John Berger, *About Looking* (New York: Pantheon Books, 1980) 50, 51.

30 Nancy, *Birth* 191, 192, 196. "This body is first an interiority dedicated to images, and to the knowledge of images; it is the 'inside' of representations, and at the same time the representation of that 'inside,'" wrote Nancy. "Literature mimes the body, or makes the body mime a signification. [. . .] In this way, in all these ways at once, sense always comes back to the book as such, that is, to literature itself, but the book is never there: it has never abolished itself in its pure presence, it has not absorbed the sign into sense, nor sense into the sign." The narrative mimes the eye in photographs.

31 Roland Barthes, *Camera Lucida* 6, 87.

32 Rennard Strickland, *The Indians of Oklahoma* (Norman: University of Oklahoma Press, 1980) 46, 47.

33 Christopher Lyman, *The Vanishing Race and Other Illusions* (New York: Pantheon Books in association with the Smithsonian Institution Press, 1982) 19, 20, 21. "Just as it was difficult for Curtis to see Indians for what they were through the veil of his culture at the time, so is it difficult for us to see him and his work for what *they* were through the bias of our time. Roughly stated, Curtis's generation believed that Indians were only real Indians when they behaved as they were imagined to have behaved prior to contact with Whites. Scientists of his generation therefore studied Indians largely in those terms. These general beliefs led to the creation and perpetuation of stereotypes of 'Indianness' still prevalent in American culture [. . .]. By choosing to specialize in

rather mythical imagery of 'the Indian,' Curtis presented an allegory which appealed strongly to a sense of Americanness."

34 Herman Viola, *The Indian Legacy of Charles Bird King* (New York: Doubleday & Company and Smithsonian Institution Press, 1976) 13. "No artist of King's time or earlier pictured Indian leaders of more different tribes, with the single exception of George Catlin, who traveled widely in the Indian country beyond the frontiers of white settlement to paint likenesses of leaders of more than forty tribes. Although in his travels Catlin met Indians of lower status, he too preferred to picture prominent chiefs and members of their families. They owned the finest costumes and cut the finest figures in their dress clothing. Catlin, too, was driven by a common motivation to picture Indians for posterity. He believed their picturesque cultures were disappearing before the advance of white settlement and the exposure of Indians to white men's wars, diseases, and vices." See also Andrew Cosentino, *The Paintings of Charles Bird King* (Washington: Smithsonian Institution Press for the National Collection of Fine Arts, 1977).

35 Richard Brilliant, *Portraiture* (Cambridge, MA: Harvard University Press, 1991) 106, 107.

36 Sontag, *Photography* 64.

37 Dorothy and Thomas Hoobler, *Photographing the Frontier* (New York: G. P. Putnam's Sons, 1980) 117.

38 Julie Inness, *Privacy, Intimacy, and Isolation* (New York: Oxford University Press, 1992) 7, 42.

39 M. M. Bakhtin, *Art and Answerability*, ed. Michael Holquist and Vadim Liapunov (Austin: University of Texas Press, 1990) 126.

40 M. M. Bakhtin, *Speech Genres and Other Late Essays*, edited by Caryl Emerson and Michael Holquist (Austin: University of Texas Press, 1986) 146, 147. "To what degree is it possible to combine *I* and *other* in one neutral image of a person," wrote Bakhtin. "I enter into a spatial world, but the other has always resided in it. The differences between space and time of *I* and *other*. They exist in living sensation, but abstract thought erases them. Thought creates a unified, general world of man, irrespective of *I* and *other*. In primitive, natural self-sensation, *I* and *other* merge. There is neither egoism nor altruism here."

41 Gisèle Freund, *Photography & Society* (Boston: David R. Godine, 1980) 4, 35, 78. "Every great technical discovery causes crises and catastrophes," wrote Freund. "The invention of photography began an evolution which ultimately rendered obsolete the art of the portrait as it was then practiced by painters, miniaturists, and engravers. Those who had adopted the old trades in response to the needs of a rising bourgeoisie rapidly lost their means of support. Many of these artists became the first photographers. Economic necessity led the artists who had once attacked photography as an artless tool 'without a soul or spirit' to adopt the new profession when their own trades were threatened with extinction. Their previous experiences as artists and craftsmen was partly responsible for the high quality of the photographic industry during its early days." With the invention of photography came a new agency, the power of images, and a shift from narratives that are heard as the native real to

material realities that are seen and written. The tribes were discovered in scripture and *interimage* portraiture and then captured as the objects of the new *seen* in photographs.

References

Abu-Laban, Yasmeen. "The Politics of Race, Ethnicity and Immigration: The Contested Arena of Multiculturalism into the Twenty-First Century." *Canadian Politics*. Ed. James P. Bickerton and Alain-G. Gagnon. 3rd ed. Peterborough: Broadview Press, 1999. 463-83.

Abu-Lughod, Janet. "Going Beyond Global Babble." *Culture, Globalization and the World-System: Contemporary Conditions for the Representation of Identity*. Anthony D. King. Binghampton: SUNY Press, 1991. 131-7.

Acosta, Oscar Zeta. *The Revolt of the Cockroach People*. San Francisco: Straight Arrow Books, 1973.

Alkana, Joseph. "Cohesion, Dissent, and the Aims of Criticism." Introduction to *Cohesion and Dissent in America*. Ed. Carol Colatrella and Joseph Alkana. Albany: State University of New York Press, 1994. ix-xxi.

Antonette, Lesliee. *The Rhetoric of Diversity and the Traditions of American Literary Study: Critical Multiculturalism in English*. Wesport: Bergin and Garvey, 1998.

Anzaldúa, Gloria. *Borderlands/La Frontera: The New Mestiza*. San Fransisco: Spinster/Aunt Lunte, 1987.

Appadurai, Arjun. "Global Ethnoscapes: Notes and Queries for a Transnational Anthropology." *Recapturing Anthropology: Working in the Present*. Ed. Richard G. Fox. Santa Fe: School of American Research, 1991. 191-210.

Appiah, Kwame Anthony. "The Uncompleted Argument: DuBois and the Illusion of Race." *"Race," Writing, and Difference*. Ed. Henry Louis Gates, Jr. Chicago: University of Chicago Press, 1986. 21-37.

---. *Identity Against Culture: Understandings of Multiculturalism*. Berkeley: Doreen B. Center for the Humanities, 1994.

---. "The Multiculturalist Misunderstanding." *New York Review of Books* 9 Oct. 1997: 30-6.

Babb, Valerie. *Whiteness Visible: The Meaning of Whiteness in American Literature and Culture*. New York: New York University Press, 1998.

Bader, Veit. "Citizenship and Exclusion: Radical Democracy, Community and Justice, or, What is Wrong with Communitarianism?" *Political Theory* 23.2 (May 1995): 211-46.

---. "The Cultural Conditions of Transnational Citizenship." *Political Theory* 25.6 (December 1997): 771-813.

Bakhtin, M. M. *Speech Genres and Other Late Essays*. Ed. Caryl Emerson and Michael Holquist. Austin: University of Texas Press, 1986.

---. *Art and Answerability*. Ed. Michael Holquist and Vadim Liapunov. Austin: University of Texas Press, 1990.

Bannas, Günter."Ausnahmen bestätigen noch die Regel der Einbürgerung." *Frankfurter Allgemeine Zeitung* 7 April 1993: 5

---. "Die Regel ist die Ausnahme: In Europa und auch in Deutschland wird Mehrfach-Staatsangehörigkeit hingenommen." *Frankfurter Allgemeine Zeitung* 16 August 1996: 10.

Barry, Iris. "Melodrama, Tract, Good Story." *New York Herald Tribune Books* 12 July 1941: 3.

Barthes, Roland. *Image Music Text*. New York: Hill and Wang, 1977.

---. *Camera Lucida*. New York: Hill and Wang, 1981.

---. "Semiology and the Urban." 1970. Rpt. in *The City and the Sign: An Introduction to Urban Semiotics*. Ed. M. Gottdiener and Alexandros Ph. Lagolopoulos. New York: Columbia University Press, 1986. 87-98.

Bauböck, Rainer. "Cultural Minority Rights for Immigration." *International Migration Review* 30.1 (1996): 203-50.

Baudrillard, Jean. *Simulations*. New York: Semiotext(e), 1983.

---. "The Precession of Simulacra." 1983. Rpt. in *Art After Modernism: Rethinking Representation*. Ed. with an introduction by Brian Wallis. Foreword by Marcia Tuctio. Boston: Godline, 1984. 253-82.

---. "Simulacra and Simulations." *Jean Baudrillard: Selected Writings*. Ed. and introd. Mark Poster. Stanford: Stanford University Press, 1988. 166-84.

Beitz, Charles. *Political Theory and International Relations*. Princeton: Princeton University Press, 1979.

Benjamin, Walter. "On Language as Such and on the Language of Man." *One-Way Street and Other Writings*. Trans. Jephcott Edmund and Kingsley Shorter. New York: Verso, 1985.

Bennett, David, ed. *Multicultural States: Rethinking Difference and Identity*. London and New York: Routledge, 1998.

Bennington, Geoffrey. "Postal Politics and the Institution of the Nation." *Nation and Narration*. Ed. Homi K. Bhabha. London: Routledge, 1990. 121-37.

Bercovitch, Sacvan. *The Puritan Origins of the American Self*. New Haven: Yale University Press, 1975.

---. *The American Jeremiad*. Madison: University of Wisconsin Press, 1978.

---. "The Rites of Assent: Rhetoric, Ritual, and the Ideology of American Consensus." *The American Self: Myth, Ideology, and Popular Culture*. Ed. Sam Girgus. Albuquerque: University of New Mexico Press, 1981. 5-42.

---. *The Rites of Assent: Transformations in the Symbolic Construction of America*. New York: Routledge, 1993.

Berger, John. *About Looking*. New York: Pantheon Books, 1980.

Berlant, Lauren. *The Anatomy of National Fantasy: Hawthorne, Utopia, and Everyday Life*. Chicago: University of Chicago Press, 1991.

Bhabha, Homi K. *The Location of Culture*. London: Routledge, 1994.

---. "On Cultural Choice." *The Turn to Ethics*. Ed. Marjorie Garber et al. New York and London: Routledge, 2000. 181-200.

Bissoondath, Neil. *Selling Illusions: The Cult of Multiculturalism in Canada*. Toronto: Penguin Books, 1994.

Boelhower, William. "Ethnographic Politics: The Uses of Memory in Ethnic Fiction." *Memory and Cultural Politics: New Approaches to American Ethnic Literatures*. Ed. Amritjit Singh et al. Boston: Northeastern University Press, 1996. 19-40.

Borja, Jordi, and Manuel Castells. *Local and Global: Management of Cities in the Information Age*. London: Earthscan Publications, 1997.

Bourdieu, Pierre. *Distinction: A Social Judgement of Taste*. Trans. Richard Nice. Cambridge, MA: Harvard University Press, 1984.

---. "The Forms of Capital." *Handbook of Theory and Research for the Sociology of Education.* Ed. John G. Richardson. New York: Greenwood Press, 1986. 241-58.

Bourne, Randolph. "Trans-National America." 1916. Rpt. in *Theories of Ethnicity: A Classical Reader.* Ed. Werner Sollors. Basingstoke: Macmillan, and New York: New York University Press, 1996. 93-108.

Bourque, Gilles, et al. "De l'universalisme au particularisme: droits et citoyenneté." *L'Amour des Lois.* Ed. Josiane Bon Lad-Ayoub et al. Sainte-Foy/Paris: Presses de l'Université Laval/ L'Harmattan, 1996. 233-56.

---, and Jules Duchastel. "La représentation de la communauté." *L'identité fragmentée.* Montréal: Éditions Fides, 1996. 29-51.

Braidotti, Rosi. *Nomadic Subjects: Embodiment and Sexual Difference in Contemporary Feminist Theory.* New York: Columbia University Press, 1994.

Brecher, Jeremy, et al., eds. *Global Visions: Beyond the New World Order.* Boston: South End Press, 1993.

Breinig, Helmbrecht. "(Hi)storytelling as Deconstruction and Seduction: The Columbus Novels of Stephen Marlowe and Michael Dorris/Louise Erdrich." *Historiographic Metafiction in Modern American and Canadian Literature.* Ed. Bernd Engler and Kurt Müller. Paderborn: Schöningh, 1994. 325-46.

Brennan, Timothy. *Salman Rushdie and the Third World: Myths of the Nation.* New York: St. Martin's Press, 1989.

Breton, Raymond. "Multiculturalism and Canadian Nation-Building." *The Politics of Gender, Ethnicity and Language in Canada.* Ed. Alan C. Cairns and Cynthia Williams. Toronto: University of Toronto Press, 1986. 27-66.

Brilliant, Richard. *Portraiture.* Cambridge, MA: Harvard University Press, 1991.

Brod, Richard, and Bettina J. Huber. "Foreign Language Enrollments in United States Institutions of Higher Education, Fall 1995." *ADFL Bulletin* 28.2 (Winter 1997): 55-60.

Brooks, David. "Bully for America." *The Weekly Standard* 23 June 1997: 16-7.

Browdy de Hernandez, Jennifer. "The Plural Self: The Politicization of Memory and Form in Three American Ethnic Autobiographies." *Memory and Cultural Politics: New Approaches to American Ethnic Literatures.* Ed. Amritjit Singh et al. Boston: Northeastern University Press, 1996. 41-59.

Brubaker, Rogers. *Citizenship and Nationhood in France and Germany.* Cambridge, MA: Harvard University Press, 1992.

Bruce-Novoa, Juan. *RetroSpace: Collected Essays on Chicano Literature, Theory, and History.* Houston: Arte Público, 1990.

Busia, Abena. "What is your Nation?" *Changing Our Own Words: Essays on Criticism, Theory, and Writing by Black Women.* Ed. Cheryl A. Wall. New Brunswick: Rutgers University Press, 1989. 196-211.

Butler, Judith. "Merely Cultural." *Social Text* 52/53 (Fall/Winter 1997): 265-77.

---. *Excitable Speech: A Politics of the Performative.* New York: Routledge, 1997.

Bühl, Walter L. "Kultur als System." *Kultur und Gesellschaft: Kölner Zeitschrift für Soziologie und Sozialpsychologie.* Sonderheft 27. Ed. Friedrich Neidhardt et al. Opladen: Westdeutscher Verlag, 1986. 118-44.

Cagidemetrio, Alide. "Introduction to Luigi Donato Ventura, *Peppino* (1885)." *The Multilingual Anthology of American Literature.* Ed. Marc Shell and Werner Sollors. New York: New York University Press, 2000. 214-8.

Caldwell, Gary. "Immigration et la nécessité d'une culture publique commun." *L'Action Nationale* 78.8 (1988): 704-11.
Canovan, Margret. *Nationhood and Political Theory*. Brookfield, Vt.: Edward Elgar, 1996.
Cardinal, Linda and Claude Couture. "L'immigration et le multiculturalisme au Canada: la genèse d'une problématique." *Les politiques publiques canadiennes*. Ed. Manon Tremblay. Sainte-Foy: Les Presses de l'Université Laval, 1998. 57-90.
Cardoso, Fernando Henrique. "North-South Relations in the Present Context: A New Dependancy?" *The New Global Economy in the Information Age*. Ed. Martin Carnoy et al. University Park: Pennsylvania State University Press, 1993. 149-59.
Chadwick-Joshua, Jocelyn. "The Rhetoric of the City in Toni Morrison's *Jazz*." *The City in African-American Literature*. Ed. Yoshinobu Hakutani and Robert Butler. Madison, NJ: Fairleigh Dickinson University Press, 1995. 168-80.
Chambers, Iain. "Signs of Silence, Lines of Listening." *The Post-Colonial Question: Common Skies, Divided Horizons*. Ed. Iain Chambers and Linda Curti. London: Routledge, 1996. 47-62.
Cheung, King-Kok, and Stan Yogi, eds. *Asian-American Literature: An Annotated Bibliography*. New York: Modern Language Association, 1988.
Chiawei O'Hearn, Claudine, ed. *Half and Half: Writers on Growing Up Biracial and Bicultural*. New York: Pantheon Books, 1998.
Cisneros, Sandra. *The House on Mango Street*. 1984. New York: Knopf, 1995.
Clifford, James. "Introduction: Partial Truths." *Writing Culture: The Poetics and Politics of Ethnography*. Ed. James Clifford and George E. Marcus. Berkeley: University of California Press, 1986. 1-26.
---. *The Predicament of Culture: Twentieth-Century Ethnography, Literature, and Art*. Cambridge, MA: Harvard University Press, 1988.
---. *Routes: Travel and Tanslation in the Late Twentieth Century*. Cambridge, MA: Harvard University Press, 1997.
Conolly, William. *Identity/Difference*. Ithaca: Cornell University Press, 1993.
Conolly-Smith, Peter. "The Translated Community: New York City's German-Language Press as an Agent of Cultural Resistance and Integration, 1910-1918." Diss. Yale University, 1996.
Conrad, Joseph. *Lord Jim*. New York: Norton, 1968.
Cosentino, Andrew. *The Paintings of Charles Bird King*. Washington: Smithsonian Institution Press for the National Collection of Fine Arts, 1977.
Couser, G. Thomas. "Oppression and Repression: Personal and Collective Memory in Paule Marshall's *Praisesong for the Widow* and Leslie Marmon Silko's *Ceremony*." *Memory and Cultural Politics: New Approaches to American Ethnic Literatures*. Ed. Amritjit Singh et al. Boston: Northeastern University Press, 1996. 106-20.

D'Souza, Dinesh. *The End of Racism: Principles for a Multiracial Society*. New York: Free Press, 1995.
Deleuze, Gilles. *Différence et répétition*. 1968. English version: *Difference and Repetition*. Trans. Paul Patton. London: Athlone Press, 1994.
---, and Michel Foucault. *Der Faden ist gerissen*. Trans. Walter Seitter and Ulrich Raulf. Berlin: Merve, 1977.
---, and Félix Guattari. "What Is a Minor Literature?" *Kafka: Toward a Minor Literature*. Trans. Dana Polan. Minneapolis: University of Minnesota Press, 1986. 16-27.

---, and Félix Guattari. *Mille Plateaux: Capitalisme et Schizophrénie.* 1980. English version: *A Thousand Plateaus: Capitalism and Schizophrenia.* Trans. Brian Massumi. Minneapolis: University of Minnesota Press, 1987.

Derrida, Jacques. "La différance." *Margins of Philosophy.* Trans. Alan Bass. Chicago: University of Chicago Press, 1982. 1-28.

---. *The Other Heading.* Trans. Pascale-Anne Brault and Michael B. Nass. Bloomington: Indiana University Press, 1991.

---. *Specters of Marx: The State of the Debt, the Work of Mourning, and the New International.* Trans. Peggy Kamuf. New York: Routledge, 1994.

Dorris, Michael, and Louise Erdrich. *The Crown of Columbus.* New York: Harper Collins, 1991.

Dumont, Fernand. "La fin d'un malentendu historique." *Raisons Communes.* Montréal: Éditions du Boréal, 1995. 33-48.

Early, Gerald. "American Education and the Postmodernist Impulse." *American Quarterly* 45.2 (June 1993): 220-9.

Edwards, Elizabeth, ed. *Anthropology and Photography 1860-1920.* New Haven: Yale University Press, 1992.

Elam, Diane. *Feminism and Deconstruction.* Routledge: London and New York, 1994.

Elshtain, Jean. "The Sovereign State." *Notre Dame Law Review* 66 (1991): 1355-84.

Die Emmigranten. St. Louis, Mo.: Aug. Wiebusch & Son Printing Company, 1882.

Escoffier, Jeffrey. "The Political Economy of the Closet: Toward an Economic History of Gay and Lesbian Life before Stonewall." *American Homo: Community and Perversity.* Berkeley: University of California Press, 1998. 65-78.

Fabre, Michel. *From Harlem to Paris: Black American Writers in France, 1840-1980.* Urbana and Chicago: University of Illinois Press, 1991.

Falk, Richard. "The Global Promise of Social Movements: Explorations at the Edge of Time." *Explorations at the Edge of Time: The Prospects for World Order.* Philadelphia: Temple University Press, 1992. 125-55.

---. "Evasions of Sovereignty." *Explorations at the Edge of Time: The Prospects for World Order.* Philadelphia: Temple University Press, 1992. 196-213.

Fanon, Frantz. *The Wretched of the Earth.* Trans. Constance Farrington. Preface by Jean-Paul Sartre. Harmondsworth: Penguin, 1979.

Festinger, Leon. *A Theory of Cognitive Dissonance.* 1957. Stanford: Stanford University Press, 1962.

Fiedler, Leslie A. *The Inadvertent Epic: From* Uncle Tom's Cabin *to* Roots. New York: Simon & Schuster, 1979.

Fisher Fishkin, Shelley. "Interrogating 'Whiteness,' Complicating 'Blackness': Remapping American Culture." *American Quarterly* 47.3 (1995): 428-66.

Fishman, Joshua. "Language Maintenance." *The Harvard Encyclopedia of American Ethnic Groups.* Ed. Stephan Thernstrom. Cambridge, MA: Harvard University Press, 1980. 629-38.

Fluck, Winfried. *Das kulturelle Imaginäre: Eine Funktionsgeschichte des amerikanischen Romans 1790-1900.* Frankfurt/M.: Suhrkamp, 1997.

Foucault, Michel. "Ariane s'est pendue." *Le Nouvel Observateur* 229 (1969).

---. "Of Other Spaces." *Diacritics* 16.1 (1986): 22-7.

Frankenberg, Ruth, ed. *White Women, Race Matters: The Social Construction of Whiteness*. Minneapolis: University of Minnesota Press, 1993.

Franklin, Benjamin. "Observations concerning the Increase of Mankind, Peopling of Countries, &c." *The Papers of Benjamin Franklin*. Ed. L. W. Labaree et al. Vol. 4. New Haven: Yale University Press, 1961. 225-34.

Fraser, Nancy. "Women, Welfare, and the Politics of Need Interpretation." *Unruly Practices: Power, Discourse and Gender in Contemporary Social Theory*. Minneapolis: University of Minnesota Press, 1989. 144-60.

---. "Struggle Over Needs." *Unruly Practices: Power, Discourse and Gender in Contemporary Social Theory*. Minneapolis: University of Minnesota Press, 1989. 161-87.

---. "A Rejoinder to Iris Young." *New Left Review* 223 (May/June 1997): 126-9.

---. "From Redistribution to Recognition? Dilemmas of Justice in a 'Postsocialist' Age." *New Left Review* 212 (July/August 1995): 68-93. Rpt. in Nancy Fraser. *Justice Interruptus: Critical Reflections on the "Postsocialist" Condition*. New York: Routledge, 1997. 11-40.

---, and Linda Gordon. "A Genealogy of 'Dependency': Tracing A Keyword of the US Welfare State." *Signs* 19.2 (Winter 1994): 309-36. Rpt. in Nancy Fraser. *Justice Interruptus: Critical Reflections on the "Postsocialist" Condition*. New York: Routledge, 1997. 121-50.

---. "Heterosexism, Misrecognition, and Capitalism: A Response to Judith Butler." *Social Text* 52/53 (Fall/Winter 1997): 279-89.

Freedberg, David. *The Power of Images*. Chicago: University of Chicago Press, 1989.

Freire, Paolo. *Pedagogy of the Oppressed*. New York: Continuum, 1993.

Freud, Sigmund. *Jokes and Their Relation to the Unconscious*. Trans. and ed. James Strachey and Angela Richards. New York: Pelican, 1976.

Freund, Gisèle. *Photography & Society*. Boston: David R. Godine, 1980.

Gagnon, Alain-G. "Fédéralisme et identités nationales: Le passage obligé de l'État-nation à l'État plurinational." *L'État-nation au tournant du siècle: les enseignements de l'expérience canadienne et européenne*. Ed. Panayotis Soldatos and Jean-Claude Masclet. Université de Montréal: Chaire Jean Monnet, 1997. 293-317.

Gans, Eric. *Originary Thinking*. Stanford: Stanford University Press, 1993.

Geertz, Clifford. "The Uses of Diversity." *Michigan Quarterly Review* 25.1 (1986): 105-23.

Genocchio, Benjamin. "Discourse, Discontinuity, Difference: The Question of Other Spaces." *Postmodern Cities and Spaces*. Ed. Sophie Watson and Kathrine Gibson. Cambridge: Blackwell, 1995. 35-46.

Gilroy, Paul. "Route Work: The Black Atlantic and the Politics of Exile." *The Post-Colonial Question: Common Skies, Divided Horizons*. Ed. Iain Chambers and Linda Curti. London: Routledge, 1996. 17-29.

Giroux, Henry. *Theory and Resistance in Education: A Pedagogy for the Opposition*. New York: Bergin and Garvey, 1983.

---. "Cultural Studies, Resisting Difference and the Return of Critical Pedagogy." *Border Crossings: Cultural Workers and the Politics of Education*. New York: Routledge, 1992. 161-79.

Giroux, France. "Le nouveau contrat national est-il possible dans une démocratie pluraliste? Examen comparatif des situations française, canadienne et québécoise." *Politique et Sociétés* 16.3 (1997): 129-47.

Gitlin, Todd. *The Twilight of Common Dreams: Why America is Wracked by Culture Wars*. New York: Owl Paperback/Henry Holt, 1996.

Glazer, Nathan. *We Are All Multiculturalist Now.* Cambridge, MA: Harvard University Press, 1997.
Gleason, Philip. "Identifying Identity." *Theories of Ethnicity: A Classical Reader.* Ed. Werner Sollors. Basingstoke: Macmillan, and New York: New York University Press, 1996. 460-87.
Gogolin, Ingrid. "Sprache und Migration." *Ethnische Minderheiten, Volk und Nation: Soziologie inter-ethnischer Beziehungen.* Ed. Friedrich Heckmann. Stuttgart: Enke, 1992. 488-90.
Golfman, Noreen. "Locating Difference: Ways of Reading Multiculturalism." *Mosaic* 29.3 (September 1996): 175-85.
Gómez-Peña, Guillermo. *The New World Border: Prophecies, Poems and Loqueras for the End of the Century.* San Francisco: City Lights, 1996.
Gonzales, Rodolfo. *I Am Joaquín/Yo soy Joaquín.* New York: Bantam Books, 1972.
Goody, Jack. *The Domestication of the Savage Mind.* Cambridge: Cambridge University Press, 1977.
Goonetilleke, D.C.R.A. *Salman Rushdie.* London: Macmillan, 1998.
Gosewinkel, Dieter. "Die Staatsangehörigkeit als Institution des Nationalstaats. Zur Entstehung des Reichs- und Staatsangehörigkeitsgesetzes von 1913." *Offene Staatlichkeit: Festschrift für Ernst-Wolfgang Böckenförde zum 65. Geburtstag.* Ed. Rolf Grawert. Berlin: Duncker & Humblot, 1995. 359-78.
Gouvernement du Québec, Conseil des relations interculturelles. "Culture publique commune et cohésion sociale: le contrat moral d'intégration des immigrants dans un Québec francophone, démocratique et pluraliste." *Gérer la diversité dans un Québec francophone, démocratique et pluraliste: principes de fond pour guider la recherche d'accommodements raisonnables* (1994): 11-37.
---. Ministère des Communautés culturelles et de l'Immigration du Québec, Direction des communications. *Au Québec pour bâtir ensemble. Énoncé de politique en matière d'immigration et d'intégration* (1990).
---. Ministère des Communautés culturelles et de l'Immigration du Québec. *La gestion de la diversité et l'accommodement raisonnable* (1993).
Grafton, Anthony. *New Worlds, Ancient Texts.* Cambridge, MA: Harvard University Press, 1992.
Gramsci, Antonio. *A Gramsci Reader: Selected Writings 1916-1935.* Ed. David Forgacs. London: Lawrence and Wishart, 1988.
Grentrup, Theodor. "Die Reichstagsdebatte 1912 über die Mischehen in den deutschen Kolonien." *Die Rassenmischehen in den deutschen Kolonien.* Paderborn: Ferdinand Schöningh, 1914. 38-47.
Grewal, Gurleen. "Memory and the Matrix of History: The Poetics of Loss and Recovery in Joy Kogawa's *Obasan* and Toni Morrison's *Beloved.*" *Memory and Cultural Politics: New Approaches to American Ethnic Literatures.* Ed. Amritjt Singh et al. Boston: Northeastern Press, 1996. 140-74.
Grossberg, Lawrence. "The Space of Culture, The Power of Space." *The Post-Colonial Question: Common Skies, Divided Horizons.* Ed. Iain Chambers and Linda Curti. London: Routledge, 1996. 169-88.
Grund, Francis J. *The Americans in Their Moral, Social and Political Relations.* 1837. New York: Kelley, 1971.
Guralnik, David B., ed. *Webster's New World Dictionary of the American Language: 2nd College Edition.* New York: The World Publishing Co., 1968. 1509.

Habermas, Jürgen. *Ecrits politiques*. Paris: Cerf, 1990.
Halifax, Joan. *The Fruitful Darkness*. New York: HarperCollins Publishers, 1993.
Hall, Stuart. "For Allon White: Metaphors of Transformation." *Stuart Hall: Critical Dialogues in Cultural Studies*. Ed. David Morley and Kuan-Hsing Chen. London: Routledge, 1996. 287-305.
Hannerz, Ulf. *Transnational Connections: Culture, People, Places*. London and New York: Routledge, 1996.
Harlow, Barbara. *Resistance Literature*. New York: Methuen, 1987.
Harvey, David. *Justice, Nature and the Geography of Difference*. Oxford: Blackwell, 1996.
Harvey, Julien. "Culture publique, intégration et pluralisme." *Relations* (October 1991): 239-41.
Haskell, Edward F. *Lance: A Novel About Multicultural Men*. New York: John Day Company, 1941.
Haygood, Wil. "A Black Writer's Journey into Poor White America." *The Boston Globe Magazine* 25 July 1999: 1, 14-23, 31-43.
Heckmann, Friedrich. *Ethnische Minderheiten, Volk und Nation: Soziologie inter-ethnischer Beziehungen*. Stuttgart: Enke, 1992.
Held, David. *Democracy and the Global Order*. Cambridge, MA: Polity Press, 1995.
---. "Democracy and Globalization." *Re-imagining Political Community: Studies in Cosmopolitan Democracy*. Ed. Daniele Archibugi et al. Cambridge, MA: Polity Press, 1998. 11-27.
Hettling, Manfred. "Schritt nach vorn zurück: Das erste Gesetz zur deutschen Staatsangehörigkeit." *Frankfurter Allgemeine Zeitung* 7 August 1996: N6.
Hildebrandt, Mathias. *Multikulturalismus und* Political Correctness *in den USA*, forthcoming.
Hill, Mike, ed. *Whiteness: A Critical Reader*. New York: New York University Press, 1997.
Hollinger, David A. *Postethnic America: Beyond Multiculturalism*. New York: Basic Books, 1995.
---. "How Wide the Circle of the 'We'? American Intellectuals and the Problem of the Ethnos since World War II." *American Historical Review* (April 1993): 317-37.
"Hommage à Julien Harvey: Le Québec, société plurielle en mutation?" *Globe* 1.1 (1998).
Hong Kingston, Maxine. *Tripmaster Monkey: His Fake Book*. New York: Knopf, 1989.
Honneth, Axel. *The Struggle for Recognition: The Moral Grammar of Social Conflicts*. Trans. Joel Anderson. Cambridge, MA: Polity Press, 1995.
Hoobler, Dorothy, and Thomas Hoobler. *Photographing the Frontier*. New York: G. P. Putnam's Sons, 1980.
hooks, bell. *Yearning: Race, Gender, and Cultural Politics*. London: Turnaround, 1991.
Hughes, Robert. *Culture of Complaint: The Fraying of America*. Oxford: Oxford University Press, 1993.
Hutcheon, Linda. *The Politics of Postmodernism*. London and New York: Routledge, 1989.

Inness, Julie. *Privacy, Intimacy, and Isolation*. New York: Oxford University Press, 1992.
Irmscher, Christoph. "Crossblood Columbus: Gerald Vizenor's Narrative 'Discoveries.'" *Amerikastudien/American Studies* 40.1 (1995): 83-98.

Jackson, Sandra, and José Solís, eds. *Beyond Comfort Zones in Multiculturalism: Confronting the Politics of Privilege*. Westport: Bergin & Garvey, 1995.
Jameson, Frederic. "Modernism and Imperialism." *Nationalism, Colonialism, and Literature*. Ed. Terry Eagleton et al. Minneapolis: University of Minnesota Press, 1990.

---. *The Geopolitical Aesthetic: Cinema and Space in the World System.* Bloomington: Indiana University Press, 1992. 43-68.

---. "On 'Cultural Studies.'" *Social Text* 34.1 (1993): 17-52.

Jarvis, Brian. *Postmodern Cartographies: The Geographical Imagination in Contemporary American Culture.* London: Pluto Press, 1998.

Jay, Gregory S. *American Literature and the Culture Wars.* Ithaca: Cornell University Press, 1997.

Johnson, Mark. *The Body and the Mind: The Bodily Basis of Meaning, Imagination, and Reason.* Chicago: University of Chicago Press, 1987.

Jung, Carl Gustav. "Your Negroid and Indian Behavior." 1930. Rpt. in *Theories of Ethnicity: A Classical Reader.* Ed. Werner Sollors. Basingstoke: Macmillan, and New York: New York University Press, 1996. 191-201.

Juteau, Danielle. "Citoyenneté, intégration et multiculturalisme canadien." *Dual Images: Multiculturalism on Two Sides of the Atlantic.* Ed. Kálmán Kulcsár and Denis Szabo. Budapest: Institute for Political Science of the Hungarian Academy of Sciences, 1996. 162-78.

Kaldor, Mary. "European Institutions, Nation-States and Nationalism." *Cosmopolitan Democracy: An Agenda for a New World Order.* Ed. Daniele Archibugi and David Held. Oxford: Polity Press, 1995. 68-95.

Kallen, Evelyn. "Multiculturalism: Ideology, Policy and Reality." *Journal of Canadian Studies* 17.1 (1982): 51-63.

Karrer, Wolfgang. "Nostalgia, Amnesia, and Grandmothers: The Uses of Memory in Albert Murray, Sabine Ulibarri, Paula Gunn Allen, and Alice Walker." *Memory, Narrative & Identity: New Essays in Ethnic American Literatures.* Ed. Amritjit Singh et al. Boston: Northeastern University Press, 1994. 128-44.

Katz, Stanley N. "The Legal Framework of American Pluralism: Liberal Constitutionalism and the Protection of Groups." *Beyond Pluralism: The Conception of Groups and Group Identities in America.* Ed. Wendy F. Katkin et al. Chicago: University of Illinois Press, 1998. 1-27.

Keats, John. "Letter to George and Thomas Keats." 28 December 1817. *The Complete Works of John Keats.* Ed. H. Buxton Forman. Vol. IV. New York: Thomas Y. Crowell & Co., n.d. 49-51.

Keith, Michael, and Steve Pile. "Introduction Part 1: The Politics of Place." *Place and the Politics of Identity.* Ed. Michael Keith and Steve Pile. London: Routledge, 1993. 1-40.

Kellman, Steven G. "Translingualism and the Literary Imagination." *Criticism* 33.4 (Fall 1991): 527-41.

Kiss, Elizabeth. "Five Theses on Nationalism." *NOMOS XXXVIII: Political Order.* Ed. Ian Shapiro and Russell Hardin. New York: New York University Press, 1996. 288-332.

Knopff, Rainer, and F.L. Morton. *Charter Politics.* Scarborough: Nelson Canada, 1991.

Knop, Karen. "Re/Statements: Feminism and State Sovereignty in International Law." *Transnational Law and Contemporary Problems* 3.2 (Fall 1993): 293-344.

Kristeva, Julia. *Strangers To Ourselves.* New York: Columbia University Press, 1991.

Kroeber, Alfred L., and Clyde Kluckhohn. *Culture: A Critical Review of Concepts and Definitions.* Papers of the Peabody Museum of American Archaeology and Ethnology 47. Cambridge, MA: Harvard, 1952.

Kroker, Arthur. *The Possessed Individual.* New York: St. Martin's Press, 1992.

Kymlicka, Will. *Liberalism, Community and Culture.* Oxford: Oxford University Press, 1989.

---. *Multicultural Citizenship: A Liberal Theory of Minority Rights.* New York: Oxford University Press, 1995.
---. "Ethnicity in the USA." *The Ethnicity Reader: Nationalism, Multiculturalism and Migration.* Ed. Montserrat Guibernau and John Rex. Cambridge, MA: Polity Press, 1997.

Lacan, Jacques. *The Four Fundamental Concepts of Psycho-Analysis.* Ed. Jacques-Alain Miller. Trans. Alan Sheridan. Harmondsworth: Penguin, 1986.
Lange, Bernd-Peter. "Dislocations: Migrancy in Nabokov and Rushdie." *Anglia* 117.3 (1999): 395-411.
Lefebvre, Henri. *The Production of Space.* Trans. Donald Nicholson-Smith. Oxford: Blackwell, 1991.
Lefort, Claude. *The Political Forms of Modern Society: Bureaucracy, Democracy, Totalitarianism.* Ed. John B. Thompson. Cambridge, MA: Polity Press, 1986.
Lenz, Günter H. "Historians, Histories, and Public Cultures: Multicultural Discourses in the United States and Germany." *Transatlantic Encounters: Multiculturalism, National Identity and the Uses of the Past.* Ed. Günter H. Lenz and Peter J. Ling. Amsterdam: VU University Press, 2000. 63-103.
Lévinas, Emmanuel. *Collected Philosophical Papers.* Trans. Alphonso Lingis. Dordrecht and Boston: Martinus Nijhoff Publishers, 1987.
Levine, Lawrence. *The Opening of the American Mind.* Boston: Beacon Press, 1996.
Levy, Jacob. "Classifying Cultural Rights." *NOMOS XXXIX: Ethnicity and Group Rights.* Ed. Ian Shapiro and Will Kymlicka. New York: New York University Press, 1997. 22-68.
Lipschuts, Ronnie D. "Reconstructing World Politics: The Emergence of Global Civil Society." *Millennium* 21:3 (1992): 389-420.
Lösch, Klaus. *Interkulturalität: Kulturtheoretische Prolegomena zum Studium der neueren indianischen Literatur Nordamerikas.* ZAA Studies. Tübingen: Stauffenburg, 2002.
Lorde, Audre. *Zami: A New Spelling of My Name.* Watertown: Persephone Press, 1982.
Lowe, Donald. *History of Bourgeois Perception.* Chicago: University of Chicago Press, 1982.
Luhmann, Niklas. *Soziologische Aufklärung: Aufsätze zur Theorie sozialer Systeme.* Vol. 1. Opladen: Westdeutscher Verlag, 1970.
Lyman, Christopher. *The Vanishing Race and Other Illusions.* New York: Pantheon Books in association with the Smithsonian Institution Press, 1982.

MacCormick, Neil. "Liberalism, Nationalism and the Post-Sovereign State." *Political Studies* XLIV (1996): 553-67.
Marlowe, Stephan. *The Memoirs of Christopher Columbus.* New York: Scribner's, 1987.
Maslin, Janet. "Tom Hanks as an Innocent Interloper in History." *The New York Times* 6 July 1994.
McLaren, Peter. "White Terror and Oppositional Agency: Towards a Critical Multiculturalism." *Multiculturalism: A Critical Reader.* Ed. David Theo Goldberg. Oxford: Blackwell, 1994. 33-70.
McWilliams, John P. *Hawthorne, Melville, and the American Character: A Looking-Glass Business.* Cambridge: Cambridge University Press, 1984.
Michael, Martina. "Postcolonial Literatures: Use or Abuse of the Latest Post-Word." *Postkoloniale Literaturen: Peripherien oder neue Zentren? Gulliver* 33 (1993): 6-23.
Michaels, Walter Benn. *Our America: Nativism, Modernism, and Pluralism.* Durham: Duke University Press, 1995.

Miller, John J. *The Unmaking of Americans: How Multiculturalism Has Undermined the Assimilation Ethic.* New York: Free Press, 1998.

Miller, David. *On Nationality.* Oxford: Oxford University Press, 1995.

Minh-ha, Trinh. "The Undone Interval: Trinh T. Minh-ha in Conversation with Annamaria Morelli." *The Post-Colonial Question: Common Skies, Divided Horizons.* Ed. Iain Chambers and Linda Curti. London: Routledge, 1996. 3-16

Minow, Martha. *Making All the Difference.* Ithaca: Cornell University Press, 1990.

Mitchell, William. "When Is Seeing Believing?" *Scientific American* (February 1994): 68-73.

Mohamed, Abdul Jan, and David Lloyd. "Introduction: Towards a Theory of Minority Discourse: What Is To Be Done?" *The Nature and Context of Minority Discourse.* New York: Oxford University Press, 1990. 1-16.

Momaday, N. Scott. *The Way to Rainy Mountain.* Albuquerque: University of New Mexico Press, 1969.

Morris, Christopher. *An Essay on the Modern State.* Cambridge: Cambridge Universtiy Press, 1998.

Morrison, Toni. *Song of Solomon.* New York: Knopf, 1977.

---. "City Limits, Village Values: Concepts of the Neighborhood in Black Fiction." *Literature and the Urban Experience: Essays on the City and Literature.* Ed. Michael C. Jaye and Ann Chalmers Watts. Manchester: Manchester University Press, 1981. 35-43.

---. *Jazz.* New York: Signet, 1992.

---. *Playing in the Dark: Whiteness and the Literary Imagination.* New York: Random House, 1992.

---. "The Site of Memory." *Inventing the Truth: The Art and Craft of Memoir.* Ed. William Zinsser. Boston: Houghton Mifflin, 1998. 185-200.

Mouffe, Chantal. "Democracy, Power and the 'Political.'" *Democracy and Difference.* Ed. Seyla Benhabib. Princeton: Princeton University Press, 1996. 246-56.

Murdock, Graham. "Mass Communication and the Construction of Meaning." *Reconstructing Social Psychology.* Ed. Nigel Armistead. Harmondsworth: Penguin, 1974. 205-20.

Murray, David. "Crossblood Strategies in the Writings of Gerald Vizenor." *The Yearbook of English Studies* 24 (1994): 213-27.

Mydin, Iskander. "Historical Images – Changing Audiences." *Anthropology and Photography 1860-1920.* Ed. Elizabeth Edwards. New Haven: Yale University Press, 1992. 249-52.

Nancy, Jean-Luc. *The Birth to Presence.* Stanford: Stanford University Press, 1993.

Nedelsky, Jennifer. "Reconceiving Autonomy: Sources, Thoughts and Possibilites." *Yale Journal of Law and Feminism* 1.1 (1989): 7-16.

---. "Law, Boundaries, and the Bounded Self." *Law and the Order of Culture.* Ed. Robert Post. Spec. issue of *Representations* 30 (1990): 162-89. Berkeley: University of California Press, 1991.

Nei, Masatoshi, and Arun K. Roychoudhury. "Genetic Relationship and Evolution of Human Races." *Evolutionary Biology* 14 (1983): 1-59.

Nelson, Robert M. "Place and Vision: The Function of Landscape in Ceremony." *Journal of the Southwest* 30 (1988): 281-316.

Nussbaum, Martha. "Patriotism and Cosmopolitanism." *For Love of Country: Debating the Limits of Patriotism.* Ed. Joshua Cohen. Boston: Beacon Press, 1996. 2-17.

O'Connell, David. "Victor Séjour: Ecrivain Américain de langue française." *Revue de Louisiane* 1.2 (Winter 1972): 60-1.

Olson, Charles. "Projective Verse." *Selected Writings*. Ed. Robert Creeley. New York: New Directions, 1966. 15-26.

O'Neill, Onora. "Justice and Boundaries." *Political Restructuring in Europe: Ethical Perspectives*. Ed. C. Brown. London: Routledge, 1994. 69-88.

---. *Towards Justice and Virtue: A Constructive Account of Practical Reasoning*. Cambridge: Cambridge University Press, 1996.

Ortiz Taylor, Sheila. *Faultline*. Tallahassee: Naiad Press, 1982.

Ortner, Sherry B. "Gender Hegemonies." *Cultural Critique* 14.4 (1990): 35-80.

O'Toole, Fintan. "The Meanings of Union: Taking the Trouble Out of the Troubles." *The New Yorker* 27 April 1998: 54.

Pagé, Michel. "Intégration, identité ethnique et cohésion sociale." *Pluriethnicité, éducation et société: construire un espace commun*. Ed. Fernand Ouellet and Michel Pagé. Québec: Institut Québécois de Recherche sur la Culture (IQRC), 1991. 119-53.

Paquet, Gilles. "Political Philosophy of Multiculturalism." *Ethnicity and Culture in Canada: The Research Landscape*. Ed. J.W. Berry and J.A. Laponce. Toronto: University of Toronto Press, 1994. 60-80.

Paredes, Américo. *With a Pistol in his Hand: A Border Ballad and Its Hero*. Austin: University of Texas Press, 1958.

Parekh, Bhikhu. "The Politics of Nationhood." *Cultural Identity and Development in Europe*. Ed. Keebet von Banda-Beckman and Maykel Verkuyten. London: University College of London Press, 1994.

Pease, Donald E. "National Identities, Postmodern Artefacts, and Postnational Narratives." *National Identities and Post-Americanist Narratives*. Durham: Duke University Press, 1994. 1-13.

Pettit, Philip. *Republicanism*. Oxford: Oxford University Press, 1997.

Pflägling, Wilhelm. *Zum kolonialrechtlichen Problem der Mischbeziehungen zwischen deutschen Reichsangehörigen und Eingeborenen*. Berlin: Universitäts-Buchdruckerei Gustav Schade, 1913.

Philpott, Daniel. "Sovereignty: An Introduction and Brief History." *Journal of International Affairs* 48.2 (Winter 1995): 353-68.

Pogge, Thomas. "Cosmopolitanism and Sovereignty." *Ethics* 103 (October 1992): 48-75.

---. "Creating Super-National Institutions Democratically: Reflections on the European Union's 'Democratic Deficit.'" *Journal of Political Philosophy* 5.2 (June 1997): 163-82.

Polanco, Héctor Díaz. *Indigenous Peoples in Latin America: The Quest for Self-Determination*. Trans. Lucia Rayas. Boulder: Westview Press, 1997.

Poster, Mark. "Introduction" *Jean Baudrillard: Selected Writings*. Ed. and introd. by Mark Poster. Stanford: Stanford University Press, 1988. 1-9.

Pratt, Mary Louise. *Imperial Eyes: Travel Writing and Transculturation*. London: Routledge, 1992.

---. "Comparative Literature and Global Citizenship." *Comparative Literature in the Age of Multiculturalism*. Ed. Charles Bernheimer. Baltimore and London: Johns Hopkins Press, 1995. 58-65.

Pinney, Christopher. "The Parallel Histories of Anthropology and Photography." *Anthropology and Photography 1860-1920*. Ed. Elizabeth Edwards. New Haven: Yale University Press, 1992. 74-95.

Ray, Jane. *The Story of Creation: Words from Genesis*. New York: Dutton Children's Books, 1993.

Raz, Joseph. "Multiculturalism: A Liberal Perspective." *Ethics in the Public Domain: Essays in the Morality of Law and Politics*. Oxford: Clarendon Press, 1994. 155-76.
Rich, Adrienne. *Blood, Bread, and Poetry: Selected Prose 1979-1985*. New York: Norton, 1986.
Rittstieg, Helmut, ed. *Deutsches Ausländerrecht*. 10th ed. München: dtv, 1996.
Rocher, François, et al. "Pluriethnicité, citoyenneté et intégration: de la souveraineté pour lever les obstacles et les ambiguïtés." *Cahiers de recherche sociologique* 25 (1995): 213-45.
Rorty, Richard. *Achieving Our Country: Leftist Thought in Twentieth Century America*. Cambridge, MA: Harvard University Press, 1997.
Rößler, Hans-Christian. "Man kann seine Identität nicht von heute auf morgen aufgeben: Viele eingebürgerte Türken behalten ihre alten Pässe." *Frankfurter Allgemeine Zeitung* 29 July 1997: 3.
Roth, Paul. "Ethnography without Tears." *Current Anthropology* 30.5 (1989): 555-61.
Ruggie, John Gerard. "Territoriality and Beyond: Problematizing Modernity in International Relations." *International Organization* 47.1 (Winter 1993): 139-74.
Rushdie, Salman. *Imaginary Homelands*. London: Granta, 1992.

Saldívar, José David. *Border Matters: Remapping American Cultural Studies*. Berkeley: University of California Press, 1997.
Sahlins, Marshall. *Historical Metaphors and Mythical Realities: Structure in the Early History of the Sandwich Islands Kingdom*. Ann Arbor: University of Michigan Press, 1981.
Salins, Peter. *Assimilation: American Style*. New York: Basic Books, 1997.
Schlesinger, Arthur M., Jr. *The Disuniting of America: Reflections on a Multicultural Society*. New York: Norton, 1992.
Schlikker, Michael. "Ausländerrecht." *Ethnische Minderheiten, Volk und Nation: Soziologie interethnischer Beziehungen*. Stuttgart: Enke, 1992. 187-9.
Schmidt, Alvin J. *The Menace of Multiculturalism: Trojan Horse in America*. Westport, Ct.: Praeger Publishers, 1997.
Schwartz, Hillel. *The Culture of the Copy*. New York: Zone Books, 1996.
Scott, Craig. "Indigenous Self-determination and Decolonization of International Imagination: A Plea." *Human Rights Quarterly* 18 (1996): 814-20.
Semprini, Andrea. *Le Multiculturalisme*. Paris: Presses Universitaires de France, 1997.
Sennett, Richard, and Jonathan Cobb. *The Hidden Injuries of Class*. New York: Knopf, 1973.
Shell, Marc, and Werner Sollors, eds. *The Multilingual Anthology of American Literature*. New York: New York University Press, 2000.
Shostak, Debra. "Maxine Hong Kingston's Fake Books." *Memory, Narrative & Identity: New Essays in Ethnic American Literatures*. Ed. Amritjit Singh et al. Boston: Northeastern University Press, 1994. 233-60.
Siemerling, Winfried and Katrin Schwenk. *Cultural Difference and the Literary Text: Pluralism and the Limits of Authenticity in North American Literature*. Iowa City: University of Iowa Press, 1996.
Silko, Leslie Marmon. *Ceremony*. New York: Signet, 1977.
---. *Almanac of the Dead*. New York: Simon & Schuster, 1991.
Singh, Amritjit, et al., eds. *Memory, Narrative, and Identity: New Essays in Ethnic American Literatures*. Boston: Northeastern University Press, 1994.
---. *Memory and Cultural Politics: New Approaches to American Ethnic Literatures*. Boston: Northeastern University Press, 1996.
Smith, Patrick. *Warhol: Conversations about the Artist*. Ann Arbor: UMI Research Press, 1988.

Soja, Edward. "Heterotopologies: A Remembrance of Other Spaces in the Citadel-LA." *Postmodern Cities and Spaces*. Ed. Sophie Watson and Kathrine Gibson. Cambridge: Blackwell, 1995. 13-34.

Sollors, Werner. "Ethnicity." *Critical Terms for Literary Study*. Ed. Frank Lentricchia and Thomas McLaughlin. Chicago: University of Chicago Press, 1990. 288-305.

---. "For a Multilingual Turn in American Studies." *American Studies Association Newsletter* (June 1997): 13-5.

---. *Neither Black Nor White Yet Both: Thematic Explorations of Interracial Literature*. New York: Oxford University Press, 1997.

---. "Multiculturalism in an Age of Xenophobia: An Introduction." *Multiculturalism in an Age of Xenophobia: Canadian, American, and German Perspectives*. Ed. Abraham J. Peck and Reinhard Maiworm. CD-ROM. Cincinnati: American Jewish Archives and Goethe-Institut B VISTA InterMedia Corporation, 1997.

---. *Multilingual America: Transnationalism, Ethnicity, and the Languages of American Literature*. New York: New York University Press, 1998.

Sontag, Susan. *On Photography*. New York: Farrar, Straus and Giroux, 1973.

Soyinka, Wole. "This Past Must Address Its Present." Nobel Lecture, Swedish Academy, Stockholm, 8 Dec. 1986 <http://www.nobel.se/literature/laureates/1986/soyinka-lecture.html>.

Stefanski, Valentina Maria. "Die polnische Minderheit." *Ethnische Minderheiten in der Bundesrepublik Deutschland: Ein Lexikon*. Ed. Cornelia Schmalz-Jacobsen and Georg Hansen. München: C.H. Beck, 1995. 386-91.

Strickland, Rennard. *The Indians of Oklahoma*. Norman: University of Oklahoma Press, 1980.

Sullivan, Teresa. "Immigration and the Ethics of Choice." *International Migration Review* 30.1 (1996): 90-104.

Swann, Edith. "Laguna Symbolic Geography and Silko's *Ceremony*." *American Indian Quarterly* 12.3 (1988): 229-49.

Tagg, John. *The Burden of Representation*. Amherst: University of Massachusetts Press, 1988.

Tamir, Yael. *Liberal Nationalism*. Princeton: Princeton University Press, 1993.

Taylor, Charles. "The Deep Challenge of Dualism." *Québec: State and Society*. Ed. Alain-G. Gagnon. 2nd ed. Toronto: Nelson Canada, 1993. 82-95.

---. "Multiculturalism and the Politics of Recognition." *Multiculturalism: Examining the Politics of Recognition*. Ed. Amy Gutmann and Charles Taylor. Expanded pb. ed. Princeton: Princeton University Press, 1994.

Thompson, Hunter S. *Fear and Loathing in Las Vegas: A Savage Journey to the Heart of the American Dream*. New York: Random House, 1971.

Trent, William Peterfield, et al. *The Cambridge History of American Literature*. Vol. 3. New York: Macmillan, and Cambridge: Cambridge University Press, 1943.

Tully, James. *Strange Multiplicity: Constitutionalism in the Age of Diversity*. Cambridge: Cambridge University Press, 1995.

Tylor, Edward B. *Primitive Culture: Researches into the Development of Mythology, Philosophy, Religion, Art, and Custom*. Vol. I. London: J. Murray, 1871.

Vauthier, Simone. "Textualité et stéréotypes: Of African Queens and Afro-American Princes and Princesses: Miscegenation in *Old Hepsy*." *Regards sur la littérature noire américaine*. Ed. Michel Fabre. Paris: Publications du Conseil Scientifique de la Sorbonne Nouvelle B Paris III, 1980. 65-107.

Viola, Herman. *The Indian Legacy of Charles Bird King*. New York: Doubleday & Company and Smithsonian Institution Press, 1976.

Virilio, Paul. "Critical Space." *The Virilio Reader*. Ed. James Der Derian. Oxford: Blackwell, 1998. 58-72.

Vizenor, Gerald. *Crossbloods: Bone Counts, Bingo and Other Reports*. Minneapolis: University of Minnesota Press, 1990.

---. *Interior Landscapes: Autobiographical Myths and Metaphors*. Minneapolis: University of Minnesota Press, 1990.

---. *The Heirs of Columbus*. Hanover: Wesleyan University Press, 1991.

---. *Manifest Manners: Postindian Warriors of Survivance*. Hanover: Wesleyan University Press, 1994.

---. *Fugitive Poses: Native American Indian Scenes of Absence and Presence*. Lincoln: University of Nebraska Press, 1998.

---. *Manifest Manners: Narratives on Postindian Survivance*. Lincoln: University of Nebraska Press, 1999.

Volz, Robert, ed. *Reichshandbuch der deutschen Gesellschaft: Das Handbuch der Persönlichkeiten in Wort und Bild*. Introd. Ferdinand Toennies. Berlin: Deutscher Wirtschaftsverlag, 1931.

Wagner, Roy. *The Invention of Culture*. Rev. ed. Chicago: University of Chicago Press, 1980.

Waldron, Jeremy. "Minority Cultures and the Cosmopolitan Alternative." *The Rights of Minority Cultures*. Ed. Will Kymlicka. Oxford: Oxford University Press, 1995. 93-119.

Walker, R.B.J., and Saul H. Mendovitz, eds. *Contending Sovereignties: Redefining Political Community*. Boulder: Lynne Reiner, 1990.

Walzer, Michael. *Spheres of Justice*. New York: Basic Books, 1983.

---. *Thick and Thin: Moral Arguments at Home and Abroad*. Notre Dame: Notre Dame University Press, 1994.

Weber, Max. "Ethnic Groups." Rpt. in *Theories of Ethnicity: A Classical Reader*. Ed. Werner Sollors. Basingstoke: Macmillan, and New York: New York University Press, 1996. 52-66.

Weinfeld, Morton. "Myth and Reality in the Canadian Mosaic: 'Affective Ethnicity.'" *Études ethniques au Canada/Canadian Ethnic Studies* 13.3 (1981): 80-100.

Welsch, Wolfgang. "Transculturality: The Puzzling Form of Cultures Today." *California Sociologist* 17/18 (1994): 19-39.

---. "Transkulturalität: Zur veränderten Verfassung heutiger Kulturen." *Hybridkultur: Medien, Netze, Künste*. Ed. I. Schneider and C.W. Thompson. Köln: Wienand, 1997. 67-90.

Wendt, Alexander. "Collective Identity Formation and the International State." *American Political Science Review* 88:2 (June 1994): 384-96.

Whitman, Walt. "Song of Myself." *Leaves of Grass*. Ed. Sulley Bradley and Harold W. Blodgett. New York: Norton, 1973. 28-89.

Wilmer, Franke. *The Indigenous Voice in World Politics*. Newbury Park, Cal.: Sage Publications, 1993.

Wilson, Vince Seymour. "The Tapestry Vision of Canadian Multiculturalism." *Canadian Journal of Political Science* 26.4 (1993): 645-69.

---. "Canada's Evolving Multicultural Policy." *Canada's Century: Governance in a Maturing Society*. Ed. C.E.S. Franks et al. Montreal: McGill-Queen's University Press, 1995. 165-84.

Wolf, Eric. *Europe and the People Without History*. Berkeley: University of California Press, 1982.

Wolfe, Alan. *One Nation, After All: What Middle-Class Americans Really Think About God, Country, Family, Racism, Welfare, Immigration, Homosexuality, Work, The Right, The Left, and Each Other*. New York: Viking Press, 1998.

Wolfe, Alan, and Jytte Klausen. "Identity Politics and the Welfare State." *Social Philosophy and Policy* 14.2 (Summer 1997): 231-55.

Wulffen, Thomas, ed. *Der gerissene Faden: Nichtlineare Techniken in der Kunst*. Spec. issue of *Kunstforum* 155 (June-July 2001): 46-298.

Xu, Ben. "Memory and the Ethnic Self: Reading Amy Tan's *The Joy Luck Club*." *Memory, Narrative & Identity: New Essays in Ethnic American Literatures*. Ed. Amritjit Singh et al. Boston: Northeastern University Press, 1994. 261-77.

Yeatman, Anna. "Beyond Natural Right: The Conditions for Universal Citizenship." *Postmodern Revisionings of the Political*. New York: Routledge, 1994.

---. "Feminism and Citizenship." *Culture and Citizenship*. Ed. Nick Stevenson. London: Sage, 1998. 138-52.

Young, Iris Marion. *Justice and the Politics of Difference*. Princeton: Princeton University Press, 1990.

---. "A Multicultural Continuum: A Crititque of Will Kymlicka." Constellations 4.1 (April 1997). 48-53.

---. "Together in Difference: Transforming the Logic of Group Political Conflict." *The Rights of Minority Groups*. Ed. Will Kymlicka. Oxford: Oxford University Press, 1995. 155-76.

---. "Unruly Categories: A Critique of Nancy Fraser's Dual Systems Theory." *New Left Review* 222 (March/April 1997): 147-60.

Young, Era Brisbane. "An Examination of Selected Dramas for the Theater of Victor Séjour Including Works of Social Protest." Diss. School of Education, Health, Nursing, and Arts Professions. New York University, 1979.

Zalewski, Daniel. "Tongues Untied: Translating American Literature into English." *Lingua Franca* (December/January 1996/97): 61-5 <http://www.fas.harvard.edu/~lowinus/>.

Zapf, Harald. *Dekonstruktion des Reinen: Hybridität und ihre Manifestationen im Werk von Ishmael Reed*. Würzburg: Königshausen & Neumann, 2002.

Index

Abu-Laban, Y. 125, 132n25, 134n32
Abu-Lughod, J. 207n76
Adams, H. 168
Alkana, J. 155
Allen, P.G. 198n26
Amin, S. 108n31
Anderson, E. 69n1
Antonette, L. 156n7
Anzaldúa, G. 204n56, 218
Appadurai, A. 206, 207, 210n85, 214, 216
Appiah, K.A. 14-17
Archibugi, D. 97n13, 115n40
Aristotle 149
Armistead, N. 19n26
Armony, V. 136
Augustine 149
Austin, M. 182

Babb, V. 15n9
Bader, V. 93n5
Bakhtin, M.M. 187, 241, 242
Bannas, G. 172n22
Barry, I. 165n7, 165n8
Barthes, R. 209, 234, 235, 237
Bauböck, R. 57, 119
Baudrillard, J. 212, 229-231
Beitz, Ch. 100, 106, 107
Benhabib, S. 104n23
Benjamin, W. 56
Bennett, D. 12, 16n13
Bennington, G. 208n78
Bercovitch, S. 151-153, 155, 197n16

Berger, J. 237
Berlant, L. 197n14
Bernheimer, Ch. 182n37
Bernstein, R.J. 69n1
Berry, J.W. 132n24
Bhabha, H.K. 8, 29, 66, 196n7, 197n13, 198n25, 203n52, 205n61, 208n78, 208n79, 216n104, 217n107, 218n113
Bhargava, R. 61
Bickerton, J.P. 125n3
Bissoondath, N. 136, 137
Blodgett, H.W. 211n87
Bloom, A. 166
Bobrow, D. 119
Bodmer, K. 239
Boelhower, W. 198n23, 199n28, 203n49
Bon Lad-Ayoub, J. 136
Borja, J. 115n40
Bourdieu, P. 19
Bourne, R. 14, 172
Bourque, G. 136n37
Bradley, S. 211n87
Bragdon, K. 163
Braidotti, R. 24n40
Brandt, W. 171
Brecher, J. 196n6
Breinig, H. 10, 213n91
Brennan, T. 196n9
Breton, R. 132, 133
Brilliant, R. 239, 240
Brod, R. 182n35
Brooks, D. 39n8
Browdy de Hernandez, J. 201n42

Brown, C. 101n21, 106n29
Brown, J. 175
Brubaker, R. 170n18, 171n19, 171n20
Bruce-Novoa, J. 9, 217, 218n109
Buchwald, N. 182
Bühl, W.L. 19n27
Busia, A. 198
Butler, J. 58, 69n1, 77n5, 84n9
Butler, R. 209n84
Buxton Forman, H. 23n39

Cabeza de Vaca, A.N. 154, 155
Cagidemetrio, A. 187n45
Cairns, A.C. 133
Caldwell, G. 137n42
Canovan, M. 93n13, 97, 98n15
Cardinal, L. 133, 134n31
Cardoso, F.H. 108n31
Carnoy, M. 108n31
Castells, M. 115n40
Catlin, G. 239n34
Chadwick-Joshua, J. 209n84
Chambers, I. 196n5, 198n24, 203n51, 204n55, 204n57, 208n79, 212
Chametzky, J. 163
Chen, K.-H. 61n25
Cheney, L. 45
Chesnutt, Ch. 178n29
Cheung, K.-K. 183n39
Chiawei O'Hearn, C. 21n33
Christensen, P. 198n26
Cisneros, S. 203
Clark, V. 198n21
Clifford, J. 20, 196n6, 198n19, 202n44, 203n54, 217n107
Clinton, B. 49
Cobb, J. 73n3
Cohen, J. 93n5

Colatrella, C. 155n5
Columbus, Ch. 213n91, 214
Connolly, W. 104n23
Conolly-Smith, P. 163, 190
Conrad, J. 54, 55, 61, 63
Cosentino, A. 239n34
Cossé Bell, C. 163
Couser, T. 201, 202
Couture, C. 133, 134n31
Creeley, R. 20n30
Crèvecoeur, M.G. de 14
Cultrone, R. 233
Cunningham, F. 119
Curti, L. 196n5, 198n24, 203n51, 204n57
Curtis, E. 239

D'Souza, D. 131n18
Da Ponte, L. 182
Dahbur, O. 119
de Bry, T. 231, 232
Dean, J. 147
Deleuze, G. 22n34, 23n35, 24, 197n12
Der Derian, J. 196n4
Derrida, J. 24, 29, 55, 56n5, 91, 231n8
Dewey, J. 168
Döblin, A. 209
Dorris, M. 213n91
Douglass, F. 44
DuBois, W.E.B. 15n8, 44
Duchastel, J. 136n37
Dumas, A. 175
Dumont, F. 136n37
Dunton, A.D. 132

Eagleton, T. 205n61
Early, G. 182
Edwards, E. 230, 232n14

Elam, D. 32
Ellison, R. 44
Elshtain, J. 111n37
Emerson, C. 242n40
Engler, B. 213n91
Erdrich, L. 213n91
Erikson, E. 165n6
Escoffier, J. 85n11

Fabre, M. 163n2, 175n26
Falk, R. 105n25, 117n44
Fanon, F. 65, 196n8, 196n9
Faust, A.B. 182
Festinger, L. 23
Fiedler, L. 166, 167n13
Fisher Fishkin, S. 216
Fishman, J. 190
Fluck, W. 18n24
Flynt, L. 233
Ford, G. 17
Forgacs, D. 61n28
Forst, R. 69n1
Fortier, E.J. 182
Foucault, M. 19, 22, 205, 206, 231n8
Fox, R.G. 206n66
Frankenberg, R. 15n9
Franklin, B. 13, 44
Franks, C.E.S. 125n4
Fraser, N. 8, 73n2, 77n5, 84n9, 85n10
Freedberg, D. 235
Freire, P. 156n7
Freud, S. 63-65, 165n6
Freund, G. 242

Gagnon, A.-G. 9, 125n3, 136n36
Gans, E. 230, 236
Garber, M. 66
Gates, H.L., Jr. 15n8, 163, 174

Geertz, C. 57, 58
Genocchio, B. 206n63
Gibson, K. 206n63
Gilroy, P. 196, 202n44, 203, 204n59, 205n62
Girgus, S. 197n16
Giroux, F. 136, 139
Giroux, H. 156n7
Gitlin, T. 38
Glazer, N. 8, 11, 12n3, 14, 16, 37, 131, 166, 167, 173
Gleason, P. 165n6
Gogolin, I. 181n33
Goldberg, D.T. 198n19
Golfman, N. 125
Gómez-Peña, G. 31, 203n54
Gonzales, R. 157n10
González-Berry, E. 163
Goody, J. 231
Goonetilleke, D.C.R.A. 218n110
Gordon, L. 85n10
Gosewinkel, D. 170n18
Gottdiener, M. 209n84
Grafton, A. 231, 232
Gramsci, A. 61-63
Grawert, R. 170n18
Grentrup, T. 179n30
Grewal, G. 200n32
Grossberg, L. 198n24, 203n50, 208n80, 216n105
Grund, F. 197n15
Guattari, F. 23n35, 197n12
Guibernau, M. 131
Gutmann, A. 16n13, 94n6, 128n11

Habermas, J. 131
Hakutani, Y. 209n84
Haley, A. 166, 200
Halifax, J. 231, 233, 234
Hall, S. 61, 199n27

Hanks, T. 230n3
Hannerz, U. 31
Hansen, G. 171n19
Hanssen, B. 66
Hardin, R. 92n3
Harlow, B. 198
Harvey, D. 205n62
Harvey, J. 125, 137n42, 139n49, 141
Haskell, E.F. 165, 166, 172
Hawthorne, N. 197n15
Haygood, W. 11
Heckmann, F. 173n24
Held, D. 97n13, 115n40
Hettling, M. 170n18
Higham, J. 168
Hildebrandt, M. 14n6
Hill, M. 15n9
Hobsbawm, E. 171
Hodge, B. 205n62
Hoffman, A. 119
Hollinger, D. 164-166, 178, 183, 191
Holquist, M. 241n39, 242n40
Honig, B. 61
Honneth, A. 69n1, 79n6, 83n7
Hoobler, D. 240
Hoobler, T. 240
hooks, b. 198n18
Huber, B.J. 182n35
Hughes, R. 38
Hugo, V. 175
Hutcheon, L. 235

Iacovino, R. 125
Inness, J. 241
Irmscher, Ch. 213n92, 215n97
Isajiw, W.W. 127

Jackson, S. 207n75

Jameson, F. 26, 202n45, 205n61, 217
Jarvis, B. 197n15, 198n24, 200n32, 204n58, 209n83, 216n101
Jay, G.S. 155, 156
Jaye, M.C. 209n81
Jefferson, T. 157
Johnson, M. 23n37
Jospin, L. 170
Jung, C.G. 186
Juteau, D. 125, 126

Kafka, F. 197n12
Kaldor, M. 97n13
Kallen, E. 127n10, 133
Kallen, H.M. 14
Karrer, W. 198n26, 199n28, 203n53
Katkin, W.F. 130n15
Katz, S.N. 130
Keats, J. 23
Keith, M. 195n2, 195n3, 198n19, 203n53, 216n102
Kellman, S.G. 188n46
Kennedy, J.F. 49, 230
Keynes, J.M. 37
King, A.D. 207n76
King, Ch.B. 239
Kingston, M.H. 211, 212, 217
Kiss, E. 92n3
Klausen, J. 100n19
Kluckhohn, C. 18n19
Knop, K. 111n37
Knopff, R. 135n34
Koditschek, T. 69n1
Kogawa, J. 200n32
Kohl, H. 126
Kohler, M. 115n40
Kristeva, J. 91n2
Kroeber, A.L. 18n19

Kroker, A. 229n1
Kunow, R. 9
Kymlicka, W. 92-97, 103n22, 104n23, 109n32, 109n33, 126n7, 127, 131, 132

Labaree, L.W. 13n5
Labelle, M. 138
Lacan, J. 60
Laclau, E. 61
Lagolopoulos, A.P. 209n84
Lange, B.-P. 217n107
Laponce, J.A. 132n24
Laurendeau, A. 132
Lee, A. 180
Lefebvre, H. 195, 206n63
Lefort, C. 59, 60n24, 61n26, 62n31
Lentricchia, F. 18n17
Lenz, G. 16, 17, 168
Lévinas, E. 53n1
Levine, L. 38, 166
Levy, J. 109n33
Liapunov, V. 241n39
Lind, M. 168
Ling, P.J. 17n14
Lipschuts, R.D. 117n44
Lloyd, D. 198n19, 204n59
Locke, J. 149
Lorde, A. 201, 202, 203n53
Lösch, K. 10, 18n18
Lowe, D. 234
Luhmann, N. 24
Lukes, S. 69n1
Lyman, Ch. 239n33

MacCormick, N. 104n24
Macedo, S. 119
Maiworm, R. 190
Mandela, N. 204
Mansbridge, J. 69n1

Marcus, G.E. 20n29
Marlowe, S. 213n91
Marshall, P. 202n43
Marx, K. 56, 72, 83n8
Masclet, J.-C. 136n36
Maslin, J. 230n3
Mazurek, K. 125
McKay, N. 174
McKenzie, S. 147
McLaren, P. 198n19, 205n62
McLaughlin, T. 18n17
McWilliams, J.P. 197n15
Means, R. 231, 233
Meléndez de Avilés, P. 157
Melkevik, B. 136
Melville, H. 197n15
Mencken, H.L. 182, 183
Mendovitz, S.H. 105n25
Michael, M. 205n62
Michaels, W.B. 167, 183, 191
Miller, D. 92-97, 99n16, 99n17
Miller, J.-A. 60n23
Miller, J.J. 38, 129, 131n18
Minh-ha, T. 204, 205n62, 217
Minow, M. 104n23
Mishra, V. 205n62
Mitchell, W. 229, 230n2
Mohamed, A.J. 198n19, 204n59
Momaday, S. 203
Morelli, A. 204n57
Morley, D. 61n25
Morris, Ch. 105n26, 106n28
Morrison, T. 15n9, 199, 200, 203, 204, 207-210, 212, 217
Morton, F.L. 135n34
Mouffe, Ch. 61, 104n23
Müller, K. 213n91
Mulroney, B. 134
Murdock, G. 19n26
Murray, A. 198n26

Murray, D. 215n96-98, 215n100
Mydin, I. 232

Nabokov, V. 217n107
Nancy, J.-L. 237
Napoléon 175
Nedelsky, J. 111n37
Nei, M. 15n8
Neidhardt, F. 19n27
Nelson, R.M. 201n38
Nhat Hanh, T. 234
Nicholson, L. 69n1
Nicholson-Smith, D. 195
Nixon, R. 37
Nussbaum, M. 93n5

O'Connell, D. 175n26
O'Neill, O. 100, 101, 106
O'Toole, F. 56
Olson, Ch. 20
Ortiz Taylor, S. 157, 158
Ortner, S.B. 18n22
Orwell, G. 168
Ostendorf, B. 163
Ouellet, F. 140
Øverland, O. 163

Pagé, M. 140
Paquet, G. 132n24, 137
Paredes, A. 157
Parekh, B. 58, 93n4
Parker, Q. 238
Pasqua, Ch. 170
Pastorius, F.D. 182
Pearson, L.B. 132
Pease, D.E. 196n10, 197n12, 197n15, 200n36
Peck, A.J. 190
Pérez de Villagrá, G. 156
Pettit, P. 112, 113

Pflägling, W. 179n30
Phillips, A. 69n1
Philpott, D. 105n27
Pile, S. 195n2, 195n3, 198n19, 203n53, 216n102
Pinney, Ch. 232
Pochmann, H.A. 183
Pogge, T. 100, 105n26, 106, 115, 116n43
Polanco, H.D. 110n34
Post, R. 111n37
Poster, M. 231n7, 231n8
Prakash, G. 205n61
Pratt, M.L. 182n37, 208n79
Presley, E. 147
Priewe, M. 201n38
Puzo, M. 152

Ralston, K. 230
Ray, J. 180
Raz, J. 58, 59
Reagan, R. 49
Reed, I. 29
Renan, E. 141
Rex, J. 131
Rich, A. 195
Richards, A. 63n36
Richardson, J.G. 19n28
Rittstieg, H. 170n18
Robert, P. 136
Rocher, F. 138, 140
Rocher, G. 138
Roosevelt, T. 39, 43, 49
Rorty, R. 167, 168, 173
Rößler, H.-C. 173n23
Roth, P. 229n1
Rowan, S. 186
Roychoudhury, A.K. 15n8
Ruggie, J.G. 115n41

Rushdie, S. 196n9, 217n107, 218n110, 218n111

Sahlins, M. 18n23
Saldívar, J.D. 206n63
Salins, P. 38
Sartre, J.-P. 196n8
Schlesinger, A.M., Jr. 16, 37, 46, 131n18, 132
Schlikker, M. 173n24
Schmalz-Jacobsen, C. 171n19
Schmidt, A.J. 131n18
Schneider, I. 29n44
Schwartz, H. 230
Schwenk, K. 164
Scott, C. 111n36
Séjour, V. 174, 175, 177, 178, 180, 182, 184
Séligny, M. 175
Semprini, A. 126n8
Sennett, R. 73n3
Shapiro, I. 92n3, 109n33, 119
Shell, M. 163n1
Shore, E. 186
Shostak, D. 212n88
Siemerling, W. 164
Silko, L.M. 200, 201n37, 201n38, 202, 214
Singh, A. 198n23, 198n26, 199n27, 199n28, 200n32, 201n42, 202n43, 207n73, 212n88
Smith, P. 233n16
Soja, E. 206n63
Soldatos, P. 136n36
Solf, H. 179
Solís, J. 207n75
Sollors, W. 9, 10, 18n17, 163n1, 165n6, 174n25, 177n27, 191
Sontag, S. 236, 240
Soyinka, W. 204, 205, 208

Spiller, R. 183
St. Thomas 149
Staden, H. 232
Stefanski, V.M. 171n19
Stephens, J. 180n32
Stevenson, N. 111n37
Strachey, J. 63n36
Strickland, R. 238
Suárez, S. 159
Sullivan, T. 57
Swann, E. 201n38

Tagg, J. 236
Tamir, Y. 92-94, 98, 103n22, 115n40
Tan, A. 207n73
Taylor, Ch. 16n13, 57, 93, 94n6, 127, 128, 136n36
Thernstrom, S. 190n47
Thompson, C.W. 29n44
Thompson, H. 157
Thompson, J.B. 59n20
Thompson, S. 183
Toennies, F. 179n30
Tremblay, M. 133
Trent, W.P. 182n38
Trudeau, P.E. 133-135
Tully, J. 104n23, 136n36
Turner, F.J. 197
Turner, T. 148
Tylor, E.B. 18

Ulibarri, S. 198n26

Vauthier, S. 163, 177
Ventura, L.D. 187n45
Verkuyten, M. 93n4
Villanueva, T. 163
Viola, H. 239n34
Virilio, P. 196n4, 196n6, 216n105

Vizenor, G. 9, 31, 152, 156n8, 213-215, 217, 233n15
Volz, R. 179n30
von Banda-Beckman, K. 93n4
von Reizenstein, L. 186

Wagner, R. 18n20
Waldron, J. 93n5
Walker, A. 198n26
Walker, R.B.J. 105n25
Walkowitz, R.L. 66
Wall, Ch.A. 198n21
Wallis, B. 212
Walzer, M. 14, 100n18, 116n42
Warhol, A. 233
Watson, S. 206n63
Watts, A.C. 209n81
Wayne, J. 213
Weber, M. 72, 171n19
Weber-Jaric, G. 186n42
Weinfeld, M. 135
Weldon, L. 119
Welsch, W. 28, 29n44
Wendell, E.J. 184
Wendt, A. 115n40, 119
White, J. 232
Whitman, W. 168, 211
Williams, C. 133
Wilmer, F. 110n35
Wilson, V.S. 125n4, 128n12, 134, 135n34
Wolf, E. 18n25
Wolfe, A. 48, 100n19
Wright, E.O. 69n1, 77n4
Wulffen, T. 22n34

Xu, B. 207, 211

Yeatman, A. 111n37
Yogi, S. 183n39

Young, E.B. 175n26, 178n29
Young, I.M. 8, 84n9, 106n29

Zalewski, D. 186n44
Zangwill, I. 14
Zapf, H. 29n46
Zaretsky, E. 69n1
Zeta Acosta, O. 157
Zinsser, W. 199n29